Changing Methodologies in TESOL

Jane Spiro

© the chapter their several authors, 2013

Edinburgh University Press Ltd
22 George Square, Edinburgh EH8 9LF

www.euppublishing.com

Typeset in 10/12 Minionby
Servis Filmsetting Ltd, Stockport, Cheshire,
printed and bound in the United States of America

A CIP record for this book is available from the British Library

ISBN 978 0 7486 4620 3 (hardback)
ISBN 978 0 7486 4619 7 (paperback)
ISBN 978 0 7486 7762 7 (webready PDF)
ISBN 978 0 7486 7764 1 (epub)

CONTENTS

USEFUL ABBREVIATIONS

BANA	British, Australasian, North American (Holliday 1995)
BNC	British National Corpus
BAWE	British Academic Writing in English Corpus
CANCODE	Cambridge-Nottingham Corpus of Discourse in English
CLIL	content and language integrated learning
CLL	Community language learning (Curran 1983)
CLT	Communicative language teaching
EAP	English for Academic Purposes
EIL	English as an International Language
ELF	English as a Lingua Franca
ELT	English Language Teaching
ENL	English as a Native Language
ESP	English for Specific Purposes
HOT	Higher order thinking
ICT	Information communication technology
LAB	Language Aptitude Battery (Pimsleur 1966)
LAD	Language Acquisition Device (Chomsky 1965)
LL	language learning
LT	language teaching
MLAT	Modern Languages Aptitude Test (Carroll and Sapon 1955)
PPP	Presentation Practice Performance
SLA	Second Language Acquisition
TBL	Task-based learning (Ellis 2003; Eckerth and Siekman 2008)
TESEP	Tertiary, Secondary and Primary (Holliday 1995)
TPR	Total Physical Response (Asher, Kusudo and de la Torre 1983)

TEACHING CASE STUDIES

SERIES EDITORS' PREFACE

Editors Joan Cutting, University of Edinburgh and Fiona Farr, University of Limerick

This series of textbooks addresses a range of topics taught within **TESOL programmes** around the world. Each volume is designed to match a taught 'core' or 'option' course (identified by a survey of TESOL programmes worldwide) and could be adopted as a prescribed text. Other series and books have been aimed at Applied Linguistics students or language teachers in general, but this aims more specifically at students of ELT (English Language Teaching – the process of enabling the learning of English), with or without teaching experience.

The series is intended primarily for college and university students at third or fourth year undergraduate level, and graduates (pre-service or in-service) studying TESOL on Masters programmes and possibly some TESOL EdDs or Structured PhDs, all of whom need an introduction to the topics for their taught courses. It is also very suitable for new professionals and people starting out on a PhD, who could use the volumes for self-study. The **readership level** is **introductory** and the tone and approach of the volumes will appeal to both undergraduates and postgraduates.

This series answers a need for volumes with a special focus on **intercultural awareness**. It is aimed at programmes in countries where English is not the mother tongue, and in English-speaking countries where the majority of students come from countries where English is not the mother tongue, typical of TESOL programmes in the UK and Ireland, Canada and the US, Australia and New Zealand. This means that it takes into account physical and economic conditions in ELT classrooms round the world and a variety of socio-educational backgrounds. Each volume contains a number of tasks which include examples from classrooms around the world, encourage comparisons across cultures and address issues that apply to each student's home context. Closely related to the intercultural awareness focus is a minor theme that runs throughout the series, and that is language analysis and description, and its applications to ELT. Intercultural awareness is indeed a complex concept and we aim to address it in a number of different ways. Taking examples from different cultural contexts is one, but we also plan to look at many other educationally relevant cultural dimensions such as sociolinguistic influences, gender issues, various learning traditions (e.g. collectivist vs individualistic), culturally determined language dimensions (e.g. politeness conventions). Taking examples from different cultural contexts is one way of tackling the issue of intercultural awareness, but the volumes in the series also look at many other educationally relevant cultural dimensions such as sociolinguistic influences, gender issues, various learning traditions (e.g. collectivist vs individualistic), culturally determined language dimensions (e.g. politeness conventions).

TESOL students need **theory clearly related to practice**. This series is practical and is intended to be used in TESOL lectures and workshops, providing group tasks and independent activities. Students are invited to engage in critical thinking and to consider applications of concepts and issues to their own particular teaching contexts, adapting the tendencies and suggestions in the literature to their own countries' educational requirements. Each volume contains practical tasks to carry out individually, in small groups or in plenary in the classroom, as well as suggestions for practical tasks for the students to use in their own classrooms. All the concepts and issue encountered here will be translatable into the ELT classroom. It is hoped that this series will contribute to your improvement as a teacher.

The series presents ELT concepts and research issues **simply**. The volumes guide students from the basic concepts, through the issues and complexities, to a level that should make them alert to past and recent teaching and research developments in each field. This series makes the topics accessible to those unaccustomed to reading theoretical literature, and yet takes them to an exam and Master's standard, serving as a gateway into the various fields and an introduction to the more theoretical literature. We also acknowledge that **technology** is a major area within TESOL and this series is aware of the need for technology to feature prominently across its volumes. Issues of technological integration and implementation are addressed in some way in each of the volumes. The series is based on state-of-the-art research. The concepts and issues raised are intended to inspire students to undertake their own research and consider pursuing their interests in a PhD.

Editorial Advisory Board

As well as the two editors, the series has an Editorial Advisory Board, whose members are involved in decisions on commissioning and considering book proposals and reviewing book drafts. We would like to acknowledge and thank members of the Board for all of their work and guidance on the Textbooks in TESOL series:

- Prof. David Bloch, University of London, UK
- Dr Averil Coxhead, Victoria University of Wellington, New Zealand
- Prof. Donald Freeman, University of Michigan, USA
- Mr Peter Grundy, Northumbria University, UK
- Ms Annie Hughes, University of York, UK
- Prof. Mike McCarthy, University of Nottingham, UK
- Dr Liam Murray, University of Limerick, Ireland
- Dr Anne O'Keeffe, Mary Immaculate College, University of Limerick, Ireland
- Dr Jonathon Reinhardt, University of Arizona, USA
- Prof. Randi Reppen, North Arizona University, USA

- Assoc. Prof. Ali Shehadeh Ali ShehadehAli Shahadeh, UAE University, United Arab Emirates
- Assoc. Prof. Scott Thornbury, the New School, New York, USA
- Prof. Steve Walsh, Newcastle University, UK

ACKNOWLEDGEMENTS

These materials were evolved with and for teachers in multiple settings, sponsored by British Council Teacher Development in India, Japan, Poland, Mexico, China, Hungary; Klubschule Migros in Switzerland; Oxford University Press in Finland, Sweden, Ireland, Croatia; BA programmes for Malaysian teachers with MPIK Malaysia. Also thanks are due to the four cohorts of MA teachers at Oxford Brookes University School of Education who piloted these materials and shared their teaching experiences and stories, and who have helped to enrich this book. In particular they have contributed stories from Chile, China, Egypt, Greece, Kuwait, Hungary, India, Lebanon, Saudi Arabia, St. Maarten, Taiwan, Turkey and the Ukraine.

The Changing Methodologies project was supported by a National Teaching Fellowship (Higher Education Academy) which funded the resources and Oxford Brookes University which provided the time essential to the development of this book.

Editors, fellow writers, students and colleagues have also read drafts of this book and fed their insights into its creation. These include Judit Zerkowitz in Budapest, Crystal Ashley in Olympia, US, and Anna Furman in London. Especial thanks are due to Fiona Farr for thorough and painstaking editing and James Dale for meticulous guidance and support in its production.

The text of this book has been enriched by extracts from *English Language Teaching Journal (ELTJ)*, *TESOL Quarterly*, *Applied Linguistics*, *Language Teaching*, *Reading Research Quarterly*, *Language Learning*, for which many thanks to journal editors. In addition thanks to Judit Sollosy for her translation of Istvan Orkeny in Chapter 6.

Special thanks are due to my co-contributors, fellow teachers and TESOL practitioners who brought their huge professional and scholarly expertise into this book: Liam Murray, John Eyles, Lynn Errey, and most especially Paul Wickens whose kindness and technical skills during the production process were a lifeline.

Finally heartfelt thanks to my husband John who has waited patiently while time has been consumed by this book, and has nourished us both with his creative insights, cooking and kindness.

THE AUTHOR

Jane Spiro is Reader in Education and TESOL at Oxford Brookes University

CONTRIBUTORS

Lynn Errey was Principal Lecturer in Applied Linguistics and Learning and Teaching co-ordinator at Oxford Brookes University

John Eyles is creator of the online language learning programme *English to Go*, and a pioneering project teaching English by mobile phone.

Liam Murray is Lecturer in French and Associate Head of School at the University of Limerick.

Paul Wickens is Senior Lecturer in English Language and Communication at Oxford Brookes University.

THE MEANING OF METHODS

INTRODUCTION

Changing Methodologies for TESOL is aimed at the student, student teacher and practising teacher of TESOL interested in how the English language is experienced, taught and learnt in the twenty-first century worldwide. It takes account of the fact that language is not only taught and learnt in classrooms, but at home, on the street, and through cyberspace. It also explores the way our ideas about language, teaching and learning have changed as a result of changes in the wider world: attitudes to language, development of learning technologies, and rapid, global and shared ways of communicating. The book aims to help student teachers to negotiate the multiple factors involved in teaching English to speakers of other languages, and make sense of this multiplicity for their own learning/teaching contexts.

The book is divided into three key sections:

- **Methods and the Language Learner** starts with the impact of learner needs, context and culture on language, learning and teaching approaches, and considers the way theories about language learning have impacted on classroom practice. It answers the question: how do my methods take account of the learner, and theories of how languages are learnt?
- **The Language in Methods** explores knowledge of language and its impact on methods, from the word to whole texts, including the written word, the spoken word, and pedagogic approaches to vocabulary and grammar. It answers the question: how do my methods take account of language, and changes to the English language in the twenty-first century?
- **The World in the Classroom** explores multiple competences for the modern world, including what we need to know and do in order to function successfully in, between and across cultures, including the cultures of work and study. It answers the question: what other skills and capabilities are we developing when we learn a language, and how can the teacher's methods take account of these?

Each chapter includes:

- **An introduction** telling you the key questions about learning and teaching which are addressed in the chapter

- **Discussions** connecting current debates in the profession with real teachers in practice
- **Case studies** of real teachers and learners describing their own experiences with TESOL
- **Tasks** that you can complete either as part of discussion with others, or on your own. These include: investigative classroom tasks; reading tasks that guide you through a significant article; analysis of teacher case studies in relation to your own experiences; web activities that invite you to explore online resources connected with each section and topic
- **Further and guided readings** for each topic and chapter so you can encounter TESOL debates through the voices of researchers, practitioners, materials writers and other significant contributors to the profession. **Further readings are available as additional material at: http://www.euppublishing.com/page/TESOL/ AdditionalResources/Spiro. Online resources will be indicated with the icon** 💻.

These sections and chapters do not need to be read sequentially or comprehensively. Each task, table and section is self-contained so you can use the book to select and dip into parts that interest you or are relevant to particular questions that concern you.

1.1 DEFINING METHODS

This chapter asks the questions:

- What do the terms 'methods' and 'methodology' mean, and why do they matter?
- How do methods and methodology connect with what teachers actually do in the classroom?

In a research study in 2007, Bell asked teachers to explain what they meant by the term 'methods'. These are some of their answers:

Teacher views of methods
- 'Method applies to a structured idea that a teacher follows – combining theory and practice that best suits their learners' needs.' (Bell 2007: 139)
- 'Knowing methods is useful to decide our practices. We need to know methods in order to make our choices.' (Bell 2007: 139)
- 'The teacher should use a teaching method or group of methods that suit his/her personality, the classroom atmosphere, and the student's proficiency and interests.' (Bell 2007: 140)

Although their answers are all different, they suggest a similar understanding; that 'methods' are the choices and decisions teachers make in the classroom. In 1993, Richards, Platt and Platt defined methods as 'the practices and procedures used in teaching' (Richards, Platt and Platt 1993: 228). In their analysis, practices and procedures entail what actually takes place in the classroom. This includes, for example, which activities and materials are chosen, the kind of interaction that happens between students and teacher in class, the balance and nature of classroom talk, and the way in which instructions are given. According to the teachers in Bell's survey, as well as Brown (1994) and Richards (2001), 'methods' answer the question: *what do I do in the classroom?*

The first teacher in Bell's survey also mentions that methods 'combine theory and practice'. Every teaching decision is driven by underlying beliefs and principles, whether the teacher is conscious of this or not: beliefs about how languages are learnt, what the roles of teachers and learners are, and what the goal of the language lesson is. There will, for example, be a reason why one teacher stands at the front of the class and gives explanations of grammar rules, whilst another teacher leads learners to find out the rules for themselves. One teacher may believe the goal of the lesson is to teach learners the intellectual skills of grammar analysis, and his or her role is to be the informer who imparts this knowledge. Another teacher may believe the goal of the lesson is to give learners confidence to communicate naturally in the target language, and his or her role is to lead learners to make discoveries for themselves about language. There are other factors, too, that impact on beliefs, such as learner expectations, the availability of resources, the requirements of the test or syllabus, the demands of an employer or head teacher. A composite of all these factors leads a teacher to make choices about methods. The question: *what are my reasons for what I do in the classroom?* leads us to answers which are both connected with external factors, and are also deep and integral to the teacher. Richards (2001) describes this deep layer as 'methodology'.

The search for a methodology that works has caused teachers and researchers to question every aspect of the language teaching process: the learner, the teacher, the language, learning and teaching materials and learning itself. Researchers and teachers have asked questions such as: *does second language learning parallel the way a mother tongue is learnt? How and how far should learning involve a learner's personal and life experiences, as well as intellectual learning? How can language be divided into teachable chunks? How often should a teacher correct errors?* Yet we have come to understand that there can never be finite answers to these questions, nor a single answer to the questions: *which methods work? Which ones work best?* Our understanding constantly changes in the light of new information, new ideas, and new technology. More importantly, the questions *what, why* and *how* are different in every classroom and with every teacher. Teachers will make different choices depending on where they are, who their learners are, and what the social and cultural world within which they teach is. Every teacher needs to be a methodologist, finding his or her own answers to professional questions and choosing appropriate opportunities to create the optimal learning conditions for his or her own classes. Brown calls this kind of teacher the 'enlightened eclectic' (Brown 1994: 74). This kind of teacher knows about different methods, and is able to select from them critically or reject them entirely, without being tied to any specific orthodoxy.

Not all teachers and researchers use terminology in the same way. For example, Larsen-Freeman (2000) uses 'method' interchangeably with the term 'approach'. Bell (2007), in his interviews with teachers, found that they made little distinction between the terms 'methods' and 'approaches'. Terminology is not in itself critical, as long as teachers and researchers are able to understand one another. In this book, we will be making the distinction throughout between methods, or surface activities and procedures, and methodology, which refers to the theories and systems which underlie these choices. Each chapter will bring together background theories and the research studies which generated them, case studies of real teachers, practical methods and teaching ideas. As a reader, you will be asked to make connections between these for yourself, and think about how the ideas are or are not uniquely helpful for classrooms you have experienced as a learner or as a teacher. In other words, this book will help you too to become an 'enlightened eclectic', able to pick what is best for your own classroom in full knowledge of the range of options available to you.

1.2 PRACTICE BEFORE METHODS

We have suggested in the section above that there is no 'best' method for teaching, because this will vary not just from classroom to classroom but from learner to learner, lesson to lesson. We can never be sure that a particular method, coursebook or activity will work; each one needs to be negotiated anew by the teacher. To illustrate this, we will now turn to two real participants in the classroom.

Our first example is Wei Wei, a student of English in a Malaysian high school. For her, English is simply one subject amongst many at school. Our second example is Ursula, a teacher of English in a Swiss private language school. Ursula's students are trainee business executives who need to pass a company test in order to progress in their careers. Both were asked the following questions:

- Can you identify a moment when you understood something for the first time or 'something happened' as a result of teaching?
- Can you identify how this change took place? How did you know learning was really happening?

A learner answers:

> I had an hour of homework every night translating and learning grammar rules.
> I hated it but the teacher said always this is the way you will learn [sic]. Then I
> just stopped doing it. Instead I texted my friends, and listened to English songs
> on YouTube. I did so much better afterwards. In my test the teacher
> congratulated me after.
> – Wei Wei (student of English in Malaysia)

A teacher answers:

> I was trying so hard to make activities exciting in class, set up games and
> role-plays and brought in pictures, I was working harder and harder and the
> students were doing less and less. Then I said, 'what's the matter?' and they said,
> 'will this help us pass the test?' I realised I had tried to ignore the tests and make

English fun, but I wasn't thinking about what they wanted. When I began to use the tests either to start or finish the lesson they really relaxed. I think they felt safer that way, when all along I had thought 'fun' would make them feel safer.
– Ursula (teacher of English in Switzerland)

These two stories tell us a number of interesting things. Firstly, they tell us that a way of teaching (or a method) is neither right nor wrong. It depends on what the learners need, and what the goals and aims of the lesson are. Wei Wei learnt through non-instructed informal contexts such as texting her friends and exploring YouTube. Ursula's learners felt unsafe in 'fun' contexts and needed exactly the kind of learning Wei Wei had rejected; they wanted clear, focused tasks related to the exam syllabus.

Secondly, they show us that methods can only be evaluated when they are contextualised; that is, we can only determine whether they are useful or not by looking at learners, teachers, the syllabus, the institution, the cultural setting. For example, in Ursula's case the students who needed to pass a company test had limited study time and their approach was practical and instrumental. In Wei Wei's case, realising that English connected her with friends and the outside world was a much greater incentive than passing the test.

Thirdly, both stories suggest that what learners and teachers are 'told' to do is often in conflict with what really assists learning. Wei Wei's teacher was using a formal method of learning through rules and patterns, which was congruent with the way she was trained and taught herself. In contrast, Ursula was trained using communicative and humanistic approaches, where grammar was not taught explicitly, but through lifelike, even gamelike activities. In both cases the learners were seeking to learn successfully *in spite* of the teacher, rather than because of her.

Principles and beliefs tell us about the 'deep' layer beneath the surface. They are the core views about language and learning which determine our choices in class. Wei Wei's teacher above tends to 'lecture' and demonstrate rules on the blackboard. She may have the belief that learners need to 'receive' knowledge intact, and that the goal of the teacher is to communicate 'what I know' as informant and 'expert'. This kind of teacher may tend to use 'explanation' a great deal in the language lesson, and may spend longer talking in class than her students. In answer to the question *why*, she might also say that students need maximum exposure to correct forms of the language, and that some questions need explanation and mediation by a teacher because they are too difficult for students to answer for themselves.

In contrast, Ursula might have the belief that language is best learnt through active engagement in the way children learn their mother tongue; and that the goal of the classroom is to encourage learners to learn independently, and develop problem-solving skills which will serve them outside the classroom too. This kind of teacher may set up activities in which students work on their own or together, and arrive at an understanding of language concepts through 'discovery'. There could be layers beyond this too, which explain a teacher's methodology. It could be that it reflects his or her own experience as a teacher or as a learner, or that it is imposed by the context – the coursebook, the exam syllabus or the institution. It could also be the only methodology the teacher has encountered, and one he or she continues to adopt even whilst sensing it is not ideal.

1.3 METHODS AND POST-METHODS

What do the stories of Wei Wei and Ursula (and others like them) mean for our understanding of methods and methodologies? We see from them that 'following the method' does not always lead to success, and that both learners and teachers find their own ways to learn successfully. Senior (2006) describes a research project conducted by Clark (1969) in which three methods of language teaching were compared. She reports on the surprise findings of this research, which are given in Extract 1 below.

Extract 1: The effect of methods on student learning: interesting findings

In 1970 large-scale research was conducted in the USA on the effects on student learning of three different foreign language teaching methods. The major conclusion came as a surprise to everyone (and a disappointment to those who had assumed that the audiolingual approach would prove to be more effective): there was no significant difference in the levels or achievement of the students in the different groups. In other words, all three methods were equally effective. However, certain incidental findings were intriguing. One was that numbers of teachers admitted that they had not adhered strictly to the approach they were meant to be using, but had taught in the ways they thought best. This finding highlights the fact that teachers find it extremely difficult to limit themselves to teaching in prescribed ways: pedagogic eclecticism is, it seems, a key feature of effective teaching. (Senior 2006: 141)

Discussion questions
1. What are these surprise results?
2. What are the implications for teachers of these findings?

Senior's research seems to support the information we have from teachers and learners on the ground: that 'set' methods, orthodoxies and fashionable ideas do not necessarily work, and that both learners and teachers tend instead to seek answers for themselves about what works best. Kumaravadivelu (2006) coined the term 'post-methods' to describe this move away from a single-method approach and towards 'pedagogic eclecticism', where teachers make their own choices and draw on multiple methods to do so. For example, Ursula in Section 1.2 above now chooses a number of methods for her learners: grammar-focused tasks preparing for the test which meet the learners' own expectations; communicative games to prepare them for using English in interaction with others; and some activities based on drama and role-play, because this is her own specialist interest and she feels confident her own enthusiasm will enthuse her students too, as long as their test-related needs are also being met. In other words, Ursula's realisation is not that an interactive and communicative method is inappropriate, but rather that using this approach exclusively does not meet her learners' needs, so she needs to combine this with other approaches too.

In Extract 2, Kumaravadivelu explains in more detail what he means by a post-methods approach, and why he feels it has arisen.

Extract 2: Developing a new approach to methods: beyond methods

Considering the more significant trend-setting shifts that have marked the 1990s, we can claim with some justification that we have now reached a much higher level of awareness. We might even say, with a good measure of poetic license, that we have moved from a state of awareness toward a state of awakening. We have been awakened to the necessity of making methods-based pedagogies more sensitive to local exigencies, awakened to the opportunity afforded by postmethod pedagogies to help practicing teachers develop their own theory of practice, awakened to the multiplicity of learner identities, awakened to the complexity of teacher beliefs, and awakened to the vitality of macrostructures – social, cultural, political, and historical – that shape and reshape the microstructures of our pedagogic enterprise'. (Kumaravadivelu 2006: 81)

Discussion questions
1. Kumaravadivelu describes a series of 'awakenings' for teachers in the past ten years. What have they awakened to?
2. How does this change our approach to 'methods'?

The term 'post-methods' has evolved to describe an approach in which the teacher places the learner and the learning context at the centre of their choices. Rather than relying on the coursebook or a prescribed method, teachers will draw on any ideas, materials or procedures that meet the needs of their learners at any one time or in any one lesson. They have responded to 'top-down' prescriptions by making their own choices where they can.

1.4 CONCLUSION

This chapter has answered the following questions:

What do the terms 'methods' and 'methodology' mean and why do they matter?
Teachers often refer to 'methods' as surface activities, procedures and practices. They are important because these are the concrete events that are part of a teacher's daily practice, even though teachers may label and describe them in different ways.

'Methodology' refers to the beliefs and attitudes to learning, language and teaching which underlie what teachers do in the classroom. Appreciating the way methodology leads to methods is important because this helps us to understand our teaching decisions, and review and critique them in the light of new information and experience.

How do methods and methodology connect with what teachers actually do in the classroom?

Methods are about what teachers actually do in the classroom. Thus there can be no fixed or single idea of 'methods that work', because every teacher, class and learner is different. A post-methods approach to teaching takes account of this diversity and places *what teachers really do* at the centre of our understanding.

Similarly, methodology – our underlying beliefs and attitudes – has changed as a result of teacher experience in real classrooms, and will continue to do so as we learn more and more about what really happens in language learning situations, and learn from the diversity and complexity of these.

SECTION ONE: METHODS AND THE LANGUAGE LEARNER

2

LEARNING THEORIES AND METHODS

INTRODUCTION

This chapter asks the questions:

- How do beliefs and attitudes to learning affect language teaching methods?
- How have theories about language learning influenced the actual practice of language teachers?

We explore teaching methods as responses to questions researchers and teachers have asked about the language learning process; and consider them not as historical artifacts, but as opportunities for eclectic teachers to make informed choices about what will suit their learners best.

2.1 AN OVERVIEW OF LEARNING THEORIES: BELIEFS AND PRACTICES

We saw in Chapter 1 that there are theories which lie behind teacher actions, whether these actions are the teacher's free choice or prescribed by an institution, syllabus or coursebook. We also saw in Chapter 1 that teachers test these theories beside the realities of their own learners, and find that what is prescribed is not necessarily what is best for their learners. This chapter looks at these underlying theories, and how they impact on practice. What actually happens in the classroom if a teacher believes, or is required to act on the basis of, Theory A rather than Theory B – or if a school favours Argument A rather than Argument B in response to a professional question?

Every aspect of the teaching process has been questioned by researchers and teachers: the learner, the language, the teacher and the learning process. Below are some of these key questions, and the opposing positions which have been taken in answer to them. There are, of course, multiple positions between these two opposites. As you read, you might consider what your own position is in response to each of the questions, and whether you would follow argument A, argument B, or an interim position between the two.

- Do we all learn a new language in the same way, or are there differences depending on our first language?

- Should the way we teach a second language be informed by the way we acquire a first language?
- Should learning a language involve engagement with the whole self, or is it a predominantly intellectual activity?
- How far should a teacher intervene in the learning process?

Language learning dilemma 1: do we all learn a new language in the same way, or are there differences depending on our first language?

Argument 1a	Argument 1b
Every learner follows parallel patterns of learning and development, irrespective of his or her first language. This idea is based on the notion of a **universal grammar** – that every human being has an internal capacity to process and pattern language (Chomsky 1965). The **natural order of acquisition** hypothesis suggests that all language is learnt using similar stages; for example simpler structures are learnt before the more complex ones, and grammatical changes to words seem to be learnt in a similar sequence. (Brown 1973; Pienemann, Johnston and Brindley 1988). Other findings suggest that words which convey content (such as *car, apple, mummy*) are learnt before grammatical words which are empty of meaning (such as *it, was, on*). Many language teaching materials are structured on the basis of this belief, that some aspects of the language system are intrinsically more 'difficult' and later learnt, irrespective of the learner's first language.	There are patterns of development specific to each language. This idea is based on a notion of **contrastive analysis**, which suggests that it is possible to predict what a learner will find difficult in a second language by comparing this with his or her first language. (Lado 1957; Wardhaugh 1970). Materials based on a contrastive view of learning explore the ways in which English is and is not different from a learner's first language. *Learner English*, for example (Swan and Smith 2001), compares English with eighteen other languages, asking questions such as 'how is time expressed (in the verb form? using adverbials?)' and 'how are sound and spelling related?' The underlying belief is that understanding a learner's first language will help the teacher predict and understand errors.
Examples: So for example, we know that the -s ending in the third person is slowly learnt by learners of all first languages – even though this is not an intrinsically 'difficult' grammatical feature.	**Examples:** So for example, we know that the present perfect is difficult for Mandarin speakers because there is no equivalent in their language, and difficult for French speakers because there *is* an equivalent form in French, but it has a different function.
Teaching implications If you believe that there is a 'natural order' in which all learners learn a language, it also follows that a structure or language item	**Teaching implications** The teacher of a monolingual class may select language points which represent specific contrasts between the L1 and L2 –

taught too early will simply not be 'acquired'. The teacher must allow for errors, and wait for the learner to internalise the language point. What a teacher can do, however, is to provide the *opportunity* for learning the correct form through examples, repetition and exposure.

Materials writers develop programme/course materials which are 'staged' to matched the natural order of acquisition: for example, simple verb forms such as *I am a ---, I live in --- come first, and more complex verb forms such as *I should have known --- come much later.

for example the sound contrast between /l/ and /r/ for Mandarin speakers.

Some resources, such as Swan and Smith (2001), specifically look at the differences between English and other languages such as Swahili, Hindi, Arabic and Turkish, identifying ways in which the languages are different. Teachers can use this as a resource to help them plan the syllabus for a specific group of language speakers.

Language learning dilemma 2: should the way we teach a second language be informed by the way we acquire a first language?

Argument 2a	Argument 2b
One view of acquiring a first language suggests children learn to use language to convey important messages about feelings and everyday needs. The adult 'scaffolds' or stages learning so the child can move gradually from what is familiar to what is new. (Vygotsky 1978; *see also* dilemma 4, below). One aspect of this theory of learning is that adults modify their language to give the child **comprehensible input** (Krashen 1985). Krashen and Terrell (1992) called this **the natural approach**, and it has formed the basis for a view of second language learning.	Another view of the way a child learns a first language is that it is a process of forming habits. It is formed by modelling correct language, imitation and practice, so the 'correct' language becomes automatic and habitual. This theory of learning led to the **audiolingual approach** and was based on research by Skinner (1961). He found that pigeons could be taught habits through positive reinforcement and rewards. It was believed language might be learnt in the same way. For example, a baby will have the sounds 'mamama' reinforced by the positive responses of the parent. The word 'mama' becomes a habit and these sounds become fixed in the baby's linguistic repertoire.
Examples In the classroom informed by Krashen's theory, the language will be modified by the teacher so all the language examples are tuned to the learner's level. A key principle of this lesson is that language will be personalised so learners use language purposefully and meaningfully to communicate their everyday needs.	**Examples** In the audiolingual lesson, the teacher will model correct language and will then ask the students to imitate and repeat ten or more times so the form becomes automatic. The language might be in 'chunks' which are not explained but which have useful functions in everyday life, for example: 'What's your name? What's your name?' 'I'm a student! I'm a student!'

Teaching implications Teachers who strictly follow this view of language learning will not teach grammar explicitly, but through discovery and exposure to the language. This kind of lesson/teacher will also allow errors, as these are seen as a natural part of the learning process. This view of learning forms the basis of **humanistic approaches**, which model the support and nurturing a child has when he/she learns the mother tongue.	**Teaching implications** If the student makes errors, this means the 'habit' has not been correctly learnt. The teacher will structure the lesson so that the possibility of error is minimised, and her goal will be total accuracy. Errors are corrected, as they are considered evidence of incomplete learning. The language is learnt in 'chunks' mechanically through drills and repetition, with the whole class progressing together and at the same pace.

Language learning dilemma 3: should learning a language involve engagement with the whole self, or is it a predominantly intellectual activity?

Argument 3a	Argument 3b
Some educators both within and outside language learning (for example, Gertrude Moscowitz within, and Carl Rogers outside) believe that learning is most effective when it engages the whole person. **Humanistic learning theory** is founded on the argument that the child learns a first language in (ideally) loving and supported settings, using language to express core needs and feelings, and so all learning should take place in this way. The humanistic teacher's position is that the learner's emotional responses, or 'affect', are as important in the classroom as intellectual processes. (Arnold 1999)	**The cognitive learning theory** recognises that language learning involves the development of thinking – for example, memorising both sight and sound (Pickett 1978), using reasoning and deduction to recognise rules and patterns (Rubin 1987) and applying strategies such as organising, labelling, recording, using labels and terminology about language (Oxford 1990, 2011). These thinking capacities are essential for the good language learner, and may be missed out if they are not specifically developed.
Examples A teacher who believes in a humanistic learning theory may include the following activities and objectives on the syllabus: Building self-esteem as a learner Team-building: feeling safe within the group Recognising signs of stress Dealing with anger Arnold's book (1999) has sections that focus on learner anxiety, memory, autonomy and self-esteem.	**Examples** A teacher who believes in the predominantly intellectual or cognitive role of the lesson may include the following activities and objectives on the syllabus: Ways of storing and remembering vocabulary Using the dictionary Spelling patterns
Teaching implications The teacher who follows a humanistic approach may adopt one or more of these methods:	**Teaching implications** The teacher conducting a lesson that draws from a cognitive learning theory, may adopt one or more of these methods:

A five-minute meditation at the start or close of the class A five-minute 'visualisation' activity, in which learners sit with their eyes closed and follow the teacher's voice taking them on an internal journey Encourage learners to write a personal journal and discuss these daily in class Set up co-mentoring partnerships, in which learners counsel one another in pairs	Identify, explain and analyse patterns and rules in the language (grammar processes) Focus on the study and analysis of written texts Compare the first and second language (translation processes) This focus on language learning as an intellectual activity, including comparisons between first and second language, was called the **grammar-translation method** and was the predominant method of language teaching until the 1960s.

Language learning dilemma 4: how far should the teacher intervene in the learning process?

Argument 4a	Argument 4b
The **social constructivist** approach to language learning suggests that people learn a second language through interaction with, and focused guidance from, an informed 'other' (Vygotsky 1978). As a theory of learning, this is based on the idea that language is a means of social interaction. The 'guide' or teacher moves learners from their current knowledge to their *potential* knowledge. The teacher with this learning approach will be careful to draw on what the learner already knows, and will use this as a starting point for establishing learning needs and goals. This teacher will also differentiate between learners, and provide each with a framework for learning step by step, recognising what is feasible and achievable as a future learning goal. The teacher will then bridge the gap between current and potential knowledge, through guided steps, or 'scaffolding'. The zone of proximal development (ZPD) is the distance between the *actual* development level of the child, as determined through problem solving, and the level of *potential* development, as determined through problem solving under adult guidance or in collaboration with more capable peers.	The **learner autonomy** approach to language learning suggests 'the ideal situation is for the students to take over their own learning – in other words to do it without having to be shown how by the teacher' (Harmer 2007: 399). This position emerges partly from research suggesting that successful learners tend to take responsibility for their own learning, and do not depend on the teacher or the classroom for learning opportunities (Oxford 2011). Autonomous language learners make decisions for themselves, and manage their own learning.

Examples Wood (1998) suggests that teachers can scaffold children's learning in various ways: suggesting, praising the significant, encouraging rehearsal, being explicit about organisation, reminding, modelling, providing part-whole activities.	**Examples** The autonomous learner would: decide what he or she wants to study; decide what resources he or she needs; plan his or her own activities; formulate his or her own questions and seek ways of answering them. In other words, the autonomous learner is the one who makes decisions, and the teacher acts as a bystander providing the conditions for learning (Benson 2007).
Teaching implications A criticism of this approach is that it does not account for the capacity of learners to find solutions to problems for themselves. A practical criticism is that the close and supportive setting implicit in the scaffolding of learning suggests parent: child situations and is unworkable in the typical classroom, where teachers have large numbers of learners and prescribed learning goals.	**Teaching implications** The teacher who believes in learner autonomy may: invite learners at the start of the class to draw up their own goals and learning objectives; set up a class library so learners can choose reading materials for themselves; set up a self-access resource where learners can choose what they want to study for themselves; provide free class time for learners to work at their own pace on their own projects and activities

As we have discussed, the teacher does not need to adopt just one approach; an eclectic teacher will find something interesting in each one, and may make decisions about the class depending on what age the learners are, what their goals are, or where the class is taking place. Below are examples of typical questions that language teachers ask, and a variety of answers they might arrive at depending on the learners, the learning situation, or even the particular lesson.

Should I correct errors or accept that errors are part of the natural learning process?

If you believe in the natural order of acquisition, you will allow learners to correct errors for themselves in their own time, when they are ready to learn a specific rule. If you are teaching using the audiolingual method, using, for example, drills and repetitions, your focus will be on accuracy and you will correct errors in order to cultivate appropriate language habits.

If you are teaching with an underlying belief in the cognitive learning theory, you might respond to an error by analysing its cause and revisiting the rule or pattern which it relates to.

Should I teach grammar rules explicitly, or lead learners to acquire rules subconsciously through practice?

If you believe learners learn a second language in the same way as their mother tongue, you will not teach rules or patterns explicitly, but rather model patterns through example and exposure to the language.

If you are conducting a humanistic lesson, your goal will be building confidence, or allowing learners to talk about themselves, so grammar rules will not be relevant to your lesson.

If you are conducting an audiolingual lesson, you will be inviting learners to practise and repeat language in chunks, and will not need to analyse these chunks or explain the rules.

Should I use the mother tongue in the classroom, or only the target language?

If you are following the grammar-translation method you will explicitly use the mother tongue to make comparisons between the first and the second language.

If you are using the audiolingual approach you will use just the target language in the classroom, to provide the maximum opportunity for correct models of the language.

If you are adopting a number of different humanistic approaches you will include the mother tongue in order to lower the anxiety of the learners and bring their whole selves into the classroom.

What should my role as a teacher be in the classroom?

If you are following a humanistic teaching approach, you will allow learners to occupy most of the talking time, while you act as a guide and facilitator.

If you are conducting an audiolingual lesson you will provide a model for the learners and be the 'conductor' orchestrating the repetition and imitation of correct forms.

If you are conducting a grammar-translation lesson you will be the 'informer' of the class, providing information the learners need to understand rules and patterns.

Task 2.1 Classroom task: examining key concepts

Below are descriptions of two different classrooms: one is Roxanna's secondary-level classroom in Romania, the other is Fayad's primary-level classroom in Kuwait. Read these brief snapshots of their classrooms and imagine you are invited to teach one lesson to each class.

  A. What would your answers be to each of these questions?

- Should I correct errors, or accept that errors are part of the natural learning process?
- Should I teach grammar rules explicitly, or lead learners to acquire rules subconsciously through practice?
- Should I use the mother tongue in the classroom, or only the target language?
- What should my role as a teacher in the classroom be – guide, facilitator, informer, friend or parent?

B. As a teacher, how might you adapt your approach so it is appropriate for each case study group?

Teaching case study 1: a secondary school in Romania	Teaching case study 2: a primary school in Kuwait
The learners are 15–16 years old and have studied English for six years, through the grammar-translation approach. There are 35 in the class. They work with texts, including literary texts, and keep notebooks of grammar rules and vocabulary lists. They are preparing for a school leaving exam which is very important for their future career. The test will include translating sections of the texts, comprehension questions about detailed meaning, and grammar questions. They have a set coursebook with instructions and translations written in Romanian, and it is a requirement to work through the coursebook by the end of the school year. The learners are very motivated, although they do not hear English in their daily lives and do not know any native speakers. They see English as an opportunity to study, travel, and possibly work in other countries.	The learners are 6–7 years old. They are in a primary school in Kuwait where there is a policy of English language education from an early age. Higher education is in the medium of English, and many official roles in the country are conducted in English, so they are likely to hear the language spoken around them. However, the children have only learnt English for one year, and are also learning to read and write in their mother tongue. The school is also new to them. There are no set coursebooks or resources and the teacher is free to make her own choices about what to do in the classroom.

Task 2.2 Research: conduct your own research into a language learning dilemma

Think about one activity or experience since your childhood in which you were fully engaged, and as a result of which you learnt something or changed.

Was there a teacher involved in the process? If so, how did the teacher help to facilitate the experience? If there was no teacher involved, what was the stimulus or starting point for the activity? What motivated you to continue?

Now ask the same question of five peers, friends or relations.

Use the information you have discovered to form some initial responses to the question: **How far should the teacher intervene in the learning process?**

Task 2.3 Explore teaching method approaches online 💻

Compare the clips below of two teaching methods in action and notice how these examples do, or do not, demonstrate the characteristics of different methods outlined in Arguments 1a and 1b in Section 2.1.

Communicative method (Argument 1a): <http://www.youtube.com/watch?v=5bW1 5RpON9M&feature=related>

Audiolingual method (Argument 1b): <http://www.youtube.com/watch?v=AJ1tr8kK kGU&feature=related>

2.2 AN OVERVIEW OF TEACHING METHODS: METHODS INTO PRACTICE

Section 2.1 considered the way teachers and researchers have responded to professional dilemmas, and what they actually do in the classroom as a result. Section 2.2 looks at how methods cluster together depending on their approach to the learner. It aims to answer the following questions:

- What methods should we follow if we believe language is a form of communication?
- What methods should we follow if we believe the teacher can accelerate learning?
- What methods should we follow if we believe that learners should be at the centre of teaching decisions, not the syllabus or the coursebook?
- What methods should we follow if we believe the whole learner should be engaged in the language classroom?

Teaching for communication

This section considers different teaching approaches which derive from the view that learning a language involves communication and social interaction, rather than the manipulation of rules and patterns.

The **communicative approach** derived from the view that the purpose of language is to communicate meaning and messages. Argument 2a above suggested that a child acquires a language in order to express early needs and feelings, and this is a prime and burning incentive for learning. The communicative approach is also based on the notion that the role of language is to communicate genuine information. Typical communicative lessons include personalising language so students are talking about their real lives, opinions, needs and feelings rather than mechanically manipulating language forms. The topics in Table 2.1 illustrate the difference between lessons that emphasise communicative interactions, and lessons that emphasise language forms.

However, there is more than one approach to communicative learning and teaching. Howatt (1984) and Ellis (2003) describe the 'weak' and the 'strong' approach, and teachers are likely to make choices along a spectrum of possibilities between the two.

Table 2.1   Communicative lesson topics and grammar lesson topics

Communicative lesson topics	Grammar lesson topics
Telephone talk: phrases for opening and closing telephone conversations Buying clothes: what do you say in a clothes shop? How to apply for summer jobs: what do you write? What do you say? What should you read?	Question forms: *wh-* questions and subject/verb reversal (e.g. *Who's speaking?* v. *Could I speak to Annette, please?*) Comparisons: *-er* and *-est* suffixes v. more/most (e.g. *cheaper/cheapest* v. *less expensive/more expensive*) Simple present and the modal 'can' to describe abilities (e.g. *I speak two languages. I can drive.*)

Table 2.2   Analytical and communicative lesson stages

Analytical stage
Next week; In a day's time; At the moment; Once; Last year
1. What do all these phrases have in common? (They are all adverbials of time)   2. What is different about them? (Two of them refer to future time, one to present time, two to past time)
Communicative stage
1. Write one true sentence about yourself and two untrue sentences beginning *At the moment; Last year; Next week*   2. Ask your partner to guess which one is true

The 'weak' approach to communicative language teaching is influenced by the argument that language learning involves conscious cognitive strategies such as recognising, classifying, labelling and memorising patterns (argument 3b above). A teacher who adopts a 'weak' approach to the communicative language classroom will analyse the components of language in the traditional way, focusing on accuracy and form. But this teacher will then practise the forms using communicative methods: activities that focus on meanings, interaction, and the exchange of information. In other words, this teacher will start with an analytical stage in which cognitive skills are the focus, followed by a communicative stage in which communication of meaning is the focus, as in Table 2.2.

The teacher might then discuss the statements, firstly from the point of view of meaning, memory and exchange of experiences, and secondly from the point of view of verb form, comparing which tenses each adverbial introduces.

The 'strong' approach to communicative teaching, in contrast, is influenced by the idea that learners will discover the language system for themselves if given sufficient opportunity, as they did with their first language. The teacher who adopts a strong approach will involve students in sharing, interacting, and exchanging information, and the teacher will act in these lessons as a guide, facilitator or mentor, rather than as the source of knowledge. Defining or explaining the key language might emerge (if at all) as a result of student need, during or after the activity, or would be arrived at without teacher intervention by the students themselves. The teacher adopting a lesson with a 'strong' approach would start with the second activity in Table 2.2, and omit the analytical stage in which meanings and usage of time adverbials are discussed. However, he or she might then develop the second activity in one of the ways below:

- Ask your partner questions about the true story.
- Ask your partner questions about the false story. You can ask:
  - Why did you tell this story? Is any part of the story true?
  - What have you learnt now about your partner?

Table 2.3   Strong and weak approaches to language teaching

Strong approaches ←——————————————————————→ weak approaches

Learners will discover the language system for themselves if given sufficient opportunity	Language learning involves conscious cognitive strategies which need to be explicitly developed

Task 2.4 Reflecting on your teaching position

If you were a teacher, would you choose to offer both the analytical and the communicative stages of the task in Table 2.2, or just one of these, or would your answer be 'it depends'? In other words:

Do you believe it is the teacher's job to explain grammar and language features, or to lead students to discover these features for themselves?

In Table 2.3 are two opposite responses to this question. Where do you sit along the spectrum? Can you explain your position?

Task-based learning

Task-based learning emerged from the 'strong' approach to communicative teaching. As with the communicative approach, it is influenced by views of learning which might on the surface appear to be in conflict with one another. On the one hand, it is influenced by the view that learning should engage the whole person and go beyond the manipulation of discrete language items. On the other hand, it is also influenced by the view that the cognitive (or thinking) skills involved in learning a language need the opportunity for development. Willis describes the task-based approach as combining 'the best insights from communicative language teaching with an organized focus on language form' (Willis 1996: 1). Its key principle is the engagement of the learner with real-world tasks that entail problem-solving, collaboration with others, and the integration of all four skills. Another important principle is that the task focuses on 'meaning to obtain an objective' (Bygate, Skehan and Swain 2007), rather than the conscious acquisition of language. There are different kinds of task-based activities, based on different notions of the task itself. The following are some examples:

- The class has a one-week project researching the way a newspaper is put together and the kind of items and text types found on each page. The task is to produce a class paper including each text type, such as feature page, letters to the editor, classified ads and captioned photos. This task type matches the kind described by Prabhu (1977), which includes pre-tasks, detailed preparation and meaning-focused activities.
- Interview a partner about his or her learning journey this term and draw together a 'map' showing the highs, lows and plateaux. You can choose together to represent and label this in any way you like. Moskowitz (1978) would describe this as a task with an 'affective' goal, designed to bring the whole learner into the classroom.
- The class is asked to draw up a language syllabus for one week of class, in which

Table 2.4   Do learners really need teachers? Three responses

Strong view	Partial view	Traditional view
A strong view suggests that learners learn best when they choose what to learn and how to learn for themselves. The way we learn basic life skills can be taken as evidence of this view. We learn to walk or to ride a bicycle outside a formal instructed context, by trial and error and with a strong incentive to succeed.	A partial view suggests that learners might need the guidance of teachers, but not necessarily carefully progressive materials which control each step of the learning journey. A parallel to this is using a recipe book. We might learn the basic skill of baking a cake from a recipe book, then use the basic skills to invent new recipes for ourselves.	A traditional view takes the position that a learner needs the guidance of the teacher to be successful in learning. Teachers are necessary in the learning process to guide learners from current to new knowledge. Teachers have the overview of what learners need to learn and how to arrive there.

they come to a consensus about what they would like to study. The task includes working first in pairs, then groups, then as a whole class to draw up a set of class priorities for their learning. These outcomes are to be presented to the teacher at the end of the task. This task is the kind in which teacher and students negotiate what is to happen in class, and is described as a 'process' activity by Breen and Candlin (1987).

These three different tasks all share a communicative purpose and prioritise meaning over explicit language learning. They also go one stage further than the communicative approach, in giving learners the opportunity to work independently of the teacher once the initial task has been shaped. In fact, the task-based syllabus is one of the drivers that has encouraged us to ask: do we really need the teacher at all? Could it be possible that the learner actually works better when given the opportunity to be entirely independent? Table 2.4 above gives three answers to this question.

Accelerated learning

This section will look at a number of methods which aim to make learning achievable rapidly. They do so by engaging the whole human being through sound, movement and emotions, rather than by developing language as an intellectual capacity alone.

Total physical response, or TPR, was developed by James Asher in the 1960s. Its main principle is that learners internalise language when they connect it with physical actions and movements. The method mirrors ways in which a parent interacts with a child, using repetition and actions to illustrate meaning. The TPR teacher gives the learners commands or instructions, and the learners respond to these in groups. It allows learners to hear the language without needing to reply, and to act as a group rather than being individually exposed. It is also a way of illustrating the meaning of instruction verbs and related nouns through demonstration and movement. Here are some examples of what the teacher might say, model and then instruct the class to do:

Stand up!
Sit down!
Stand on the chair!
Move the book onto the desk!
Open the door!
Close the door!

TPR lends itself particularly to instructions and commands which can be demonstrated, rather than other sentence types. It might seem to be a disadvantage of the TPR approach that it does not lead naturally into other language forms. However, Asher has suggested that 'most grammatical features ... can be nested into the imperative form' (Asher et al. 1983: 62). He gives as examples commands such as these, which include reference to other verb forms and to abstract as well as concrete vocabulary:

- *Marie, pick up the picture of the ugly old man and put it next to the picture of the government building.* (Asher et al. 1983: 64)
- *When Luke walks to the window, Marie will write his name on the blackboard.* (Asher 1983: 62)

Task 2.5 Exploring a TPR lesson 💻
View the Total Physical Response lesson in the clip below.
Notice what the teacher is doing and saying.
Notice what the students are doing and saying.
Do you think this is a useful way to teach language?
<http://www.youtube.com/watch?v=ikZY6XpB214&feature=related>

Suggestopedia was developed in the 1960s by a Bulgarian medical doctor, Georgi Lozanov. It drew on the combined principles of Soviet automatic learning techniques and Indian yogic practice of relaxation. In the central part of the Suggestopedia lesson students lie back comfortably in soft chairs, relax peacefully and listen to the teacher reading the text or language for study. This reading is conducted slowly and gently by the teacher three times. During the third time, soothing music is played to encourage the lowering of anxiety and conscious blocks to learning.

Five years after his first encounter with the method, Stevick identified three characteristics about Suggestopedia which made it worthwhile discussing:

- Learning involves the unconscious functions of the learner as well as conscious functions
- Through this method people can learn much faster than they usually do
- Learning is held back by the norms and expectations of learning taught to us by society (Stevick 1983: 129)

He said: 'I believe that Suggestopedic factors play a role in the success of many other methods and techniques which in themselves have nothing to do with Suggestopedia' (Stevick 1983: 133). These factors, according to Stevick, lead to a number of insights about teaching which are widely meaningful and effective in the classroom. These include:

- Find out what students already know
- Say as little as possible
- Omit all information that is not demanded by students' questions
- Invite students to try out their knowledge to see whether it works
- Keep teachers' answers to no more than five or ten seconds
- Leave time and opportunity for students to answer one another's questions (Stevick 1983: 141)

Learning with the whole person
The section above looked at two methods which aim to speed the learning process by engaging the whole person. This section looks at one more method which also works on the basis that learning is best achieved when it brings the learner's life experiences and emotions into the learning process.

Community language learning
Charles Curran offers an approach to learning which places the whole person at the centre. In his view, 'any discussion of the educative process has really to start with the relation of conflict, hostility, anger and anxiety to learning' (Curran 1983: 147). In his approach, the learner/teacher relationship parallels that of counsellor/client. He sees this as having five phases in which the client/student becomes gradually independent of the counsellor/teacher:

1. The student/client is dependent on the teacher/counsellor for new language
2. The student/client acquires new confidence as new words and phrases are learnt and can be used independently of the teacher
3. The student/client acquires increased independence, though his or her output is still monitored and corrected by the teacher/counsellor, rather as an adolescent is monitored by a parent whilst exploring his/her independence
4. The teacher/counsellor is needed progressively less, for the more refined and idiomatic examples of language
5. The teacher/counsellor and student/client are independent of one another, with the student acting for him or herself while the counsellor just reinforces and fine-tunes certain aspects of language such as pronunciation (Curran 1983: 173)

The community language learning (CLL) approach emerges from this view of the student/teacher relationship. Learning is in small or large groups which are convened not as classes, but as 'communities'. The 'knower' of the target language needs to share the mother tongue of the learners. This is usually the teacher, but could also be other students in the group who can move between the mother tongue and target language as an interpreter/translator.

The learners direct the conversation, determining what it is they want to talk about and say. They whisper this in their mother tongue to one of the translators/interpreters.

The teacher then translates these utterances into the target language for the rest of the group. This translation can also be recorded, so the learner can then work with it to learn and extend the target language comments with the teacher.

A key aspect of this approach is that the utterances are interactive and shared by the whole group as part of the group process.

The interaction may end with the group discussing their experience, what they have learnt and what has been discussed. The learner is deemed in this approach to move from dependence on the 'knower' to gradual ownership of the target language.

Task 2.6 Research activity

What is your view of learners using the mother tongue as an intermediate stage in using the target language? Think about a language classroom you have experienced either as a learner or a teacher, and notice the ways in which the mother tongue was or was not included in the learning process.

If you can, talk to a group of learners and ask them:

- Do you have an idea of how often you use your mother tongue when you are in the language lesson?
- When do you like to use your mother tongue? Why?
- When do you not like to use your mother tongue? Why?

Review the description above of CLL and think about the questions below in relation to yourself as learner or teacher in a classroom you have experienced.

- What is your view of using language in the classroom to describe spontaneous feelings and ideas, without directing the topic as teacher? How comfortable would you feel with this? How comfortable would your learners feel?
- Would it be practical for you as teacher to act as interpreter/translator for your learners so they can talk in the mother tongue? Why, or why not?

2.3 THE FORCES OF CHANGE: METHODOLOGIES AND WHERE WE ARE NOW

We have seen that methods emerging in response to professional questions provide opportunities rather than orthodoxies from which teachers might critically select. Methods which might at first appear outdated and eccentric, such as Suggestopedia or audiolingual approaches, still provide insights and strategies which can inform the contemporary teacher. Just as it would be wrong to say any single method can offer conclusive answers, so equally it might be short-sighted to dismiss a method as having nothing to say to the teacher. But where are we now, in terms of the changes and developments inside and outside language education? What are some of the broader influences on the language teaching profession which we need to take account of, as we progress through the twenty-first century?

The Dogme approach

The **Dogme approach** derives from the partial view that learners do not need scaffolded and progressive learning materials determined by a coursebook or curriculum designer. Thornbury, who founded the movement, described his frustration with an approach to teaching in which 'the lesson space was filled to overflowing with *activities* at the expense of the learning *opportunities*'. He felt that 'the problem seemed to stem from an over-reliance on materials and technical aids', such as 'workbooks, tapes, transparencies, flashcards, Cuisenaire rods, and other gimmicks' (Thornbury 2009: 3).

He and his colleagues changed their approach and instituted a policy in which published materials were used minimally, replaced by materials brought in by the students themselves, 'found' inside the classroom, or made by the teachers. When this happened, they found that 'the improvement in the quality of teaching was dramatic' (2009: 3).

Thornbury's 'first commandment' of the Dogme approach is:

Teaching should be done using only the resources that teachers and students bring to the classroom – i.e. themselves – and whatever happens to be in the classroom.

Reflective practice

Teacher education programmes, and the professional literature, increasingly focus on the ways in which teachers question and learn from their own practice. They include the view that the aim of teacher development is to understand and improve practice, rather than to follow any set standards or methods. The reflective teacher will continually critique methods externally imposed by exam boards, published resources, school and national policy or teaching orthodoxies, and will seek to understand the research and theories of others in the light of his or her own experience and beliefs. The reflective teacher is thus able to evolve his or her own theories of learning and teaching. Schön describes the process of making on-going decisions about practice as 'reflection in action'. Larsen-Freeman calls this 'thought-in-action', but the principle is the same: the reflective teacher will act according to professional judgement, rather than on the basis of a specific method (Schön 1983; Moon 1999; Pollard 2008; Bolton 2010).

Appropriate methodology

Since Holliday's critique of a Westernised perception of methods (1994, 2005), the profession has revisited its assumptions about effective learning and teaching. There has been a collective recognition that methodologies developed through and in one culture do not necessarily transfer into others, and it is unsound to require or expect them to. Each learning context makes its own demands upon learner and teacher, and has its own unique combination of constraints and drivers.

Learner autonomy

We have come to understand that learners can often work very well without the explicit intervention of the teacher and that, in fact, more teaching can often lead to less learning. The link between teaching and learning has been explored in the last twenty years in such a way that teachers have begun to profoundly rethink their role in the classroom. For example, we have come to understand the importance of learners developing their own strategies for learning (Oxford 1990), and experiments with self-taught environments have shown that learners often do very well learning complex concepts without the intervention of teachers at all. Chapter 3 explores the example of the Hole in the Wall Project, where children in a slum village in India learnt to use a computer without the help of adults or teachers (Mitra 2011).

Global English

We are also questioning the kind of English being taught, recognising that it is no longer the exclusive property of native speakers, or of speakers in the English-speaking world. This means that every English language teacher needs to have a position about which English he or she is teaching, and why (Kirkpatrick 2007a, 2007b).

Intercultural competence

Given that the English language is part of a global means of communication, the teacher of English could also be seen as preparing learners to communicate within, between and across cultures. This extends the skills of the learner beyond the practice of language as a system, or even language as communication within a shared community. It demands further skills of open-mindedness and sensitivity which the language teacher may not consider part of his or her remit. However, intercultural competence has been anatomised and explored widely within educational debates, and a capacity to understand and develop these will increasingly be part of the expected skills-base of the language teacher (Byram 1997).

The digital revolution

There are now multiple ways in which we communicate and exchange messages. Text messages, Internet, Skype and social networking sites have all changed the way we read and write, and many young people have grown up with this expectation of digital and cyber-communication. Learners have access to their own rich learning resources: podcasts (Travis and Joseph 2009), Web 2.0 weblogs (Raith 2009), blogging (Rourke and Coleman 2009), YouTube (Watkins and Wilkins 2011) and technology for self-access learning (Warschauer and Liaw 2011) are just a sample. These different media provide both incentive and opportunity for language learning. Many learners have near-infinite access to information, resources for self-study and means for global communication, and are proficient in using these – often more so than their teachers. This is a development every classroom and every teacher needs to take account of, impacting as it does on our understanding of methods and materials, and the roles of both learners and teachers. Section 8.3 explores this issue in more detail and offers opportunities for teachers to evaluate digital resources and their impact on learning and teaching.

Table 2.5 Teaching methods, and your views and practice

	Audiolingual approach	Grammar-translation	Communicative approach	Humanistic approach
What the teacher does	Models correct language	Explains grammar rules	Facilitates real-life exchanges and situations	Mentors and supports individual learning
What the learner does	Mirrors and imitates examples of correct learning	Becomes a 'linguist' in understanding rules	Simulates and practises language for real-life settings outside the classroom	Negotiates personal learning goals with the teacher
Learning activities	Drilling correct language Chanting	Practising structures	Dialogues and role-play in lifelike contexts	Personalised learning
Learning goals	To use language forms correctly	To understand language rules and use them accurately	To communicate appropriately in social settings	To develop confidence and fluency in real-life settings
Your views and practice?				

Teacher narratives

As these areas of understanding have evolved, teachers' stories about their practice have entered the literature as legitimate contributions to knowledge. As a result, new ways of describing and explaining what we do have emerged, such as the analysis of critical incidents (Tripp 1995) and the exploring of commonality in teacher stories (Senior 2006, Tsui 2009). This means that when we discuss 'methods and methodologies', we need to do so with constant reference to 'real' teacher stories.

Task 2.7 Formulating your own teaching position

Table 2.5 summarises the methods presented in this chapter and some key words that characterise them. Review this chapter, and then add your own views about each method.

- Which approaches have you experienced, either as a teacher or as learner?
- What was your experience of these?
- As an 'eclectic' teacher, which strategies would you choose to use in a teaching context you are familiar with? Can you explain why or why not?

Task 2.8 Exploring Dogme online resources 🖥

The Dogme approach has generated hot debate amongst teachers. Some believe a rejection of published resources is unrealistic and impractical; others have identified with the approach fully and share their lesson plans, teaching ideas, class-created activities and materials. Explore these resources yourself by following the link: <http://www.teachingenglish.org.uk/articles/dogme-a-teachers-view>

Ask at least five teachers who you know what they think of the ideas you find on the Dogme website. See if you can find any similarities or connections between the teachers who are positive about these ideas, and any similarities or connections between those who are negative.

Task 2.9 Researching change: you and the forces of change

Explore the ways in which the English language teaching profession has changed by interviewing two or three teaching colleagues or friends. If you can, compare a teacher who is early in his or her career with another who has had ten or more years' experience in the profession.

- Ask them to tell you their professional stories: the start of the career, its challenges and changes, what was learnt on the way
- In what respects are their experiences different?
- In what respects are their experiences similar?
- In what respects have the demands, expectations, skills and approaches changed from the start of their careers to the present day?
- What are the main areas of change you have noticed? Do any of these match, confirm or contradict the 'forces of change' discussed in Section 2.3?
- Which of the changes do the teachers find energising and exciting? Which of them do they find troubling and challenging?
- How do your own experiences as a learner or teacher compare with theirs?

2.4 FURTHER READING 🖥

Explore the following further readings in the online resource for this book.

Task 2.10 Larsen-Freeman, D. (2000), 'The Dynamics of Methodological Change' (Chapter 12), *Techniques and Principles in Language Teaching*, Oxford: Oxford University Press.
Task 2.11 Bell, D. (2007), 'Do teachers think that methods are dead?', *ELT Journal* 61:2, 135–43.

2.5 CONCLUSION

This chapter asked the questions:

How do 'beliefs and attitudes to learning' affect language teaching methods?

This chapter has explored the 'chain of connection' between a teacher's view of language and learning and his or her teaching decisions in the class, and suggested that many teachers seek their own answers in response to their learners, rather than following a prescribed method. However, there is much to learn from debates about language methods as they change and evolve. Methods emerge from beliefs about how language is learnt, and how learning takes place, and offer a spectrum of views: from language as intellectual engagement with the language system, to language as a means of social interaction; from teacher as model of correct language to teacher as facilitator; and from learning as a process of error and correction to learning as an enabling process scaffolded by the teacher. These debates reveal the range of possible interpretations the teacher may have about learning and language, and the importance of making these beliefs explicit.

How have theories about language learning influenced the actual practice of language teachers?

The chapter also introduced you to the link between theories about language learning, and actual practice in the classroom such as audiolingual, grammar-translation, communicative or humanistic approaches: Suggestopedia, total physical response (TPR) or community language learning (CLL). We noted that, although each of these approaches may be critiqued, there are aspects of each which may be useful for the eclectic teacher, as long as we are able to make informed selections on the basis of our learners and our views about what is important in the classroom.

2.6 GUIDED READING

Kumaravadivelu, B. (2006), 'TESOL Methods: changing tracks, challenging trends', *TESOL Quarterly*, 40:1, 59–81

We will look in more detail at the article by Kumaravadivelu which ended Chapter 1. You are invited to read his account of the broad trends and changes over the past twenty-five years of the ELT profession.

As you read, think about the questions below:

- What do you think makes a method fashionable and what makes it fall out of fashion, according to Kumaravadivelu? (paragraphs 1 and 2)
- Kumaravadivelu critiques the audiolingual and the communicative methods in this article. What are his core criticisms? He goes on to say, in this article, that the two ended up not being that different from one another. Can you explain how it could be that two apparently different methods might in fact have much in common? (paragraphs 3 and 4)
- He ends up by making a broad claim for the profession becoming critical, and connecting 'the word with the world'. What could this phrase mean to you as a language user, as a teacher, or as a student? (paragraph 5)

Kumaravadivelu takes a historical view of the changes in teacher approaches to methods. Below are extracts from his article (2006) in which he poses the view that teachers themselves, and the varied contexts of learning and teaching, are more important than teaching orthodoxies.

Paragraph 1

This article traces the major trends in TESOL methods in the past 15 years. It focuses on the TESOL profession's evolving perspectives on language teaching methods in terms of three perceptible shifts: (a) from communicative language teaching to task-based language teaching, (b) from method-based pedagogy to postmethod pedagogy, and (c) from systemic discovery to critical discourse. It is evident that during this transitional period, the profession has witnessed a heightened awareness about communicative and task-based language teaching, about the limitations of the concept of method, about possible postmethod pedagogies that seek to address some of the limitations of method, about the complexity of teacher beliefs that inform the practice of everyday teaching, and about the vitality of the macrostructures–social, cultural, political, and historical – that shape the microstructures of the language classroom.

He starts by commenting on the supremacy of the communicative method in the 1980s.

Paragraph 2

During the 1980s, CLT (communicative language teaching) became such a dominant force that it guided the form and function of almost all conceivable components of language pedagogy. A steady stream of scholarly books appeared with the label *communicative* unfailingly stamped on the cover.

He explains this supremacy as a response to the audiolingual method:

Paragraph 3

CLT was a principled response to the perceived failure of the audiolingual method, which was seen to focus exclusively and excessively on the manipulation of the linguistic structures of the target language. Researchers and teachers alike became increasingly sceptical about the audiolingual method's proclaimed goal of fostering communicative capability in the learner and about its presentation–practice–production sequence. The proponents of CLT sought to move classroom teaching away from a largely structural orientation that relied on a reified rendering of pattern practices and toward a largely communicative orientation that relied on a partial simulation of meaningful exchanges that take place outside the classroom. They also introduced innovative classroom activities (such as games, role plays, and scenarios) aimed at creating and sustaining learner motivation. The focus on the learner and the emphasis on communication made CLT highly popular among ESL teachers.

He then goes on to critique the communicative method on the grounds that it was unable to deliver on its stated aims.

Paragraph 4

Legutke and Thomas (1991), Nunan (1987), and Thornbury (1996) reveal that the so-called communicative classrooms they examined were anything but communicative. In the classes he studied, Nunan (1987) observed that form was more prominent than function, and grammatical accuracy activities dominated communicative fluency ones. He concluded, 'There is growing evidence that, in communicative class, interactions may, in fact, not be very communicative after all' (p. 144). Legutke and Thomas (1991) were even more forthright: 'In spite of trendy jargon in textbooks and teachers' manuals, very little is actually communicated in the L2 classroom. The way it is structured does not seem to stimulate the wish of learners to say something, nor does it tap what they might have to say' (pp. 8–9).

Kumaravadivelu analysed lessons taught by teachers claiming to follow CLT, and confirmed these findings: 'Even teachers who are committed to CLT can fail to create opportunities for genuine interaction in their classroom' (Kumaravadivelu 2006: 113).

He describes the gradual disenchantment of the idea of the communicative approach, and its replacement with other ideas, such as task-based learning (TBL), 'exploratory practice' (EP) and the 'postmethod condition'. However, the broad pattern of change he describes is that of a move in the profession towards criticality.

Paragraph 5

During the 1990s, the TESOL profession took a decidedly critical turn. It is probably one of the last academic disciplines in the field of humanities and social sciences to go critical. Simply put, the critical turn is about connecting the word with the world. It is about recognising language as ideology, not just as system. It is about extending the educational space to the social, cultural, and political dynamics of language use, not just limiting it to the phonological, syntactic, and pragmatic domains of language usage. It is about realising that language learning and teaching is more than learning and teaching language. It is about creating the cultural forms and interested knowledge that give meaning to the lived experiences of teachers and learners.

The readings below will help you look further at particular methods, and critique them from your own perspective.

Swan, M. (1985), 'A critical look at the Communicative Approach', *ELT Journal*, **39:1, 2–11**

Klapper, J. (2003), 'Taking communication to task? A critical review of recent trends in language teaching', *Language Learning Journal*, **27, 33–42**

Swan identifies two core 'fallacies' of the communicative approach as follows:

The belief that students do not possess, or cannot transfer from their mother tongue, normal communication skills is one of two complementary fallacies that characterize the Communicative Approach. The other is the 'whole-system' fallacy. This arises when the linguist, over-excited about his or her analysis of a piece of language or behaviour, sets out to teach everything that has been observed – without stopping to ask how much of the teaching is a) new to the students and b) relevant to their needs. (Swan 1985, p. 10)

What is your view of the criticism that some methods try to 'teach everything that has been observed'? Which aspects of observed language behaviour do you think need not or should not be taught? Which aspects do you think should be taught?

Swan's criticisms of the communicative approach date from 1985. What additional perspective does Klapper give us in his criticism below?

With regard to theory, it is a surprise for many to discover that the so-called communicative approach has few clear links to second language acquisition research or second language acquisition theories; indeed, that it remains largely 'atheoretical' about learning. (Klapper 2003: 33)

How do these views compare with Kumaravadivelu's criticisms in the 2006 article you read above?

3

THE PLACE OF THE LEARNER IN METHODS

INTRODUCTION

This chapter asks the questions:

- Why is it important for the teacher to be aware of learner differences?
- What difference does this awareness make to the methods we choose as teachers?

Below are the stories of three learners who are all learning English; yet their reasons for learning, and the contexts within which they do so, are entirely different.

Teaching case study 3: Mexico
Ixchel is 14 years old and lives in Mexico, just near the Mexican-American border. She hears a great deal of American English through the media and through the mix of people who live locally, but her mother tongue is Spanish, and this is the language of her peer group and family. English is a compulsory subject at school, and part of the school leaving exam which will help her go to University, travel to the USA or get a good job.

Teaching case study 4: Japan
Tako is a 42-year-old Japanese businessman who works for a large Japanese company. He is required to learn English by his company if he wishes to be promoted to management level. This would require travelling and negotiating with non-Japanese clients. These clients are often not English speakers themselves, but English is the language which all the speakers use to communicate.

Teaching case study 5: UK
Vicente is six years old and has travelled from Somalia to England with his family as an asylum-seeker. He speaks French and three African languages, but only has a few words of English. He has started in a primary school in a suburb of London, and sits with children who have special educational needs such as dyslexia.

It is clear that a teacher would need to adapt approaches, methods, and materials to take account of the differences between these learners, even though core teaching philosophy might remain the same. Teachers may take different approaches to these variables. They may choose to consider, for example, the learner's age, reasons for learning the language, learning backgrounds, and whether or not there is exposure to English in his or her everyday life. There may, too, be further factors unique to the individual learner which the teacher may not be able to predict. Which of these are important? How can the teacher really take account of all of these?

This chapter will look at all the different ways we might need to interpret and respond to learner differences. In so doing, we will look at three key aspects: what is intrinsic to the learner him or herself, such as learning aptitude and personality; what is specific to the context and situation for learning (such as where, why and when teaching takes place); and finally, how these factors impact on the language itself – the kind of English language the learner needs, and its relationship to his or her community and everyday life.

3.1 THE INDIVIDUAL LEARNER AND METHODS

In a class of thirty learners, although the input and opportunities in class may be the same for all learners, it is inevitable that every learner will learn at a different pace. Some will absorb information seemingly rapidly and be able to use the language immediately in new situations; others may struggle with the same concepts and need much longer to absorb and apply them. Is it the nature of the lesson itself, or the teacher's methods or philosophy, that suits some learners and not others? Is there something specific to each individual learner, such as attitude to the language, motivation to learn, home context or classroom dynamic, which is making the difference? Are some learners just better than others? Studies in aptitude attempt to answer this last question.

Aptitude

Research into the question of aptitude has been taking place since 1955, with the introduction of the Modern Language Aptitude Test (MLAT) (Carroll and Sapon 1955) and the Pimsleur Language Aptitude Battery (LAB) (Pimsleur 1966). Carroll and Sapon identified four aspects of language learning which they considered determined aptitude:

- *Auditory ability*: such as the capacity to recognise, distinguish between, and imitate sounds
- *Grammatical sensitivity*: such as the ability to recognise patterns, analyse forms, extrapolate linguistic concepts
- *Inductive learning ability*: such as the ability to absorb language by exposure, rather than through formal and analytical learning
- *Memory*: such as the ability to retain new vocabulary items, rules and irregularities

These aptitudes may be demonstrated in a number of ways.

Imagine you are encountering an entirely new language for the first time. In Table 3.1 are some words in the new language which you might find in a dictionary.

If you were deploying the aptitude of a good memory, you might simply learn the list. If you were deploying the aptitude of grammatical sensitivity, you might make

Table 3.1   Aztec language: decoding a new language

Aztec	English
ikalwewe	big house
ikalsosol	old house
ikalcin	little house
komitwewe	big cooking pot
komitsosol	old cooking pot
petawewe	big mat
petasosol	old mat
petacin	little mat
komitmeh	cooking pots
petameh	mats
koyamecin	little pig
koyamemeh	pigs

deductions. For example, you might see samples of language as patterns and examples of the whole, and start to analyse and deconstruct.

You might have been able to find:

1. Ways in which the plural is marked in Aztec (the morpheme *meh*)
2. The Aztec items for house (*ikal*), cooking pot (*komit*), mat (*peta*), and pig (*koya*) (nouns)
3. The Aztec items for big (*wewe*), old (*sosol*), little (*cin*) (adjectives)
4. The ways in which the items in (2) are joined into one word with the items in (3) (adjectives and nouns). Aztec is agglutinative: that is, there is a tendency for words to 'grow' and attach to one another, as with big cooking pot = *komitwewe*
5. Aspects of Aztec word order: noun comes before the adjective rather than vice versa as in English
6. A sound pattern in each word of consonant/vowel/consonant/vowel

However, there are important criticisms of the aptitude argument, which have made it enter, disappear and then re-enter professional debate. In 1982, Krashen claimed that aptitude was irrelevant, as all learners followed a 'natural order' of acquisition, in which some language elements are learnt early, and others later and more slowly; and that these processes are common across all language users and abilities. Another criticism is that 'intelligence' is neither fixed, nor culturally neutral. For example, learners who have had a great deal of practice and experience in activities such as the one above are likely to find it easier than those with none. Similarly, a learner who tries out this activity in the spirit of adventure, play or experiment, may perform very differently to the learner who is presented with this as part of a test, in a formal time-limited setting which entails assessment. In other words, aptitude is not a fixed capacity, but is capable of change. The article by Hirano (2009) in Further Reading task 1 (Section 3.4) gives an example of a learner who has 'learnt' that he finds English difficult, and has had to 'unlearn' this in order to be successful.

But it is this very argument which has meant the idea of aptitude has re-entered professional conversations. Robinson writes that aptitude 'has been retheorized as a dynamic, potentially trainable concept' (Robinson 2007: 258). Recent research recognises that notions of aptitude need to be much more closely linked to the 'daily conditions of classroom learning and practice' (Robinson 2008: 270). Skehan (2002) revisited the components of aptitude identified above, connecting them instead to the way learners process a second language. He suggested four kinds of processing which happen:

Noticing the new language
Patterning the new language, so it is possible to make generalisations
Controlling the analysed knowledge in production
Lexicalising or varying the patterns to meet different communicative needs
(Skehan 2002; Robinson 2008)

Through instructed learning, there is the likelihood that these qualities of successful learning can be developed and enhanced. This presents some hope for the teacher as well as for the learner. It also gives the teacher a detailed understanding of the generic skills that may lead to success. In Table 3.2 are examples of how Skehan's four components can be developed and encouraged by the teacher.

Table 3.2   Skehan's four components of aptitude (Skehan 2002)

Skehan's four components of aptitude	Examples of teacher actions
Noticing	Notice ways in which a text refers to past time: He *used to* leave every day at 7 a.m. Every day *he would stop* in the square to drink at the fountain. She *had seen* him walk that way every day. Yet today *he didn't appear.*
Patterning	Invite learners to notice patterns (for example: past-participle endings in words such as *caught, taught, fought, thought*)
Controlling	Set up controlled activities which simulate real-life activities to practise 'noticed' language (for example:complete a diary with arrangements, and practise ways of expressing future time. Some suggestions are: *I'm busy on Monday; I'll be in school on Tuesday evening; I'm going away at the weekend*)
Lexicalising	Move towards free opportunities for learners to try out the language independently through tasks, activities, or projects (for example: interview a grandparent or older relation and ask them to tell you a story about their childhood. Write down the story, practising different ways of referring to past time)

Age

There is a common belief amongst teachers and researchers that children up to the age of seven have a 'plasticity' in their abilities which allows them to learn language rapidly and successfully. Chomsky called this capacity the LAD, or Language Acquisition Device, and Skinner called it the 'black box' (Skinner 1961). In the real classroom world, teachers and parents such as the one below offer many examples of children who learned a second language before the age of seven, apparently to native speaker standard, and without any transfer of pronunciation from the first language into the second. By contrast, older children and adults seem to retain 'interference' from their mother tongue, such as an accent. Here is one teacher, working in a primary school in north London, UK, contrasting the learning of a second language by a six-year-old boy with that of his parents.

Teaching case study 6: a Somali learner in the UK

Vicente arrived with his family from Somalia at the age of six. He spoke very little at school for the first three months, and I was concerned; but at Christmas, when Santa Claus arrived at playtime to distribute presents, I heard him talking completely fluently and confidently to Santa, asking him for a football for Christmas. He also learnt his words perfectly for the pantomime. Both his parents came to the pantomime and were clearly thrilled to see this, hugely proud. They came to thank me, and they had learnt this one line off by heart: 'Thank you teacher, we are very happy.' Vicente had now far outstripped them in his English, and was teaching them the phrases they needed to communicate.

Cook suggests this teacher story is typical: 'My new postgraduate overseas students prove this annually. They start the year by worrying whether their children will cope with English, and they end it by complaining how much better the children speak than themselves,' (Cook 1991:83). Yet these examples, though typical, are not as straightforward to interpret as they seem. Research evidence in favour of the superiority of young children has proved surprisingly hard to find. Much research, on the contrary, shows that age is a positive advantage (Cook 1991: 84).

In fact, studies with Finnish (Urponen 2004), Hungarian (Nikolov 2000) and German (Moyer 1999) language speakers suggest that age and learning capacity are quite complex. Nikolov and Djigunovic (2012) arrive at the view that a critical age hypothesis is no longer tenable, since learners in these studies were able to attain proficiency even though they began learning languages after puberty. It is possible to see that the adult learner has learning skills and a conscious understanding of language patterns and processes which make him or her 'catch up' and overtake the child learner.

The implications of this for the language teacher are promising. There are benefits to learning at each stage if the teacher is aware of these and exploits them. The child, for example, may have the tendency to enjoy learning through play, without needing conscious and explicit explanation of language. The adult may have the skills of recognising rules and patterns, making connections between the first and second language, and understanding how language works in the social world. Whilst both are important and valuable skills in the language learning process, it might be that

Table 3.3   Teaching young learners, teaching adults: what the teacher can do

The teacher of young learners	The teacher of adults
can draw on the child's capacity to 'acquire'– to learn unconsciously without needing the mediation of rules, explanations and technical language can draw on the child's desire to communicate and belong to a peer group can draw on the child's capacity to play	can draw on the adult's cognitive understanding, e.g. of patterns, rules, comparisons can draw on the adult's knowledge of the mother tongue: e.g. comparisons between L1 and L2 can draw on the adult's experience of social and cultural conventions; e.g. politeness strategies, conversational principles can draw on the adult's knowledge of the world: e.g. loan words between languages, technical words

the teacher skews the lesson to meet the expectations of the class, or what he or she knows works best with this particular group of learners (Table 3.3).

Learner strategies and the 'good language learner'
What are strategies and why are they important?

A strategy might give us insight into the question: what do learners actually do when they learn? Although this seems to be a very central and relevant question, researchers have only recently begun to search for answers to this question. The most comprehensive attempt to do so was by Oxford (2002), whose analysis of learner strategies is based on a core belief that learning is not simply determined by cognitive or intellectual capacities, but by the 'whole person'. She identified six key categories in answer to the question: what does the learner actually do, when learning?

Language learning strategies
Learners tend to:

1. seek to reduce anxiety about learning, by laughing and using praise and encouragement: (*affective strategies*)
2. learn from and with others by asking questions, sharing and exchanging ideas (*social strategies*)
3. notice and correct errors, check their progress and appreciate correction (*metacognitive strategies*)
4. develop their memories by means of grouping, visualising, patterns and rhymes (*memory strategies*)
5. analyse, summarise and practice (*cognitive strategies*)
6. find ways of dealing with 'not knowing' –asking questions, guessing, finding alternative ways of saying something (*compensatory strategies*)
   (Oxford 2002: 127)

Researchers for several decades have tried to answer the question: are there particular strategies which good language learners tend to use? Do some strategies have more likelihood of leading to proficiency in a language than others? One of the first studies investigating these questions was by Naiman et al. (1996). The researchers analysed learners who had successfully mastered a second language. They found that good language users tend to:

- find a way to learn that suits them best, irrespective of what is happening in class
- fully engage in learning activities – for example, participating in class activities, following up their learning
- be active in finding opportunities for learning that go beyond what the teacher offers them in the lesson
- continually seek to improve and develop their language knowledge, such as by asking native speakers to correct them, or checking new words in the dictionary
- be aware that language is not just a classroom subject, but a form of communication applied to the real world, involving action and interaction
- try and separate the new language from the mother tongue, so they are not trying to translate between the two, but to think and function in the second language
- not feel that their dignity or identity are threatened if they make mistakes – they are not worried about 'looking silly' when creating new sounds, or mispronouncing words
  (Cook 1991: 81)

What is interesting is that several of these strategies happen irrespective of what the teacher does. Good language learners will learn, whether or not the teacher teaches. When Nunan conducted his own research amongst 44 'good' language learners, he came to the following conclusion:

> Despite the diverse contexts and environments in which the subjects learned English, practically all agreed that formal classroom instruction was insufficient.
> (Nunan 1991: 175)

Effective learning might be seen as a halfway meeting between the learner and the teacher. 'Good learning' clearly cannot take place without learners themselves, but can it take place without a teacher? Below is an example of highly effective learning which took place without the intervention of a teacher:

Teaching case study 7: Calcutta, India
The project began by asking a question about children in the slum areas of India, starting with Calcutta. With lack of a physical location for school, or the funds to pay teachers, these children had little chance of going to school, but could schooling instead come to them?

A computer was bricked into the wall of the village square, at the height of a ten-year-old child, and a camera was trained on the computer to see if, how and when it was used over a period of three months.

During this time, more and more children of all ages gathered around the computer. The older children were lifting up the younger ones so they could see; the

Table 3.4   Research into the good language learner: implications for the teacher

Do	Don't
Provide the stimulus and opportunity for learning Allow learners the opportunity to ask the questions they choose, and provide the resources to find the answers Accept that learning can take place informally, through play and experimentation, and provide opportunities for this. Accept that what is learnt cannot be planned or predicted	Underestimate the capacity of a learner to develop new skills and strategies, if given the chance Assume or stereotype what you think a learner is capable of: 'he or she won't be able to achieve that because . . .' could well be wrong

twelve-year-old girls were planning rotas so everyone had a chance. The children had learnt to access Google, play computer games and listen to music. They were even accessing English lessons and copying the accent on screen.

All this took place with children who had had no formal education of any kind, and could not read or write before the computer appeared in their village square. There had also been no adult intervention apart from the supply of the resource itself (Mitra 2011).

Task 3.1 Learning from the Hole in the Wall Project: Learners as research resource 🖥

View this 2011 online talk from one of the founder researchers of the Hole in the Wall Project, Sugata Mitra: <www.ted.com/speakers/sugata_mitra.html>

- What does the Calcutta case study example tell us about creating a good learning environment?
- What does it tell us about what a teacher can and cannot do to make a difference?

Note down your ideas and then compare them with the implications listed in Table 3.4. These are some implications for the teacher in keeping alive the learning excitement which is often more evident outside the classroom than inside it.

Learning and learner identity

We have seen that learning a language is not as simple as following instruction in a classroom. Learners may deploy strategies which make them successful, or they may even choose not to do so because they feel success in the second language is not desirable. Ehrman and Dörnyei (1998: 184) say 'language learning frequently entails new thought processes, identity, and values that can present a threat to learners'.

Pavlenko and Lantolf (2000) describe changes in identity that take place when learning a second language. They suggest that these changes are often triggered by events which to the outsider may seem to be just small adjustments to the target language. Hoffman (1989), newly arrived from Poland, describes her first day in a new school in the United States. She (Ewa) and her sister Alina are renamed 'Eva' and 'Elaine' by the teacher. Ewa explains how, on the outside, 'nothing much has happened, except a small, seismic mental shift. The twist in our names takes them a tiny distance from us' (Hoffman 1989: 105). She describes this distance as a 'gap' which makes language increasingly less meaningful and disconnected from real life and her inner world:

> I wait for that spontaneous flow of inner language which used to be my night-time talk with myself . . . Nothing comes. Polish, in a short time, has atrophied, shriveled from sheer uselessness. (Hoffman 1989: 107)

Thus, the change in language becomes a change in self and identity; it changes what she is able to express and what it is acceptable to feel. Only gradually she finds it possible to take possession, or 'appropriate' the new language:

> Eventually the voices enter me, by assuming them I gradually make them mine. (Hoffman 1989: 219–20)

Although Hoffman's story is specific to herself, it does represent the complexity of experiences learners may have in acquiring a new language. It shows us that this is not just about linguistic development, but a much broader question of how language represents our 'selves'. Pavlenko and Lantolf (2000) describe this development as a process of 'reorganization' in which learners are

> forced to reorganize, and in some cases organize anew, the plots of their life stories in line with the new set of conventions and social relationships sanctioned by the new community in which they find themselves. The result is the formation of new ways to mean. (Pavlenko and Lantolf 2000: 219)

For teachers, this may help us to understand blocks and leaps in the learning process, which go beyond linguistic skill alone.

Task 3.2 Research task: crossing language identities

Find two or three friends, colleagues, or relations who speak more than one language. Interview them and find out:

- Are there words, concepts, ways of categorising and describing in their mother tongue or first language which do not match the second language? For example, names and nicknames, ways of addressing seniors, relations and friends?
- Are any words, concepts, ways of categorising in the second language surprising, difficult or alien in contrast to the first language?
- When do they feel most comfortable/natural/fluent speaking the mother tongue?
- When do they feel most comfortable/natural/fluent speaking the second language?

Task 3.3 Teaching task
Think about the research information you might have gathered from Task 3.2 above.

- Do you think teachers take account of ideas and experiences which might be difficult to express in the L2?
- Do you think teachers should give opportunities for learners to share their knowledge of the mother tongue in the English classroom? If so, how could this best be done to benefit all learners?

Think about your own answers, drawing upon:

- A situation in which you were a learner
- A situation in which you observed another teacher teaching language

3.2 LEARNER CONTEXTS

This section will consider the multiple reasons and motivations which lead learners to an English language classroom, and the ways these may be influenced by context. We will analyse the context of learning according to *where* it happens physically, *how* it happens professionally and *why* it happens pedagogically.

3.2.1 WHERE LEARNING HAPPENS: LOCATION

Whilst we can make many general statements about what all learners share, what teachers will find most important are the conditions unique to their classrooms. A classroom is more than simply a physical location; surrounding it is a political, geographical, economic, cultural and social context that impacts on what is happening inside the room. For some teachers, what happens outside this room is as important as, or even more important than, what happens inside.

Teaching case study 8: Hungary
In this case study we consider the dual language school in Hungary, a concept in which children experience total English language immersion in their school studies. The following are some features which are specific to the Hungarian context:

- The language is structurally and historically distinct from the Indo-European languages of its neighbours and related only to Estonian and Finnish. This means there are few opportunities to travel, work and socialise in Hungarian outside Hungary itself
- For a generation, Russian was the compulsory foreign language and contacts outside Communist/Soviet contexts were discouraged. This has been entirely supplanted, and a new generation has grown up with full opportunities within Europe and worldwide
- Opening up to the West after 1989 involved both a 'dearth of qualified professionals'

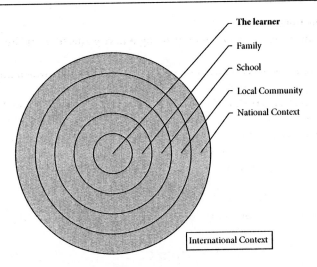

Figure 3.1   The learner's context: teaching onion

to teach English (5,000 vacancies for EFL teachers – Dörnyei 1992), a growing demand for English instruction, and a mushrooming of agencies investing in FL teaching in Hungary (Duff 1997: 21)

- The schools were fee-paying and supported by parents who found it 'increasingly important and desirable for their children to have the opportunity to learn marketable foreign languages well at school' (Duff 1997: 42)

A learner in this school, therefore, is representative of a great deal more than him or herself. Surrounding learners in this school are parents, ambitious to give the younger generation bilingual opportunities; other schools and schoolchildren who do not have the opportunity or financial resources to attend schools of this kind; the ministry and government bodies who do not recognise the International Baccalaureate qualification offered by the school. These layers of influence can be represented like an onion, with the learners at the centre and the different circles of influence around them (see Figure 3.1).

3.2.2 HOW LEARNING HAPPENS: PROFESSIONAL CULTURE

Holliday (1994) introduced an entirely different way of explaining the context of language learning, based not on regional location but rather on the *professional culture* of the learning. He described the distinction between two very different settings, which he labelled BANA (British, Australasia and North America) and TESEP (tertiary, secondary and primary):

BANA comprises an innovative, often predatory culture of integrated skills which is located in the private sector or in commercially-run centres in universities and

Table 3.5   Holliday's notions of BANA and TESEP (Holliday 1994)

	BANA	TESEP
Teacher qualifications	Multiple qualification routes, including locally based and US/UK-based such as CELTA, DELTA	State qualified through mainstream training
Relationship with national educational policies	Connected to English/US exam systems such as Cambridge ESOL, IELTS and TESOL tests	Controlled by national curriculum, educational policy, national status of English and state exams
Teacher–student link	Teacher may not share the same L1 or background culture as the learners, and may be living and working in a second culture	Likely to share the same L1 and background culture as the majority of learners, and be living and working in home culture
Resources	Teachers and schools independently able to make their own selections of resources	Controlled by school or national policy: prescribed coursebooks, tests and resources
Class demography	Could be self-funded learners with class sizes limited to an optimum: e.g. British Council limit of 16	Likely to be large classes homogeneous in age and directed towards the same prescribed learning goals

colleges in Britain, Australasia and North America. TESEP comprises a more traditional culture of collections of academic subjects, which is located in state, tertiary, secondary or primary schools throughout the world. (Holliday 2005: 3)

This distinction is useful, because there are many consequences for the teacher determined by which of these two settings he/she works within. Table 3.5 identifies some of these consequences.

However, Holliday himself has come to critique the distinction. His concern is that because the BANA professionals tend to come from the English-speaking West, they have increasingly been regarded as the 'centre' of English language learning, while the TESEP professionals have been regarded as 'peripheral' (Holliday 2005: 3).

3.2.3 WHY LEARNING HAPPENS: NEEDS ANALYSIS

In addition, our teaching is importantly determined by what it is the learner actually needs. Hutchinson and Waters (1987) suggested that learner needs could be grouped into three categories:

- *Necessities,* or 'what the learner has to know in order to function effectively in the target situation' (Hutchinson and Waters 1987: 55). For example, pilots learning Aeronautical English must crucially learn the 'lingua franca' of 'air language', such as the way letters of the alphabet are spelled out internationally (A for Alpha, T for Tango, O for Oscar and so on). Necessities can be planned by analysing and understanding in detail the target situation where the language will be used.

- *Lacks,* or the gap between the learners' current level and the level they are aiming for. For example, a learner passes a University entrance test with a 5.5 average. 6.5 is the average needed to win a place at the university. She will need to calculate in detail what skills, knowledge and competence are needed to bridge the gap between her current level and the one required.
- *Wants* may be different from both the necessities and the lacks. For example, a student might *need* to write academic English to pass a written test, but might *want* in addition to learn general and colloquial spoken English for travelling, socialising and applying for jobs.

Teaching case study 9: a middle school in Daejeon, South Korea

Below is a case study of a teacher in South Korea described by Parent (2009).
Where: the fifth largest city in South Korea, with a population of 1.5 million
Who: classes of 25 children, mostly from lower-middle-class families
What: 'All students, regardless of level, must follow the same textbook and do so at the same pace' (Parent 2009: 190)
How: through a 'textbook package' called *Middle School English*, which includes topics such as favourite foods, giving directions, and holidays. Each lesson is 14 pages long and follows the same pattern, which includes practising listening, speaking, reading and writing in that order. After every three lessons, there is a four-page test.

The issues:

- 'There is no needs analysis of the learners, because the National Curriculum effectively tells students what they need' (Parent 2009: 190)
- 'The teachers feel that the curriculum is designed with the low-level students in mind and note that high-level students tend to get bored'(Parent 2009)
- Class time is spent working through the coursebook, and there is therefore very little time for activities or materials created by the teacher to meet the needs of learners.

Task 3.4 You as teacher and needs analyst

You have been offered a post in the classroom in Daejeon described above. How would you identify the needs of the class in terms of:

- The *necessities* – what you will have to teach the class
- The possible *wants* of a child in the class
- Several of the children are failing the four-page test. What are the possible *lacks* you might try and resolve as a teacher? (Parent 2009: 190–4)

Table 3.6   Semi-structured interview topics: BANA and TESEP teaching contexts

Teacher qualifications	What are the criteria or qualifications for becoming a teacher in your school/context?
Relationship with national educational policies	Do you have to follow a national or a school curriculum?
Teacher–student link	Would you say your relationship with your learners was friendly or formal? Do you use first names or second names? How do they address you?
Resources	Are you able to choose your own resources? Are you able to plan your own materials and lessons?
Class demography	Can you describe a typical learner in your class?
Your own questions	

Task 3.5 Researching BANA and TESEP settings

If you can, interview one teacher from a BANA, or private language school setting, and another from a TESEP, or state sector school. In Table 3.6 are some questions which you might ask them, but you may want to add other questions of your own, based on Table 3.5.

Note down the differences and similarities between the two teachers.

Then compare your notes to Table 3.5 on page 46.

Task 3.6 Web task: exploring learner profiles 🖥

Explore profiles of learners in UK schools written by their teachers.
NALDIC learner profiles: <http://www.naldic.org.uk/eal-teaching-and-learning/outline-guidance/pupil-portraits>

- What information do the profiles give us about the learner variables that influence the child's experience in class – for example, their personality, learning background, home background, age?
- How do the teachers take account of the needs of the children?

3.3 LANGUAGE CONTEXTS: WHICH ENGLISH?

This section considers the way in which the positioning of English in the classroom will impact on methods and methodological choices, for example, whether English is a second or a foreign language, what the 'standard' English is considered to be – British, American, or World English – and what the relationship with an English-speaking community is perceived to be (or not to be). In addition, it will consider attitudes to the native and non-native speaking teacher and the positioning of the English language in the community, and consider how these contexts impact on methods and methodologies.

Ownership of English: who owns English?

Kachru (1985) has devised a model illustrating the use of English in the world in terms of three concentric circles:

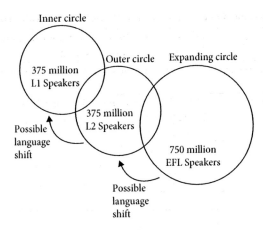

Figure 3.2   Kachru's notion of the language circles

- **Inner Circle**: territories in which English is the first or main language
- **Outer circle**: territories in Asia and Africa where English was first transported in colonial contexts and where it has coexisted with local languages
- **Expanding circle:** territories in which English has become, or is becoming, the most important foreign language

Graddol (1997), Jenkins (2012) and Seidlhofer (2011) draw from this model the following facts, which have an important impact on how we perceive ourselves as English language teachers and learners:

1. Native speakers are no longer the largest or most important users of English
2. There is a great deal of movement between the three groups, as L2 speakers of English are becoming L1 speakers, and EFL speakers are moving into ESL contexts
3. English is moving into an era where speakers of English as a first language will lose influence, as most communication will be among those using it as a second or foreign language

How will changes in the role of English affect the learner?

Learning English in the inner circle offers high potential incentives for learning, as the learner is exposed daily to the target language. It also offers opportunities for the teacher to use the 'language of the streets' as a pedagogic resource, as Sayer (2010) does in her example of Spanish language teaching in Mexico. Learning English in this context can generate views such as these:

Throughout the history of the Nation, the common thread binding those of differing backgrounds has been a common language; in order to preserve unity in diversity, and to prevent division along linguistic lines, the United States should maintain a language common to all people; English has historically been the common language and the language of opportunity in the US. By

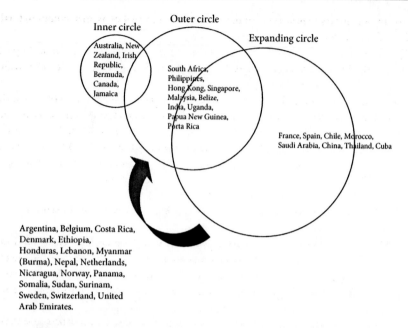

Figure 3.3   Kachru's notion of movement between inner and outer circles

learning the English language, immigrants will be empowered with the language skills and literacy necessary to become responsible citizens and productive workers in the US. – From the Bill Emerson English Language Empowerment Act, presented to the US House of Representatives on 4 January 1995

Learning English in the outer circle carries with it a linguistic history. There may be resistance to the language as one that entailed colonisation. Here is Mahatma Gandhi – a learner and user of English in his native country of India, where he grew up during the years it was a colony of the British Empire – writing in 1908:

> To give millions a knowledge of English is to enslave them . . . Is it not a painful thing that, if I want to go to a court of justice, I must employ the English language as a medium; that when I became a Barrister, I may not speak my mother tongue, and that someone else should have to translate to me from my own language? Is this not absolutely absurd? Is it not a sign of slavery?

Edge and Garton (2009) create, as an important category in understanding the learner, his or her 'ownership' of the language being learnt. They make three important points about the ownership of English, which have important implications for what and how we teach:

- The important issue is not one of native/non-native speaker as an accident of birth, but of ability to use the language internationally.
- Native speakers of national Englishes (British, US American, etc.) are only partners in the international language. They also have to learn communication strategies if they are to use it effectively (Garton and Edge 2009: 32).
- Kachru argued in 1985 that 'native speakers of this language seem to have lost the exclusive prerogative to control its standardisation: in fact, if current statistics are any indication, they have become a minority' (Kachru 1985: 30). There are not only fewer speakers of 'standard' BBC English than other regional English varieties, but also fewer native speakers of English than non-native speakers using it as a second language.

These points have important implications for teacher choices in the classroom.

- If you are a native speaker of English, it means your language variety should not be regarded as the yardstick of correctness. You might need to accommodate the English used locally where you are teaching, and the English accepted within that community as standard, even where that differs from your own notions of the standard.
- It also means that, whether you are a native speaker of English or not, the skills of effective communication need to be consciously and actively developed as part of a linguistic repertoire. These skills are discussed in Chapter 9 of this book, which focuses on competences across cultures and languages.

What does the change in ownership of English mean for teaching and learning English?

In 1985 the linguist and grammarian Randolph Quirk and the historian of language and pedagogy Braj Kachru took opposite positions on the question: which English for teachers and learners? Their position is summarised in Table 3.7. As you read you

Table 3.7   Which English? Two contrasting answers

Randolph Quirk's position	Braj Kachru's position
Quirk argued for the need to uphold standards in the use of English in both Inner Circle countries and those outside the Inner Circle. He maintained that tolerance for variation in language use was educationally damaging in Inner Circle countries, and that 'the relatively narrow range of purposes for which the non-native needs to use English is arguably well catered for by a single monochrome standard form that looks as good on paper as it sounds in speech'. (Mackay 2002: 50)	'In my view the global diffusion of English has taken an interesting turn: the native speakers of this language seem to have lost the exclusive prerogative to control its standardization: in fact, if current statistics are any indication, they have become a minority. This sociolinguistic fact must be accepted and its implication recognized'. (Kachru 1985: 30)

may like to consider how the situation has changed since 1985, and where you stand in relation to these two positions.

Task 3.7 Researching attitudes to language choice: where do you sit in the language debate?

The two views below represent opposing answers to the question, 'Which English should be taught and learnt in different parts of the world?'

'To give millions a knowledge of English is to enslave them.' – Mahatma Gandhi, 1908	'The common thread binding those of differing backgrounds has been a common language.' – Bill Emerson English Language Empowerment Act, 1995

David Crystal expands these two ideas in his book *Global English* (Crystal 2002: ix):

I believe in the fundamental value of multilingualism, as an amazing world resource which presents us with different perspectives and insights, and thus enables us to reach a more profound understanding of the nature of the human mind and spirit.	**I believe in the fundamental value of a common language**, as an amazing world resource which presents us with unprecedented possibilities for mutual understanding, and thus enables us to find fresh opportunities for international cooperation.

- Where would you place yourself, with reference to the context in which you use English, either as a teacher or as a learner?
- Can you explain your positioning?
- If you can, share these quotations with five English language teachers. Ask them to share their views about these two quotations.
- What similarities and differences did you notice in their position? Can you explain these with reference to the cultural, political, personal or educational context in which they teach English.

Task 3.8 Reflecting as a teacher in the world classroom

Pennycook, A. (2000), 'The social politics and the cultural politics of the language classroom', in J. K. Hall and W. A. Eggington (2000), *The Sociopolitics of English Language Teaching*, Clevedon: Multilingual Matters, pp. 89–103

Pennycook's key claim is that 'classrooms, both in themselves and in their relationship to the world beyond their walls, are complex social and cultural spaces' (Pennycook 2000: 89). He illustrates his claim with reference to two classrooms. Classroom 1 is described in Case Study 10 on page 53.

You as 'ethnographer' of the classroom

As you read the account below, identify what you would consider to be the key challenges here for the learner in the classroom. What would you identify as the key challenges for the English language teacher?

Canagarajah's view was that the classroom could be in some ways a safe sanctuary from the outside world, whilst being interlinked with it. He describes classrooms as a 'social and cultural domain unto themselves' which the teacher can significantly influence (Canagarajah 1993: 605).

Do you agree or disagree with Canagarajah's approach? Which aspects of the learning environment do you think you could influence for the better as a teacher?

Teaching case study 10: University of Jaffna, Sri Lanka; Suresh Canagarajah's classroom

Who: 22 first-year students, 13 female and 9 male Tamil students, mainly from rural communities and the poorest economic groups. Most come from families which have had little opportunity for education, and they have no use for English in their lives beyond the classroom.

Where: Jaffna is at the centre of the political tensions between the Sinhala government and Tamil nationalists; government bombs fall in the region of the university while university tests are taking place.

When: The university has started later in the academic year because of these 'renewed hostilities'.

What: English language is compulsory for all students at the University, and the set coursebook is *American Kernel Lessons: Intermediate* (O'Neill 1978).

Pennycook goes on to compare the Sri Lanka and the Toronto learning settings, identifying the following factors that are significant in the analysis:

Social class
Age
Ethnicity
Gender
Location

Teaching case study 11: a Chinese community centre, Toronto, Canada; Classroom 2

Who: In a class of 15, all 'claim Chinese ethnicity'; 13 from Hong Kong, 2 from Malaysia and Taiwan; 11 women and 4 men, and 12 over the age of fifty. Students enrol continuously, and groups are mixed ability with no compulsory testing. Students can stay in the class as long as they need to, so in one group there may be new arrivals and others who have been there some years. They come from a variety of different social classes.

What: The teacher has some autonomy over what is learnt and how, and can adapt these to the needs and level of the learners.

Pennycook suggests two opposing views of the politics of the classroom.

Classrooms are themselves contained social spaces. The teacher, thus, can work towards a 'democratic' classroom in which students and teachers share the power – for example, students asking questions as well as the teacher; student and teacher negotiating the content of the lesson; students learning from one another in group and pair work.	'Classrooms cannot be separated from the outside world. Whatever the teacher does, students do not leave their social relations, their rural upbringings or their relationships to their parents at the classroom door' (Pennycook 2000: 92). Thus what the teacher can do to influence power relationships is very limited.

You as reader and analyst

Where do you stand along a spectrum between these two approaches?

Do you think as a teacher you might be able to create a contained social space in the classroom? Or it impossible to change what the learners bring into the space? Or is the answer somewhere in between these two positions?

Locate yourself along the spectrum and compare your view with Pennycook's position below. Then write a statement of your own explaining your own position.

> Everything outside the classroom, from language policies to cultural contexts of schooling, may have an impact on what happens in the classroom. And everything in the classroom, from how we teach, what we teach and how we respond to students, to the materials we use and the ways we assess students, needs to be seen as social and cultural practices with broad implications. The challenge is to understand these relationships and to find ways of always focusing on the local while at the same time keeping an eye on the broader horizons. The view of our classroom walls as permeable means that what we do in our classrooms is about changing the worlds we live in (Pennycook 2000: 102).

Your position

Task 3.9 Exploring world Englishes 🖥

This website gives you an overview of corpora worldwide of English and Englishes, including English from East Africa, New Zealand, India, the Philippines, Singapore and Europe. Each corpus draws on a million or more words of written data: <http://www.corpora4learning.net/resources/corpora.html>

- Explore the ways in which English varies in different settings, cultures and countries.
- How might you use this resource in the classroom?

3.4 FURTHER READING 🖳

Explore the following further readings in the online resource for this book.

Task 3.10 Hirano, E. (2009), 'Learning difficulty and learner identity: a symbiotic relationship', *English Language Teaching Journal*, 63: 1, 33–41

Task 3.11 Barkhuizen, G. (2008), 'A narrative approach to exploring context in language teaching', *English Language Teaching Journal*, 62: 231–9

3.5 CONCLUSION

This chapter asked the questions:

Why is it important for the teacher to be aware of learner differences?
This chapter suggested that the factors influencing the individual learner are both personal and distinctive to each learner, such as their age, personality, identity and aptitude; and also external to the learner, such as the school, community and context within which the learning takes place. Being aware of these differences helps the teacher to recognise what can be enhanced and empowered in the classroom (such as attitude and aptitude); and what cannot be changed (such as the learning context), but can be accommodated.

What difference does this understanding make to the methods we choose as teachers?
Understanding learner differences can also help the teacher to choose approaches which are appropriate, and to understand why some methods work and others do not. A method is not in itself successful or effective; it is 'good or bad' as a method, only insofar as it 'fits' with the learners themselves. Thus, the more we understand about the learners and the context of learning, the better we are able to adapt, select and refine our methods.

3.6 GUIDED READING

Benson, P. and D. Nunan (2005), *Learners' Stories*, Cambridge: Cambridge University Press
This book explores the experiences of learners with a focus on 'how learners become diverse' (Benson and Nunan 2005: 2). The authors have collected their data through interview, dialogue, written stories and storytelling, offering rich insight into learner autobiographies. Their 'mission' in this project is to examine psychological and social factors

> with their development over time, with the relationship of these developments to the learners' broader life circumstances and goals, and with the ways in which they are influenced by learners' active involvement in the learning process.
> (Benson and Nunan 2005: 2)

As the authors explain, the use of autobiographical data as a research resource is relatively new, and the criteria for quality, and procedures for analysis, are still in a process of development. The authors draw on the stories by 'noticing' and analysing emerging topics: motivation, emotion, age, learning strategies and beliefs, identity and the influence of classroom, distance and self-instructional settings. Teachers and readers may be inspired through the methods of the authors to gather and explore their own examples of learner stories.

Holliday, A. (2005), *The Struggle to Teach English as an International Language*, Oxford: Oxford University Press

Simpson, J. (2007), 'Review of Holliday, A.: *The Struggle to teach English as an International Language*' in *Applied Linguistics*, 28:1, 147–50

Below is a review of Holliday's book discussed in Section 3.3 above. Note in the review what it is that the reviewer considers essential in Holliday's message, and what he considers the implications for TESOL professional practice are.

In this intriguing, uncompromising book Adrian Holliday aims to show how a dominant 'native-speakerist' attitude which espouses a culturalist, essentialist philosophy has contaminated Western TESOL. Native-speakerism divides the TESOL world into 'us' and 'them'. Its ill-effects, argues Holliday, are evident in ideology and approach to teaching, in method and materials, and in management style. Moreover, native-speakerism has the potential to pervade TESOL practice wherever English-speaking Western TESOL educators have an influence. In this respect, the book continues an established critical tradition which views native speakers as an obstacle to the development of English as an International Language. In contrast, Holliday posits as preferable an ideal 'position 2'. This position sees no distinction between 'us' and 'them'. Because of global changes in TESOL and the English-speaking world, we (inclusively) need to learn to adopt this second position. This means that we view English as international, geographically unshackling the language from the English-speaking West. In other words, English belongs to all, and local contexts of use become the norm. This thesis of dichotomy is maintained as a thread of argument throughout the book, in which much current TESOL practice is criticised as native-speakerist – sometimes very convincingly, and sometimes just a little too neatly.

SECTION TWO: THE LANGUAGE IN METHODS

4

GRAMMAR IN METHODS
Paul Wickens

INTRODUCTION

This chapter is the first in this section which looks at approaches to knowledge of language. In this chapter we will look at developments in the teaching of grammar and the linguistic understandings that underpin them. It asks the questions:

+ What should teachers know about grammar?
+ What should teachers know about how learners learn grammar?

We will then explore approaches to language description and what these might mean for methods and methodology.

A good place to start is to ask what grammar is. There are perhaps two main ways we use the term: firstly, the uncountable term 'grammar' refers to a part of the language system that we implicitly know and intuitively use in communication; secondly, there is the countable term 'a grammar', which refers to the explicit descriptions of such knowledge that we can find in grammar books. The two can often be confused, but we need to remember that the grammar descriptions in grammar books are necessarily limited attempts at describing the patterns, regularities and rules that we automatically draw on in our use of the living system of a language. Explicit descriptions of grammar can only be partial at best, and we must not confuse the useful categories and rules we find in grammar books with the reality of the language that people use to meaningfully communicate in the world around us. In TESOL, descriptions of grammar and the related explicit pedagogic explanations should be an important means to that communicative end, not an end in themselves. As Larsen-Freeman (2003) argues, if we are concerned with communication in the real world, we need a theory of grammar that will bring together form, meaning and use.

When looking for relevant descriptions of grammar we need to be aware that they vary according to the different theories of grammar they are based on and the different purposes and goals they have. Theories of grammar can be broadly divided into two: formal theories of grammar, which focus on categories of words and the rules for their possible combinations at sentence level; and functional theories of grammar, which are more concerned with the link between forms and meaning and how these operate in real-world texts. Grammars also have differing purposes or goals, such as prescriptive grammars that tell us how we ought to speak and write to be seen as educated, or pedagogic grammars that select and simplify the grammar descriptions for learners.

In linguistics, the dominant theory of grammar in the second half of the twentieth century has been generative linguistics. This is a formal theory of grammar, based on the work of Noam Chomsky, which seeks to identify the formal rules and principles which state what is and is not grammatical in a language. The rules and judgements of grammaticality are based on constructed examples that tap into an idealised knowledge or competence of the rules that an idealised speaker must be using in constructing sentences, rather than how we actually speak or write in the real world. The theory separates an ideal version of the language (competence) from the messy data of real-world language (performance), and it also separates notions of grammaticality from the meaning choices made in everyday language use. Chomsky's example of a sentence which is grammatically possible but nonsensical illustrates the areas of concern of the theory: 'Colourless green ideas sleep furiously.' The theory also assumes an innate language ability, and seeks to describe the similarities and differences between languages as a variation on an underlying universal grammar (Cook 2008).

In contrast, functionalist grammars such as Systemic Functional Linguistics (Halliday 1994) see language as a meaning-making resource which looks to identify the relationship between form and meaning. In this view grammar is not seen as innate, but has developed over time because of the way language has been used for recurring social purposes. Grammatical patterns and rules of syntax are part of a systematic resource that we choose from to make meaningful texts with meanings and language appropriate for a given context. We will explore what this means for descriptions of grammar in the following section.

As we saw with beliefs about learning in Section 2.1, Larsen-Freeman (2003: 105) argues that, 'As we know, teachers teach subject matter the way they conceptualise it.' If we perceive grammar as a formal, idealised description of rules, this leads us to a focus on **grammaticality** and the line between what is correct and what is not. If we see grammar as a way in which meaning is conveyed, then it will lead us to focus on message and appropriacy. This would influence what we choose to teach and how.

Task 4.1 Exploring attitudes to correctness in English:
Tick the sentences that you agree with.

1. Correctness is defined by grammar books and dictionaries.   ☐
2. Correctness is defined by how an educated native speaker of English
   uses the language.   ☐
3. There are clear standards of correctness and appropriateness for the
   use of English in, for example, BBC English.   ☐
4. All languages change; therefore, rules for correctness change.   ☐
5. The written form of English is the most correct form   ☐
6. Whether or not language is correct depends on the circumstances in
   which you are using it.   ☐
7. Students need to be told what is likely to be accepted as correct or
   incorrect in exams they will be taking.   ☐

We will explore some of these ideas further below, but let us briefly consider a couple of areas that these questions on correctness open up. A move from a formal to a functional perspective on language raises a number of questions about 'correctness'. Instead of a focus on what is grammatically correct or incorrect, we would need more nuanced judgements about what is possible and appropriate. If we look at real language in use rather than intuitions based around an idealised standard, we can see a greater range of structures and patterns that we may need to bring into our descriptions of grammar. The ability to access and analyse large amounts of language on computers has allowed researchers to do just this. Computer-based corpora or collections of texts are now used to provide data for learner grammars, dictionaries and textbooks in ELT (McCarthy 2004, Hughes 2010, McCarten 2010). We will track some of these changes in the description of grammar in this chapter, in Chapter 5 on vocabulary and in Chapter 7 on the spoken word.

Another idealisation that has been questioned is the focus on native speaker grammar. Questions 2–4 refer us to the choices as to which English we teach, and thus which grammar descriptions are most relevant to speakers in the contexts where the language will be used. Notions of appropriacy and correctness in grammar could thus refer to Singaporean English or English as a Lingua Franca (Seidlhofer 2005) rather than a native speaker standard. As Kuo (2006) argues in regard to the teaching of English as an International Language (EIL), it is teachers and students who ultimately need to make their own informed choices on these issues. Question 7, though, also reminds us that if the goal in your teaching context is to pass exams, and the focus of those exams is grammaticality and the explicit knowledge of rules, then a formal perspective on grammar would be more relevant.

4.1 WHAT IS GRAMMAR? EXPLORING OUR CONCEPTIONS OF GRAMMAR

The section will explore our understanding of grammar as teachers and explore the role of this knowledge as we prepare for teaching and helping our students with their understanding of grammar. Larsen-Freeman (2002: 105) claims that 'Many teachers (and students) believe grammar to be a linguistic strait-jacket. They think that grammar consists of arbitrary rules of a language, to which speakers must adhere or risk the penalty of being misunderstood or of being stigmatized . . .' Would this describe your perspective on grammar?

Task 4.2 Grammar in context
Consider the following conversation with the author of this chapter's eight-year-old son over breakfast one Saturday. Identify the grammar in the conversation:

1. A: hey dad . . . dad
2. B: yeh . . . what
3. A: that film can we see sometime
4. B: uh . . . which one

5.   A: the new harry potter
6.   B: yeh sure . . . but probably not today ok

What did you pick out to describe in terms of the grammar? You may have noted how there are few full clauses (only one verb group: *can . . . see*), and most of the utterances are very short and thus perhaps harder to describe in terms of grammar. This, as we will see in more detail later, is partly because the grammars we use have tended to be based on writing rather than speech. It is clear, though, that the choice of language is appropriate and meaningful to the participants, and the speakers are able to draw on the context and their shared knowledge to work out relevant meanings. As Carter (1998) points out, in face-to-face contexts such as this where there is substantial shared knowledge, it is full clauses that would be inappropriate (e.g. lines 4 and 5: A: *which film would you like to see*/B: *I would like to see the new Harry Potter film*), sounding rather stilted or even like a parody of over-politeness.

There certainly is grammar to describe – we could identify the Noun Group, e.g. *the new harry potter*, which has the word order determiner/adjective/noun (*harry potter new the* would be ungrammatical). The definite article (*the*) lets me know that my son thinks this is information I should already know, and the adjective *new* identifies which of the Harry Potter films it is (there were seven others at the time!). The choices made here strike a balance between making the meaning explicit whilst succinctly orienting the interactants to the relevant shared knowledge. In line 5, the author's son chose not to use what is the implied Head noun of this noun group – *film* – it is taken as given knowledge from the text in line 3. This dropping of words that can be recovered from the text or context is called ellipsis. When to use ellipsis and which words you can drop is both an important grammar and meaning choice. In line 2, I could have said *What is it? What do you want?* but I chose to shorten it to *What* – the choice of *What is . . . What do . . .* are not possible ellipsis. In this mundane conversation, we are both making **appropriate** and **systematic choices** about what language can be left out of the clause and still make sense in the interaction. These are choices of grammar, meaning and use, but they also mark out our relationship and the knowledge which we think we share.

We can see another common feature of the grammar of spoken language in the question in line 3. Word order is much less fixed than it is in written language, and the object (*that film*) has been brought to the front of the clause instead of its 'usual' place after the verb. This is something that my son frequently does with questions. He is bringing to the front of the clause the topic that he wishes to raise and to let me know (with the use of the determiner *that*) that this is a topic he thinks I should already know about and wants me to focus on. In adult speech, it is likely that the object would appear again as a pronoun at the end of the sentence – *that film, can we see it sometime* – and we might orientate ourselves to the speaker more directly – *Do you remember that film we were talking about, can we see it sometime.*

These descriptions move us away from an idea of **grammaticality** based on formal rules grounded in written language to a view of grammar that focuses on **appropriacy** of the meaning choices in that particular context. Such interpersonal meanings and their related grammar choices are one consideration for teachers to incorporate into their materials. Carter et al. (2011) show that fronting of what the speaker sees as key information is a common and highly systematic choice in spoken English. One such structure in the CANCODE corpus of spoken English they have identified as 'Tails' – *He was a great leader, **Gandhi was*** (Carter et al. 2001: 87) – which tend to serve an evaluative or emphatic function. Another similar structure they have termed 'Headers' – ***the old lady**, I really like her* (Mumford 2009: 140) is a way of fronting the key topic. Mumford (2009) argues that such structures show there is a greater flexibility in word order in speech than traditional grammars have allowed, which reflects the speaker's need to deal with ideas as they emerge and to fit them into the ongoing talk in real time. He also makes the observation that learners who produce such structures would probably be corrected, in line more with written norms of grammar. If one of your learners produced the question in line 3 in Task 4.2, would you correct it at any point? Why, or why not? And if so, when and how might you correct it?

As we need to express more complex meanings that are less situated in a shared context or shared knowledge, we need to make our meanings more explicit by drawing on the grammar. If I wanted to add an explanation to the last line of the dialogue that I knew was new information for my son, e.g. *cos we have to go round to see gran later*, then I would need to build the meanings more explicitly through more complex lexical and grammar choices. I would want him to be clear that it is a joint activity (*we*) and an action that we all need to do (*have to*) – so ellipsis of the subject and verb would not be an appropriate choice here. Note how these grammar choices take us out of the here-and-now and allow me to express more complex meanings which refer to notions of obligation in the semi-modal verb that have a realisation that is distant in time and place.

This distancing function of the grammar also works in terms of social relationships where we often need to manage social distance – being more polite/formal/hesitant/ authoritative. This also leads to us to drawing more carefully on grammar resources to construct the appropriate meanings. In the conversation in Task 4.2, if my son were staying at a friend's house and he were to ask his friend's parent if they could watch a TV programme in the evening, he would have to take account of the different relationships and lack of shared knowledge. So line 3 in Task 4.2 might need to draw on a greater range of grammatical resource: *Excuse me, could we watch Doctor Who on TV tonight? It's on at 6.*

Task 4.3 Exploring grammar in context
- Record a casual conversation with people you know, or find something similar online (TV drama, YouTube). Transcribe a short sequence as carefully as you can.
- Can you identify some of the features of spoken interaction we have briefly looked at above?
- Take a section of the conversation which is similar to the one in Task 4.2 (where there aren't full clauses) and reconstruct the clauses, trying to fill in as much of the assumed information as possible. What grammar did you draw on to do this?

Chapter 6 and the further readings in the online resource explore spoken grammar in more detail.

The example in Task 4.2 and the analysis we engaged in illustrate the nature of grammar as a **process of choice**: this process of 'languaging' (Halliday 1994) or 'grammaring' (Larsen-Freeman 2003) sees grammar as a meaning resource from which we make choices from the system which are appropriate to the context. When we can rely on the context around us, we can rely more on lexis to get our meaning across using gesture, intonation and references to the context and shared knowledge.

> [The more access we have to] knowledge and experience, the less need there is for grammar to augment the association of words [. . .] grammar is not a constraining imposition but a liberating force; it frees us from the dependency on context and the limitations of a purely lexical categorisation of reality.
> (Widdowson 1988 in Bruton 2009: 151)

When we distance ourselves from the here and now (past, future, hypothetical) or seek to express social distance (formality, politeness and authority), we use grammar to make our meanings more explicit. This mirrors the process of language acquisition in both L1 and L2, as we move from a reliance on lexis to one where we can use grammar to make relevant meanings across a range of contexts. As Thornbury (2001) points out, learners need to be given opportunities to increase not only their fluency but also the complexity of their language, with tasks that move beyond a reliance on the immediate context and allow time to engage in the process of making increasingly complex choices from the grammar, as well as time to receive some kind of feedback on the process. An increase in complexity and the need for feedback leads us to consider our knowledge of the rules and concepts of grammar that we rely on.

When is a rule not a rule?

As teachers we rely on the explicit pedagogic grammar descriptions that we find in textbooks and pedagogic grammar books. Such descriptions are a central part of language pedagogy, but as language educators we need to continue to explore the actual patterns of language in use and relate form, meaning and use in a range of contexts. Lantolf (2007: 36) warns of the dangers of pedagogic oversimplification: 'More often than not, formal linguistic knowledge is presented, particularly at the early stages of instruction, in a piecemeal, rule-of-thumb format rather than as coherent empirical and theoretically informed conceptual knowledge.' An example of this which has been noted previously is the rule of thumb for *some* and *any* (Batstone, 1994; Hedge, 2000). Let us explore our own knowledge of these words – their grammar, meaning and use – and relate it to what we can find out from corpus linguistics. This method allows us to look at large amounts of authentic language data on the computer via a concordance program to see patterns and regularities of form, meaning and use.

Task 4.4 Rules of thumb: when is a rule not a rule?

1. Write down a pedagogic rule for the use of *some* and *any* that you would teach to lower intermediate students. Try to do this without consulting a grammar book.
2. Would you adapt the rule for advanced students? How?

3. Now consult at least two pedagogic sources that you use, such as grammar books, websites or textbooks. Are they the same as yours?

The descriptions usually focus on the formal elements of the words as they operate in the syntax of the clause (with links to the grammar of un/countable and singular/plural).

- *some* used in positive statements
- *any* used in negative statements (key example is usually with 'not any')
- *any* used in questions

A number of 'exceptions' are often listed, which make some appeal to meaning and context of use (e.g. Scrivener 2010):

- *some* in questions: e.g. requests/offers, anticipating a positive response
- *any* in statements where there is a negative meaning: 'hardly . . . any', 'without . . . any'
- *any* in affirmative sentences – meaning 'it doesn't matter which'

Lewis (1985: 124) takes a meaning-based approach to give pedagogic explanations of the grammar and points out that all the following are possible forms:

I like some pop music; I don't like some pop music (part of)○

I like any pop music; I don't like any pop music (all or nothing)○●

What are the main differences with this approach, and what might be the benefits of each to students in your teaching context?

Let's look for ourselves, using a corpus of texts and a concordance program found on the Compleat Lexical Tutor (2012) website.

1. Go to Compleat Lexical Tutor website (use a search engine).
2. Choose the Concordance program and select the English Concordancer.
3. Enter the word to search for (*any/some*) in the empty box for 'keyword'.
4. Select a corpus in the 'Choose a corpus' box. We will use the corpora labelled *BNC Written* and then the *BNC Spoken* to look at variation of use in different modes. (These corpora are one-million-word samples of the main British National Corpus, which is a 100-million-word corpus that was collected in the UK in the 1980s.[1])
5. Finally, click 'Get concordance', and a concordance of the key search word will appear. Repeat for both corpora.

Below are two samples for *any* of 10 random hits from the two corpora (to get a smaller sample, at the top of the page, click 'any '10', '20', '30', and then click 'extract' button – this will give a random sample). In the samples below or in your own sample, count the use of *any* in questions, negative and positive clauses, and consider the meanings.

BNC Written

is extremely wide, and its members can, and do, act against	ANY	activity they deem hostile to the Socialist system and d of
one month the Commission will decide whether there are	ANY	serious doubts as to the merger creating or strengthening
state that a Lithuanian party member can not belong to	ANY	other party. The motive behind the Lithuanian party's hnson
denies taking any prohibited substance or engaging in	ANY	improper practice since his return to competition. Neither
ntered. In a well ordered and maintained pool these will in	ANY	event be minimal. The most important thing to remember
tational semantics, most of the laws quoted must be true in	ANY	reasonable abstract semantics for occam. We indicate hin
which an assessment could be made of the suitability of	ANY	publication, film or video cassette for public and on
filling the pool, the water level will immediately show	ANY	non- levelness in the edging surface. Fig. 1 (d) After t han
their counterparts in less remote rural areas, and that	ANY	decline in such areas is due to lower levels of immigration that
stimulate or depress economy when necessary without	ANY	deliberate policy change. As stabilisation policy

BNC spoken

in a bowl though. No, I go like that. Yeah but that ain't	ANY	good. You've gotta get the stu the smell goes in to
the for that amount of time you want a seat. You can't take	ANY	booze in there either. No. But it's best to get a seat dear,
dear, okay, no extra charge. Okay? But please if you're in	ANY	doubt have a word with your electrical contractor, unless
olice complaints authority started looking for it. Have you	ANY	idea what that refers to? Yes I have er it would refer
Alright. Erm just one thing. You don't have Brenda	ANY	more do you? No? No. Be a Christmas card. Erm r.
Well, just say to her, you know, working later, is there	ANY	more money in it? Mm. It's not That's the only thing
you t it, but now, I just lost it. First of all I never hear it	ANY	more on the continent I can't seem to hear the radio,
of peanuts so I have got a few that few, but you don't need	ANY	old bag do you? See when I don't go shopping I don't
get n Geoff get every thing out and place it, that's it well if	ANY	thing it's more likely to be at the top of the pile, not
I need. And, some vegetables. Yeah. But we can pick that up	ANY	time today can't we? Mm. Or Sunday. Certainly get looks

(data comes from The BNC Sampler (2005)[2] using the concordancer on the Compleat Lexical Tutor (2012) website)

We can see in the written corpus that out of the 10 instances, there is just one explicit negative (*not belong to any*); one where there is a preposition with a negative meaning (*without any*) and no instance of interrogatives. A look at the full sample of hits from the one million BNC written corpus shows broadly similar proportions; the majority are in positive clauses, the most common meaning being 'all' or 'it doesn't matter which'. In contrast, in the spoken corpus, there are three positive, five negative (four *n't*, one *never*) and two interrogative clauses. So we would be correct to claim, as previous studies have (Willis 1990, Batstone 1994), that the 'rule of thumb' clearly does not adequately describe the range of actual use. However, a more careful breakdown of mode shows us that we can make a distinction between spoken and written discourse which shows that the pedagogic 'rule of thumb' describes aspects of the form better in spoken than in written discourse.

So in trying to understand the way form, meaning and use map onto each other, we need to take account of the contexts of use and the kinds of meanings we tend to make in these contexts (Larsen-Freeman 2003). If we were designing a course in legal language we would need to need know that *any* is most commonly used in positive clauses with the meaning of 'it doesn't matter which': *The terms and conditions herein are to provide for any and all matters necessary* (note the contrast between *any* and *all*). For a course in academic English, we could explore the way quantifiers are used in corpora of student academic written and spoken discourse (e.g. BAWE and BASE corpora[3]).

In looking to understand the meanings and use of such features we would need to go on to explore the meanings and patterns that are most commonly used with *any*. For example, Willis (1990) notes that the use of *any* with the negative often acts as an emphatic and is structurally optional (*but that ain't any good. You can't take any booze in there*). This points us back to the way grammar works as a system of meaningful choices: grammar as process. What are the system choices we can make? Is the contrast between *some* and *any* a useful one, and are there other contrasts that would be more meaningful?

Example 4.1 below is a pedagogic task and part of a grammar explanation (example 4.2) and considers how the use of *some* and *any* as quantifiers is related to the choice of other quantifiers and determiners.

Example 4.1
Do you think these statements are true or false? Correct the ones you think are not true.

1. All animals have four legs.
2. Some animals have two legs.
3. Most birds can fly.
4. Any bird can fly.
5. Most animals live on land.
6. No birds can swim.
7. All birds lay eggs.
8. All fish live in the sea.
9. A lot of animals eat fruit.
10. Some fish can swim.
11. Any fish can swim.
12. All animals can swim.
13. Lots of birds can swim.
Willis (2003 p. 80)

Example 4.2

One supermarket	Two supermarkets	More than two supermarkets
The supermarket was closed. The supermarket wasn't open. I don't think the supermarket was open.	Both the supermarkets were closed. Neither of the supermarkets was open. I don't think either of the supermarkets was open.	All the supermarkets were closed. None of the supermarkets were open. I don't think any of the supermarkets were open.

(Learn English 2012: quantifiers)

Task 4.5 Exploring pedagogic resources
- Take one or more textbook series and a pedagogic grammar practice book. At what level are *some* and *any* introduced? Do they come back in later levels?
- Do explanations focus simply on form, or do they account for meanings and use?
- Are they taught in relation to other forms (a few, a lot of) as a system of meaningful choices (see examples 4.1 and 4.2)?
- What kinds of texts/contexts do the examples draw on (spoken/written; everyday conversation/written academic texts)? Do they make distinctions in use according to context?
- Is there a similar form to this in your students' L1? What difficulties might they have with the form-function-use mapping? How would this affect your planning for teaching these forms?

Pedagogic grammars are rightly the main source of knowledge for our teaching practice, but we need to continue to develop our own explicit knowledge and awareness of grammar by taking a more critical stance towards such sources. Willis (1990) illustrates this with an example of a well-known ELT textbook which sets out the standard rule of thumb for *some* and *any*; but when a corpus constructed from the textbook was queried, it was found that two-thirds of the instances of *any* actually used in the sample texts and the rubrics were in positive sentences. Jones and Waller (2011) show that the four conditionals traditionally described and taught in ELT materials do not relate to actual usage, and like Lantolf (2007), they argue for more appropriate pedagogic descriptions based on empirical evidence from corpus data.

4.2 WHAT SHOULD TEACHERS KNOW ABOUT LEARNING GRAMMAR?

Grammar pedagogy has been one of the more controversial areas in TESOL over the last twenty years, and so we find the literature asking some very basic questions: 'Should we teach grammar, or should we simply create the conditions by which learners learn naturally?' (Ellis 2006a: 83). As we saw in Section 3.1 and Case Study 6 regarding the language acquisition of young children, it is clearly possible to learn a language and its grammar without explicitly studying it: this is obviously the case in L1, and also in some L2 immersion contexts where learners implicitly acquire the language. L2 students who have studied through formal instruction must also be doing this as well, as it is not possible to explicitly cover all the rules, regularities and patterns that exist in a language within the time given.

Krashen (1981) took this view of implicit learning in L2 and argued further that explicit grammar teaching was irrelevant for language acquisition. What learners mainly need is *comprehensible input* for them to acquire the relevant grammar. The hypothesis was that explicit learning of declarative knowledge about language, such as grammar rules, does not lead to acquisition and procedural knowledge for using language. As we saw in Section 2.1, this was supported by a further hypothesis that there is a natural order in which L2 learners acquire grammar, and that this sequence cannot be changed through instruction. This was based on studies of the sequence of morpheme acquisition with the -*ing* and plural morphemes acquired before articles and the irregular past acquired before the regular past (Krashen 1981: 59), and on the fact that these orders did not vary for different L1 speakers. These hypotheses provided a key rationale in ELT for a move away from explicit grammar teaching and negative feedback, towards communicative language teaching.

However, evidence such as that from French immersion programmes in Canada (Lapkin, Hart and Swain 1991) showed that even in immersion contexts where there was substantial meaning-based input, a lack of grammar instruction and feedback on language errors led to poor levels of grammatical accuracy and plateaus in students' interlanguage development (Selinker 1972).

Recent overviews and meta-analyses of the research have shown that grammar instruction does make a difference in a broad range of contexts (Ellis 2006; Norris and Ortega 2000; Spada 2010; Spada and Tomita 2010). These studies point towards two broad conclusions from the research over the last twenty years in SLA:

1. '... while instructed language learning may not have major effects on the sequences of acquisition, it has facilitative effects on both the rate and the ultimate level of L2 acquisition' (Nassaji and Fotos 2004: 129)
2. '... instruction needs to ensure that learners are able to connect grammatical forms to the meanings they realise in communication' (Ellis 2006a: 101)

The question is: how do we integrate a focus on meaning in communicative contexts with a focus on grammar? Long (1991) proposed a *focus on form* which 'overtly draws students' attention to linguistic elements as they arise incidentally in lessons whose overriding focus is on meaning or communication' (Long 1991, in Doughty and Williams 1998: 3). This suits, for example, a Task-Based Learning pedagogy where meaningful task-based interaction comes first and the teacher identifies the grammar issues to work as they arise in class.

This is often contrasted with a *focus on formS*, where teaching is based on a structured syllabus of discrete grammar items. In modern textbooks, this is often related to a PPP methodology where pre-selected grammar items are explicitly Presented and these are then Practised through controlled exercises to the final step of freer practice/Performance. This assumes, though, that (a) students will quickly learn what is taught so that it will be available to use in a meaningful way in the communicative task in the final step, and (b) fluency will come quickly out of a control of accuracy. A PPP approach may work well from the teacher's perspective, but learners need time to restructure their interlanguage – to both acquire the form/function mapping and then to make it available within the time/pressure constraints of a communicative situation.

The research shows that whilst learners' acquisition of grammar tends to move through set developmental stages, progress is not linear, and the acquisition of certain features at each stage is not discrete (Larsen-Freeman 2006). Students may progress in some areas and backslide in others, and we need to be aware that individual students will progress at different rates and in different areas. Thus a set language syllabus will be unlikely to match the developmental cycles of learners, and a PPP approach in class is unlikely to result in the straight process of explicit teaching moving to fluent student production that the method implies.

Larsen-Freeman (2006), in a detailed study of five adult Chinese students in the USA over a six month period, showed that whilst there were average increases in development across the group in grammatical complexity, accuracy and fluency over the period, individual variation was substantial, with students showing improvement and then regression, and in some cases finishing with lower accuracy scores than when they started. Larsen-Freeman argues that SLA research into acquisition has tended to look for generalised patterns of acquisition and overlooked the extent of individual variation: how development is irregular over time; variation of progress in different areas of grammar acquisition; and variation between learners. The learning of grammar is part of a complex system of language acquisition, and progress is not linear or predictable. Thus, matching a pre-planned syllabus to individual learner needs may be little more than chance. However, as we have seen, explicit teaching and learning of grammar has been shown to have an effect on the rate and ultimate level of L2 acquisition. Ellis (2006a) argues that planned teaching of grammar may not lead directly to acquisition, but it gives the learner an explicit knowledge of the language that they can draw on later when they are at that stage in their interlanguage development.

Dealing with Complexity

What makes some grammatical structures more difficult to learn that others? Complexity may refer to the complexity of the explicit metalinguistic description of the rule and how well we can manage to express this with conceptual clarity (consider the example of *some* and *any* in Tasks 4.4 and 4.5), but we also need to consider learners' implicit knowledge of grammar. Both contribute to language acquisition. Ellis (2006b: 435) proposes the following five criteria as 'determinants of what makes different grammatical features easy or difficult as implicit knowledge':

1. Frequency (How frequently does the grammatical feature occur in the input?)
2. Saliency (Is the grammatical feature easy to notice in the input?)
3. Functional value (Does the grammatical feature map onto a clear, distinct function?)
4. Regularity (Does the grammatical feature conform to some identifiable pattern?)
5. Processability (Is the grammatical feature easy to process?)
   (Ellis 2006b: 435)

So, for example, whilst the third person 's' morpheme (walks) is frequent, it is not that salient, especially in speech, and this shows up in the order of acquisition, where it tends to be acquired later. In Ellis's study (2006b), learners were able to state the explicit rule for the indefinite article *a* quite well, but their implicit knowledge was low. He postulates that whilst it is frequent, it is not salient, it realises a number of discourse functions, and is difficult to process, as it depends on a range of other elements in the system (e.g. whether the associated noun is countable/uncountable).

The other element that Ellis (2006b: 461) mentions is the influence of the L1. We need to be aware of key conceptual differences between the two languages that are encoded in the grammar: for instance, the fact that articles (*a, the*) are difficult to acquire for Japanese learners of English as there is no equivalent concept in Japanese, and the corresponding problem of the distinction between the particles (*wa, ga*) for English learners of Japanese (Russell 2005) which mark topic prominence and subject in Japanese. Han's (2000) two-year longitudinal study of two advanced Chinese learners found that they continued to use a pseudo passive (*New cars must keep inside*) which reflected elements of the syntactic structure as well as the information discourse structure of their L1. What is important here is an understanding of the concepts involved and the meaning in use, rather than just a list of structures.

Task 4.6 Reflecting on grammar acquisition and grammar teaching
- What aspects of the L1 in your context need to be considered when looking at English grammar acquisition? How does this impact on your teaching?
- Consult a guide of L1/L2 contrasts such as Swan and Smith (Swan and Smith 2001). If your L1 is included, is your list the same as theirs?

Noticing the gap
The key shift in grammar teaching and learning has been a move towards an integration of explicit grammar teaching and implicit learning through study of the meaningful use of language forms in context. The claim for integration of form, function and use in meaningful contexts is not only based on a functional approach to language, but also relates to 'transfer-appropriate processing theory', which says we retrieve knowledge best in contexts that were similar to those in which we learned it (Spada 2010: 5). Long's (1991) proposal for an incidental Focus on Form is based on these ideas as the grammar teaching emerges from the problems that students have when engaging in meaningful tasks, rather than starting with a focus on grammatical form pre-selected by the teacher which is then practiced.

Krashen's (1981) hypothesis that language can be learned without some kind of conscious attention to form has generally been rejected. It is now widely agreed that the 'noticing' of forms is a necessary condition for language learning (R. Ellis 2006a, Nasaji and Fotos 2004). A prevalent model of acquisition identifies the main macro processes as: access to relevant **input** for students; **noticing** certain aspects of the language can lead to **intake** which can lead to a process of restructuring of the interlanguage (see Section 4.3 on the impact of corpus studies); language **output** allows the learner a chance to get **feedback** on their use of the language and to notice the gap between their language and the target language, particularly where a misunderstanding leads to a negotiation of meaning (Ellis 1998). So the two principles of 'noticing' are the need to:

- Focus students' attention on language
- Get students to produce language so that they can notice the gap between their language and the target language

Ellis (2008: 869) identifies four options for pedagogic intervention in this process, each of which is explained in more detail below:

1. Input-based: comprehension focus (focus on meaning/form mapping)
2. Explicit: develop explicit knowledge of language form – deductive and inductive
3. Production: text manipulation (error avoiding) – text creation (error inducing)
4. Corrective feedback: implicit (recasts, requests for clarification), explicit (metalinguistic explanation or elicitation)

Input-based options: These deliberately do not require the learner to produce language, so that processing resources can all go on comprehending the meaning and to 'noticing' relevant aspects of form. This can be done by giving students texts with lots of examples of the relevant structures in the text (input flooding) or interpretation tasks where students have to show they have processed the meaning of the target structure. For example:

In this task students listen to answerphone messages. First they listen to guess which city or country each message describes, and then they listen again to say which friends are still on holiday and which have returned.

- *Hi Jo. How are you? Great holiday! We've been to the Louvre and the Eiffel Tower, but we haven't been to Versailles yet. We'll phone you back. Bye.*
- *Joe, it's Barry. Fantastic holiday! We went everywhere – the Coliseum, St. Peter's, Hadrian's Villa – and we had great Italian food. Speak to you soon. Bye.*

(Thornbury 2001: 39)

Explicit options: This relates to either presenting explicit grammar rules (deductive) or getting students to work out the rules for themselves (inductive). The latter are often referred to as consciousness-raising (CR) tasks. In the above task we could move to a CR approach by getting students to formulate an explicit 'rule' for the present perfect/simple past contrast. Ellis (2008) cites research that shows that CR tasks are more effective with high-intermediate students than with low-intermediate – though this could be mitigated by considering the rule in the L1.

In Norris and Ortega's (2000) review of the research, the key finding was that explicit grammar instruction was more effective than implicit instruction. However, one key caveat here is that the beneficial effects of explicit instruction are tested through demonstrations of explicit knowledge and discrete item testing (gap fill, sentence completion), but there is little evidence of improvement in accuracy in free production tasks (Ellis 2006a, Lantolf 2007).

Production options: Output is not just a goal in itself, but a key part of the system of acquisition as we improve fluency, accuracy and complexity in ways appropriate to a particular context of use. It also allows students to 'notice the gap' between their output and the target language in the input, and is linked closely to 'feedback'. One technique that Thornbury (1997) outlines is reformulation. In a writing task, the teacher takes the content of the student writing and rewrites it so that it meets the expectations of the target genre. Students can then make a comparison with their own writing, and this allows for the same task to meet the specific needs of individual learners. The move from a meaning-based production to an accuracy/appropriacy focus fits into the principles of task-based learning (Willis 2003) that we looked at in Chapter 2.

Corrective feedback: Errors can be part of the process of awareness-raising, especially if students are encouraged to identify, explain and repair errors for themselves.

The reformulation described in the paragraph above is an example of teacher and learner sharing the correction process: the teacher reformulated the student writing to match the target expectations, and the student then identified the changes. Corrective feedback can entail different degrees of teacher intervention: from the teacher 'explaining' to students doing so for themselves by identifying rules or patterns that have been violated, labelling words and word functions, or providing language alternatives.

4.3 LEARNING GRAMMAR, TEACHING GRAMMAR

This section will include a discussion of the influences and theoretical foundations of pedagogic grammars and coursebooks, including the impact of Hallidayan and corpus linguistics on contemporary grammar teaching materials.

Textbooks and SLA

SLA research has put the focus back on how learners learn grammar, and considers teaching strategies based on these ideas. The focus is less on the teacher and how to present grammar, and more on individual learners and enabling them to notice and understand form/function mappings in contexts of use. There has also been a criticism of the PPP model with its focus on controlled practice and a move towards getting learners to engage with consciousness-raising activities. Textbooks are a key source of models for language teachers looking for pedagogic models for teaching grammar, and it is interesting to track the link between them and SLA research. Nitta and Gardner (2005) investigated the kind of grammar tasks used in nine ELT textbooks to identify the kinds of individual form-focused tasks they used and how these were situated in a broader pedagogic frame such as task-based learning or a PPP framework. They identified five kinds of form-focused task:

1. Consciousness-raising (CR) tasks
2. Interpretation tasks
3. Focused communication tasks (FCT)
4. Grammar exercises
5. Grammar practice activities

The first two tasks take an inductive approach to grammar: in CR tasks learners work out explicit rules based on examples of a particular language form; in Interpretation tasks the focus is on mapping meaning to form and there is little use of explicit grammatical metalanguage. In FCTs the learner is asked to engage in discussion tasks which are likely to produce the target language – a meaning-based task that tries to elicit language. The last two tasks consolidate learnt grammatical items through controlled exercises such as drills and gap fills, and freer communicative practice activities to develop fluency in a particular form. Looking at the overall structure of the grammar sections, Nitta and Gardner (2005) found that the textbooks overwhelmingly followed a PPP approach and there was no evidence of a move towards task-based learning which puts meaning-based tasks first (here FCTs) and then moves to a focus on form. One interesting development, though, within the PPP framework, seems to be a marked preference for inductive CR/Interpretation tasks in the presentation section rather than deductive tasks which simply state the grammar rule.

Task 4.7　Exploring pedagogic resources
Take the key textbooks that you rely on in your teaching and identify a sample of grammar activities.

- Is the structure of the tasks based on a move from presentation of forms to their practice and performance?
- In the presentation sections, are the tasks mainly inductive (CR or interpretation tasks) or deductive (explicit teaching of rules)?
- Are there any instances of a task-based approach which starts with meaning-based activities and then leads into a focus on form?
- Is the focus on form activity aimed at a particular form, or does the activity simply suggest a range of possible grammar issues that may emerge, and you as a teacher are left to decide what to focus on?

A linguistic perspective
Another key trend has been the shift in linguistics from more form-based theories towards usage-based theories of language that focus on the link between form, meaning and use in social contexts. Whilst the influence of structural grammar is still widespread in ELT, there is now as much attention given to meaning and function as to form, and as Ellis (2006a: 86) points out, generative theories of grammar have not proved relevant to syllabus designers and teachers. This shift has been driven by a range of theories and methodologies, but I will briefly focus here on two: Systemic Functional Linguistics (Halliday and Webster 2003), sometimes referred to as Hallidayan linguistics, and Corpus Linguistics (O'Keeffe and McCarthy 2010). Both have had substantial impacts on pedagogic grammars, dictionaries, practice grammars and textbooks.

What underpins a Hallidayan perspective on language is the link between form, meaning and use in a social context. The theory posits a clear link between the context of situation in which the language is used, the kinds of meanings we tend to make in those contexts and the kind of language choices that are *likely* to be used in those contexts. This focus on meaning in use changes the focus of the descriptions of the grammar towards notions of **appropriacy** and choice. For example, if we are looking at the passive, a description of the form of the verb (*be* + past participle) and the re-ordering of subject and object is only part of the issue; we also need to understand the semantics of the clause – with functional terms that describes which element is the 'actor' of the process (verb) which is the 'goal'. We need to know that the actor is expressed in a prepositional phrase (*by* + actor) and that this shift in form makes it possible to drop the actor from the clause. This can often be treated as a minor part of the grammatical descriptions; but it should not be, if you are aware that Leech and Sartvik (2002) claim that four out of five passives in English do not express the actor, e.g. *A police officer was killed last night in a road accident* (Leech and Sartvik 2002: 346). Then we need to know that its use varies significantly according to context – it is more common in scientific English than in informal spoken English, for example (Leech and Sartvik 2002) – but most importantly *why* it is used in those contexts. In scientific English, it allows a focus on the scientific process rather than those who do it, e.g. *A sample was taken and injected into the tube* (Carter et al. 2011: 367), and constructs scientists in their role as 'rational, disinterested, asocial seeker of truth' (Hyland 2009: 124).

Registers are the collections of meanings and language choices that we are likely to encounter in a given social context, as well as providing us with the system of choices of meanings and language we will likely draw in the production of texts in that situation. So we can talk about an academic, scientific, legalistic, journalistic, conversational register of English. Such a 'probability'-based theory of language has clear usefulness for ELT, as it gives us a rationale for the choice of structures and lexis for the situations our students are likely to need.

Descriptions of Registers have been key in the rise of English for Specific Purposes, with a large range of textbooks and materials available, from areas such as Business and Academic English (EAP) to niche areas such as English for Aviation (see the textbook *Flightpath*, Shawcross 2011). Corpus linguistics has allowed the study of large amounts of language in use in a particular context to see which grammatical forms are most relevant to teach. So in English for Academic Purposes we might note that clauses such as *It is clear that . . .* and *It is important to note that . . .* are often used to orientate the reader to a stance that the writer is taking. We can study how common they are in academic writing, where they are used and what their purpose is. We can see the range of patterns that such anticipatory 'it' clauses (Hewings and Hewings 2002) are used in, what lexical items they collocate with and the meanings they construct. For Halliday (1994), there is no principled distinction between lexis and grammar: 'There is no boundary between lexis and grammar: lexis and grammar are interdependent' (Stubbs 1996: 36).

Impact of Corpus studies

We have already seen, in our exploration of *some* and *any* in the opening section, how corpus linguistics has enabled descriptions of grammar to take account of what we actually say and write. We can see empirical evidence for the range of grammatical patterns that exist, the range of lexis that is used with those patterns and the kinds of meanings that they construct in a given context. The use of *any* is not the same in spoken as in written contexts, or in a legal contract as it is in a domestic conversation about what a family needs to get from the supermarket (McCarthy 2004).

Another area of impact is on reference and pedagogic grammars from the major publishers (and dictionaries). These now draw on corpora that cover English across a range of contexts, sometimes including corpora of ELT learner language. The *Cambridge Grammar of English* (Carter and McCarthy 2006) is a good example of this, as it draws on a large corpus of spoken and written English and looks to relate structures to meanings in contexts of use. It focuses on form/meaning relationships in key areas such as modality, and deals with discourse structuring of information of the clause in a section on 'Focus'. The lexicogrammar distinction is covered in a section called 'From words to grammar', and it looks at the grammar of words such as *during*, which are slightly idiosyncratic in their grammar. Concerns of variation of register are covered in sections on spoken grammar and the grammar of academic English.

In textbooks, corpora are used both to directly inform the materials and to provide examples for dialogues, grammar tasks and explanations – either used directly, or as a guide to aid in the construction dialogues. McCarthy (2004) gives a detailed explanation of the use of the CANCODE corpus in the Touchstone (McCarthy et al. 2005) coursebook series. He shows how frequency data is used to set priorities in what grammar items to teach, the kinds of meanings that a particular form has and the contexts in which it is used. This is illustrated with examples of the modal verbs *must* and *can*. McCarthy (2004) shows that in spoken English 90 per cent of the instances of the modal verb *must* are predictive (*you must be hungry*), only five per cent are related to obligation (*you must have a visa to enter the USA*), and five per cent in fixed expressions such as *I must say/admit*. 'Statistics of this kind help textbook writers set priorities in grammar teaching and find the most natural contexts for teaching grammar' (McCarthy 2004: 6).

Such corpora can also be used to find examples of authentic conversations that materials writers can then adapt for pedagogic purposes. It is argued that this gives teachers and students confidence, reassuring them that the materials are based on reliable and authentic sources which show how forms are used in everyday conversation. Looking at how the modal verb *can* is most typically used, as well as the common meaning of ability, the CANCODE corpus of spoken English also shows that it is very commonly used to 'talk about things that are possible in different situations and places' (McCarthy 2004: 6). The corpus data is then used to construct pedagogic conversations such as the following example:

> **Emma**: *Oh, no. It's raining! What can you do in New York on a rainy day? You can't take good pictures, that's for sure.*
> **Ethan**: *Oh, come on. You can do a million things. We can take a ferry to the statue of Liberty.*
> **Emma**: *A ferry – in this weather?*
> (McCarthy 2004: 6)

One issue of the use of corpora to inform teaching materials is that we need to be very aware of what varieties and registers the corpus represents, and whether this meets the students' target needs. Is it mainly written language or spoken? Is it a specific register such as academic English? Does it promote a particular native speaker variety as the target, when we are looking to promote an EIL model? As we have seen in Section 4.1, the use of the same grammar item can vary substantially in differing contexts.

Thornbury's (2004) *Natural Grammar* is a grammar practice book that brings together the methods of corpus linguistics with Halliday's (1994) insight that lexis and grammar are not separate, but that words are the most delicate grammar – words are associated with certain grammar patterns. It presents the 100 most common words in English (based on the British National Corpus[4]), showing the grammar patterns that each word is found in and associated meanings. For example, 'at' is used in the pattern 'at' + NP to talk about places and time as 'points' – *I'll drop you at the station at six o'clock*. More interestingly, it is also used in the pattern ADJ + 'at' + NP to talk about doing things well or badly – *I was good at tennis in school*. The book goes on to look at collocations and formulaic phrases, and then presents a series of controlled practice exercises.

Task 4.8 Exploring natural grammar online 🖥

Explore Thornbury's *Natural Grammar* in more detail in the online resource for this book, and search other online resources and the corpus for examples of natural grammar in practice.

Task 4.9 Researching attitudes to natural grammar

Select an example of naturally occurring language from the *Natural Grammar* online resources.

- Ask five English language speakers to identify whether the extract shows 'correct' English or not. If they are teachers, find out if they would 'correct' the English if it were spoken by learners in class.
- What did you find out about attitudes to different grammar patterns?

4.4 FURTHER READING 🖥

The online reading resource gives you the opportunity to read and think about the following readings:

Task 4.10 Hughes, R. and M. McCarthy (1998), 'From Sentence to Discourse: Discourse Grammar and English Language Teaching', *TESOL Quarterly*, 32:2, 263–87.
Task 4.11 Cullen, R. (2008), 'Teaching Grammar as a Liberating Force', *ELT Journal*, 62:3, 221–30.

4.5 CONCLUSION

In this chapter we started off by asking what teachers should know about grammar. The key point is that as teachers, we need to explore our own perceptions of what grammar is: 'As we know, teachers teach subject matter the way they conceptualise it' (Larsen-Freeman 2003:105). We have seen that usage-based theories of language and grammar emphasise the need to integrate descriptions of grammar, meaning and use. This in turn puts a focus on grammar as a process of choice, where we need to make judgements of what is grammatically possible/impossible, but seen within a broader framework of what is grammatically appropriate in a specific context. We have looked at what it may mean to develop the role of *teacher as language analyst* with the use of corpora to look at the forms, meaning and use of *some* and *any* across a range of registers and contexts of use, as a way to allow us to move beyond the recycling of inaccurate rules of thumb (Lantolf 2007).

In looking at what teachers should know about how learners learn grammar, we have seen that developments in SLA have put the focus back on how learners learn grammar, which includes a renewed emphasis on the explicit teaching and correction of grammar. The other key finding is that tasks need to integrate a focus on form(s) with meaningful communication, so that learners can map forms on to their functions in specific contexts of use. Beyond these two findings, key overviews in SLA grammar research (Spada 2010; Ellis 2006a) indicate that many questions about pedagogy are unresolved.

And finally, what does this mean for the teaching of grammar? Let me suggest two areas. Firstly, it is likely there will be a greater use of more targeted corpora to explore grammar in a range of contexts that are in line with students' target needs. These would include specialist corpora for English for Specific Purposes (Business, Airspeak) or which target students' specific interests (sport, film, hobbies). Secondly, if we are looking to engage student in tasks which focus on the mappings of form and function, it could be argued that this is best done from the students' perspective – relating the students' own meanings and understandings of the world around them to the relevant language choices – their lives and concerns, rather than those of materials writers. As we have seen in Chapter 2 when looking at learner-centred learning and the Dogme approach, Thornbury and Meddings (2009) argue that we need to move away from focusing on courses and published materials and get back to activities where we engage with our learners in meaningful interactions on topics they can discuss, drawing on language they need at that time. Others would rightly point out that this can be difficult for teachers, particularly with grammar, as they will not be able to plan and prepare for the grammar point that may emerge. Clearly, the key will be a sensitive integration and balancing of a range of approaches to the teaching and learning of grammar.

4.6 GUIDED READING

Larsen-Freeman, D. (2003), *Teaching Languages: From Grammar to Grammaring,*
Boston: Heinle
Consider Larsen-Freeman's argument for considering grammar as a skill rather than as a competence. What does the concept of grammaring add to your understanding of grammar and the process of learning grammar?

Find some examples that she gives for the way a usage-based theory of language adds to our understanding of the grammar choices we make: for example, on p. 57, look at the explanation for the motivation for saying *Meredith gave Jack advice* as opposed to *Meredith gave advice to Jack*. What do these examples add to your present understanding of grammar, and could these be useful insights for your students?

Spada, N. (2010), 'Beyond form-focused instruction: Reflections on past, present and future research', *Language Teaching,* **44:2, 225–36**

In this article, Spada reviews the Form-Focused Instruction research over the previous thirteen years, drawing mainly on three meta-analyses over this period (Spada 1997, Norris and Ortega 2000, and Spada and Tomita 2010). She addresses five specific questions:

1. Is form-focused instruction beneficial to second language acquisition (SLA)?
2. Are particular types of form-focused instruction more beneficial than others?
3. Is there an optimal time to provide form-focused instruction?
4. Are particular language features more affected by form-focused instruction than others?
5. Do particular learners benefit more from form-focused instruction?

Overall, the article suggests that it is still difficult for SLA research to answer these questions conclusively. It is a brief article based on a conference plenary, and does not provide much detail, but her main conclusion is similar to that of Ellis (2006b: 9): 'there is increasing evidence that instruction, including explicit FFI, can positively contribute to unanalysed spontaneous production, its benefits not being restricted to controlled/analysed L2 knowledge.'

Parrott, M. (2010), *Grammar for English Language Teachers* (2nd edn), Cambridge: Cambridge University Press

This is an up-to-date pedagogic grammar that strikes a good balance between pedagogic concerns and what Lantolf (2007) calls scientific concepts of grammar. Taking our example of *some* and *any* from Section 4.1, the book situates within the broader system choices of other quantifiers, as well as exploring issues of meaning and use. It is a good jumping-off point for further language awareness explorations of grammar in use in specific contexts.

The Internet Grammar of English, University College London, <http://www.ucl.ac.uk/internet-grammar/home.htm> (last accessed 17 January 2013)

This provides a useful resource to help teachers review their basic understanding of the systems in English grammar. Areas such as the structure of complex noun groups and the structure of the clause are often overlooked in teacher training in ELT.

> The Internet Grammar of English is an online course in English grammar written primarily for university undergraduates. However, we hope that it will be useful to everyone who is interested in the English language. IGE does not assume any prior knowledge of grammar.

Thornbury, S. (2001), *Uncovering Grammar*, Oxford: Macmillan Heinemann

Thornbury draws on usage-based theories of language in looking at grammar as an emergent system, and shows how this leads to a concern with grammar as process. 'Grammaring' (Larsen-Freeman, 2003) is the term he uses for this, and he shows how this translates into classroom practice. He looks at the role of *noticing* in the learning of grammar and the teacher's role in helping learners to 'uncover' their understandings of the regularities in the language. There are careful and well-illustrated discussions of inductive approaches such as consciousness raising and grammaring tasks. Consider Thornbury's position in terms of inductive versus deductive learning – is there room for the latter in this perspective (see pp. 78–9)? Do you think the approaches he outlines would work in your teaching context?

NOTES

1. British National Corpus: <http://www.natcorp.ox.ac.uk/> The online page has a 'sample' search function which will give 50 random sample hits (last accessed 21 April 2012).
2. 'Data cited herein have been extracted from the British National Corpus, distributed by Oxford University Computing Services on behalf of the BNC Consortium. All rights in the texts cited are reserved.'
3. British Academic Written English and British Academic Spoken English corpora are available at Sketch Engine Open <http://the.sketchengine.co.uk/open/>. Information about the corpora can be found at <http://wwwm.coventry.ac.uk/researchnet/BAWE/Pages/BAWE.aspx> and <http://wwwm.coventry.ac.uk/researchnet/base/Pages/BASE.aspx> (last accessed 21 April 2012).
4. British National Corpus.

5

VOCABULARY IN METHODS

INTRODUCTION

Many learners and linguists agree that vocabulary lies at the heart of learning a language. One learner said, 'I am quite happy to pronounce badly and make grammatical mistakes, but there is no escape from learning words' (Pickett 1978 in Hedge 2000: 111). We might learn structures and patterns, functions and notions, but without the words to cement them together they are meaningless. Yet ironically, focus on vocabulary as a discrete language learning skill did not achieve priority until the 1990s, with the arrival of the lexical approach. This turned around the focus of vocabulary as a subset of grammar learning, and instead made grammar a subset of vocabulary learning (Lewis 1993). In the past twenty years, multiple aspects of vocabulary learning and teaching have been explored, researched, trialled and practised. This chapter aims to address some of these aspects and identify what is important and useful for the teacher of second-language vocabulary. It answers the questions:

- What are the main influences on the teaching of vocabulary today?
- What does it mean to 'know' a word?
- What are useful strategies for acquiring vocabulary?
- How do the answers to these questions influence the teaching of vocabulary?

5.1 TEACHING VOCABULARY: TRENDS, INFLUENCES, UNDERSTANDINGS

The impact of corpus on vocabulary teaching

Chapter 4 introduced the idea of the corpus, and the ways in which naturally occurring language has influenced our view of grammar. In the same way, the corpus has changed the way we are able to answer questions about vocabulary. Millions of written words and thousands of hours of natural spoken language now form the foundation for dictionaries, grammars and coursebooks. This data from the corpus shows us how words are actually used in everyday speech by native speakers. Information from the corpus often differs widely from what coursebooks or pedagogic dictionaries tell us, and from what teachers might expect. For example, a straightforward teaching of the word *happy* might suggest:

- Happy is the opposite of sad.
- Happy means the same as (is a synonym of) joyful, pleased, glad, delighted.

However, the corpus shows us that, in fact, *happy* is less frequently used with its prime meaning than with other, more unexpected meanings. The examples below derive from the University of Quebec corpus, including 179,000 words taken from the press, 175,000 taken from academic writing and 175,000 words taken from fiction (Brown University of Quebec, <http://www.lextutor.ca/concordancers/>).

```
[20] y no stretch of the imagination a HAPPY choice
and the arguments against it as
[21] fiscal year, isn't making anyone HAPPY. Certainly
it isn't making the Presiden
[22] inly it isn't making the President HAPPY, and he
has been doing his apologetic
[23] eafter the audience waxed applause-HAPPY, but
discriminating operagoers reserve
[24] in fine voice, the chorines evoke HAPPY memories,
and the Little Flower rides t
[25] e fellow that kept crying for "Get HAPPY" had to
go home unhappy, about that it
[26] plause and flowers. All went home HAPPY except
the Newport police, who feared t
[27] nigh, and those deprived of their HAPPY hour at
the cocktail bar. In Newport la
[28] ts. And many advertisers have been HAPPY with the
results of
[29] (at least in England) are not the HAPPY, fine,
strong, natural, earthy people c
```

Here happy is used with several different meanings which are either significantly or subtly different from the prime meaning:

- 'a happy choice' (no. 20) suggests the meaning 'lucky'
- 'making the President happy' (no. 22) suggests pleasing the President and has a sense of servant to master subservience
- 'applause-happy' is an interesting compound suggesting excessive applause (no. 23)
- 'happy hour' suggests the notion of being merry with discounted drink (no. 27)
- 'happy with the results' suggests *satisfied with*, in that results meet expectations (no. 28)

Thus, as a teacher you can ask the questions of your coursebooks and resources:

Is the vocabulary being illustrated from real language use? What does the corpus say about the 'real-world' use of the word, and how is this different from the course-book use?

Digital media and creating new words

The Internet and digital ways of exchanging messages have also changed the way we might learn, understand and teach words. New words are being coined constantly to take account of new concepts, brands and products, activities and events in the modern world. One way this is done is to use the building blocks of words in new ways, to create new patterns and rules about the way a word is used. These building blocks are called morphemes, and are the smallest units of words which change their meaning and function: for example, *-ed* changes a regular verb into the past (*laugh/laughed*), or *s* changes a noun into the plural (*cat/cats*). This has happened throughout the history of language; but what is new is the way in which these new words now spread rapidly round the world through instant media such as mobile phones and the Internet. They have become a 'lingua franca' shared by all users of English and do not belong to, or necessarily come from, native speakers of English.

Below are some examples of words created to describe new concepts or phenomena, and whilst they are 'new' words, they in fact build on standard ones within the language.

> Affluenza: 'a blend of affluence and influenza' suggesting a 'social disease' arising from addiction to wealth and success
> Decruitment: recruitment means to acquire new staff; decruitment means to 'lay them off' or lose staff
> Flexitarian: 'a vegetarian who sometimes eats meat and fish'
> Overparenting: being excessively protective of your children to give them opportunities and make sure they are safe
> (From 'Learn English Today', <http://www.learn-english-today.com/new-words/new-words-in-english.htmlhttp://www.learn-english-today.com/new-words/new-words-in-english.html>)

International Englishes

It was mentioned above, and in Chapter 3, that new vocabulary in English is being generated by all users of English globally, and is no longer the prerogative of the native speaker. Whilst some of the language is shared rapidly through the cyber and digital world, other vocabularies belong to specific communities, and express something unique to their culture and lifestyle. Mackay (2002) suggests that these words fall into four specific categories: words describing daily life, housing, food, social relationships and institutions (Table 5.1).

Some of the words are transparent in meaning, such as 'clansman'; others can be understood within context, as in Mackay's example 'She was not prepared to be an impoverished first wife if Saiyud took a mistress, or a minor wife' (Mackay 2002: 61); whilst others require local 'insider' knowledge to be fully explained, such as 'moon cake', which is a bean curd cake, 'barnbrack', which is a bread roll, or 'outstation', which means away from home.

What should the teacher do with these variations? It is interesting for the teacher of English to be aware of the richness of this community and culture-specific vocabulary. Within monolingual or monocultural settings where the teacher shares the language, this cultural variety will form a constant subtext to the question of which

Table 5.1   Lexical variations in world Englishes (examples from Mackay 2002: 61)

Category	Lexical variations	Where?
Daily life	dirty kitchen outstation	Philippine English Singapore and Malaysia
Housing	shophouse sala	Singapore and Malaysia Philippine English
Food items	moon cakes barnbrack	China and Malaysia Ireland
Societal institutions	minor wife clansman	Thailand Hong Kong

vocabulary to teach and how? It is interesting to invite students to share variations they are familiar with and local attitude towards these variations. Mackay reports a survey conducted in 1999 in which Filipino and Thai speakers were asked if the words which were local and specific to their community should be placed in a dictionary of Asian English. Interestingly, 'most of the Filipino participants believed that local lexical items should take their place in a dictionary of Asian English' whilst Thai participants did not want to include any local English words (Mackay 2002: 62). Why do you think this is? What is it that makes a variety acceptable or not to a community? Butler's theory is this: 'the more English is used on a daily basis in a multilingual context, the more likely individuals in that country are to accept lexical innovation' (Butler 1999, in Mackay 2002: 62).

The corpus and vocabulary teaching

McCarten, J. (2007), *Teaching Vocabulary: lessons from the corpus, lessons for the classroom*, Cambridge: Cambridge University Press, available at <http://www.cambridge.org/other_files/downloads/esl/booklets/McCarten-Teaching-Vocabulary.pdf> (last accessed 22 January 2013)

McCarten identifies six ways in which we can learn about words from a corpus:

- Frequency – which words do we tend to use frequently, and which rarely?
- Differences in speaking and writing: which words do we tend to use in spoken contexts, and which in the written context?
- Contexts of use: in what situations, contexts and settings do we use certain words?
- Collocation: how do words join together, and which words tend to join?
- Grammatical patterns: how do words impact on grammar, and how does grammar impact on words?:
- Strategic use: how do words help to organise and manage discourse? (McCarten 2007: 3)

Which words do we tend use frequently, and which rarely?

Table 5.2 shows some information derived from corpus analysis in response to this question, in McCarten's booklet.

Table 5.2   Vocabulary frequency lists (McCarten 2007)

The most frequent word in English	I
The most frequent verbs	know go go mean think
The most frequent nouns	people time things
The most frequent adjective	good
High-frequency words	**Low-frequency words**
yeah little children things	yes small child thing

Table 5.3   Use of *probably* and *however* in different text types (derived from McCarten 2007)

	probably	*however*
Used most frequently	Academic writing	Academic writing
Used least frequently	Newspapers	Conversation

Task 5.1 You as corpus analyst and teacher

McCarten compares the use of the words ***probably*** and ***however*** in three different contexts: newspapers, conversations and academic texts (Table 5.3).

Do you think teachers should consult frequency lists such as these, before planning the teaching of vocabulary?

Do you see any problems in choosing to teach more frequent words earlier than the less frequent?

Which words do we tend to use in spoken contexts, and which in the written context?

Task 5.2: You as corpus analyst and researcher

Look at two different kinds of text that you read regularly, such as newspapers, magazines, novels or reports. Conduct your own corpus research by looking through and counting the occurrences of *probably* and *however* in each. Which text uses it most frequently? Which least frequently? Are your findings the same as McCarten's above?

How far do you think it is helpful to know which words are used in particular contexts?

How could you use this information to build a plan of which words to teach your class?

Task 5.3 Explore the corpus 🖥

Choose two or three vocabulary items you or your learners find interesting or challenging, and explore natural occurrences of the word from the Compleat Lexical Tutor link: <http://www.lextutor.ca/concordancers/>

Draw up your own definitions of the word, and any features you notice of how and where it is used in the sentence, according to the corpus.

Were there any surprises or differences from your expectations? From coursebook presentations of the word?

5.2 WHAT DOES IT MEAN TO KNOW A WORD?

What can the teacher do with this new knowledge? One answer is to look at the underlying characteristics of words, just as a linguist does. By becoming a linguist, the teacher also becomes an observer and analyst of language, and can pass these strategies on to his or her learners. Nation (2001) has suggested that knowing a word involves accessing nine different aspects of word knowledge (Table 5.4). As you read through these, you might notice how each of these components are explored from the perspective of the teacher, and the ways the teacher might activate this knowledge in the classroom.

Knowing how words are 'built'

The newly developed words in Section 5.1 are all recognisably part of the English language, even though they may be unfamiliar. The reason they do appear familiar is that they use familiar 'building blocks' of English vocabulary, so it is possible to decode

Table 5.4   Nine notions of 'knowing' a word (Nation 2001)

Nation's nine components of word knowledge	What the teacher should know
Orthography	How a word is spelt in its different forms How spelling may change the meaning of a word
Morphology	How a word is built How different parts of the word affect its meaning or function
Parts of speech	The different ways nouns, verbs, adjectives, adverbs, pronouns, prepositions behave and function in a sentence
Pronunciation	Where the stress or emphasised syllable comes in a word How individual sounds are pronounced and which written letters are silent
Meanings	How words change in different contexts Whether and how words have multiple meanings
Collocations	Which words are commonly found beside each other
Meaning associations	How words connect, such as general word to specific examples; or opposites; or words which mean something similar
Specific uses	Whether words belong in a specific context, such as vocabulary for airline pilots or for medical research
Register	Whether words are formal or informal, slang or taboo, and in which settings it would or would not be appropriate to use them

Table 5.5   A word-building chart

Beginning of word (prefix)	Root	End of word (suffix)
over de re flexi	parent breadcrumb cruit t	ing ment arian

Table 5.6   Word-building patterns: prefixes and suffixes

Prefixes	Suffixes
overtime oversize overweight overarching derail deconstruct devalue debase reread reword reformulate re-evaluate	amazement achievement statement octogenarian (over 80 years old) librarian vegetarian

their meaning using the knowledge of words we already have. Table 5.5 'unpicks' the different components of the words into three parts: beginning, middle, and end of words.

Each of the parts is called a **morpheme**, and these are the smallest units of lexical or grammatical meaning in English. Knowing about these building blocks can multiply opportunities for learning words. You might, for example, build patterns showing how the same morpheme is used in other words, as in Table 5.6.

Alternatively, you might look at how one word can 'grow' into many others, by adding and changing the morpheme. Figure 5.1 is a 'word spider', which shows how the 'single' word *friend* can open out into many other possibilities. These examples suggest that morphemes, the building blocks attached to the beginnings or ends of words, change not only grammatical function but also the semantic components, or meaning, of a word. Table 5.7 gives examples of how morphemes change meanings.

Once the basic concept is taught, you can cover a lot of words quite easily, and learners can record and learn these by building similar word stars. In Table 5.8 is a grid showing parts of words which can fit to the beginning or to the end of words.

- How many 'new' words you can make from the list in Column B by attaching the parts from Column A and/or Column C?

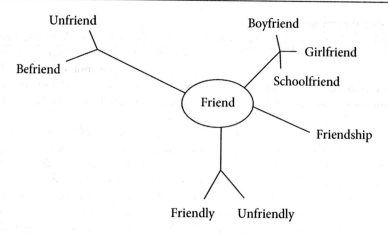

Figure 5.1   Word spider

Table 5.7   From word forms to word meanings

Changing form	Changing meaning
From *friend* to *friendship*	*-ship*: changes a concrete noun into an abstract one
From *friend* to *friendly*	*-ly*: changes a noun into an adjective (or adverb): friendly
From *friend* to *befriend*	*be-*: changes a noun into a verb
From *friendly* to *unfriendly*	*un-*: changes an adjective with positive meaning into a negative
From *friend* to *unfriend*	*un-* added to the noun creates a 'new' verb to denote striking someone off your social networking list
Creating compounds	Join the noun to a limited number of related nouns to form a new word: *boyfriend, girlfriend, schoolfriend*

Table 5.8   Word-building chart

Column A: Prefixes at the beginning of words	Column B: Roots of words	Column C: Suffixes at the end of words
en- *re-* *im-/in-/un-* *de-* *be-*	*rage* *press* *love* *light* *read* *friend*	*-able* *-ship* *-en* *-er*

- Do you need to make any spelling changes in order to create the new word?
- How is each 'new' word different from its 'root'?
- If you were invited to introduce one new word into the English language using this list, what word would that be and what would it mean?

Knowing the grammar of words

In Table 5.4, Nation mentioned amongst his nine components of 'knowing a word' the importance of knowing 'parts of speech', or the grammatical function of words inside sentences. It is useful to make a distinction between **content words**, which convey meaning about the real world, and **grammatical** words, which form links and building blocks and are empty of meaning when they stand alone. In Table 5.9 are some examples of content and grammatical words.

The words in column A are more interesting, connect with our messages and meanings, and are easier to remember, but without the words in column B it is impossible to form complete messages and convey subtleties of meaning. In fact, when we look at natural occurrences of language, it is interesting to note that we use the words in column B much more frequently than content words. Leech et al.'s frequency list (2001) showed that the fifty most frequently used words in English are grammatical words. The content words fall far behind in the amount of use, but amongst these, surprisingly, the most frequently used in Leech's list are *said* (53rd most frequent word), *time* and *people*.

There are many questions we need to ask about content words in order to appreciate their meaning, connections and 'behaviour' within a sentence or utterance. Table 5.10 suggests questions that can be asked of nouns and verbs, which are two of the main content building blocks of the sentence or utterance.

Table 5.11 is an example of how questions about a single word can lead to important information, and how this can lead into teaching ideas. There are other questions which can be asked about each part of speech. Table 5.12 suggests questions which can be asked about verbs. The answers and noticing processes this entails help you to 'build' language. Asking these questions is also valuable to model as a teacher and to develop in your learners. In Table 5.12, the verbs in Group A are all modals. They do not change when attached to different pronouns (I/you/he/she/we/they). They also do not have their own forms in the past and future, so need to 'borrow' from other verbs. For example: *must* in the future becomes – you *will have to*. If you reported the words 'You may come in' in past time, it would become 'She said I could come in', or a variation of this. All of these verbs also express the notion of permission and obligation.

Group B comprises verbs which need another word to complete them – a noun, a pronoun or another verb. These are called **transitive** verbs.

Table 5.9   Word functions (derived from Bloomer, Griffiths and Merriman 2005: 141)

Column A: Content words – categories	Column B: Grammatical words – categories
Concrete nouns: people, creatures, things	Prepositions: *of, in, by, from*
Abstract nouns: ideas, feelings	Articles: *a, an, the*
Adverbs: times, places	Demonstratives: *this, that*
Adjectives: qualities	Pronouns: *I, you, he, she, it, we, they*
Verbs: actions	Auxiliaries: *is, has, can, ought, might, may*

Table 5.10   Questions to ask about nouns

Teacher/student as linguist: questions to ask about nouns
Is it concrete or abstract? *friend* or *friendship*?
Is there a plural form? *hair* or *hairs*?
If there is a plural, how is it formed? *mouses* or *mice*?
Are there other words which are similar in meaning? *garbage, rubbish, refuse* or *trash*?
Is it a general word, or a specific one? *flower* or *rose*? *bird* or *lesser spotted grebe*?
Does the word have more than one pronunciation and if so, does this change the meaning? e.g. *reFUSE* and *refuse*
Does the word suggest a particular geographical region? *bairn* (Scottish), *child* (neutral)
Is the word archaic, or does it suggest a particular time? *Twitter* as a noun has changed its meaning since 2010 from birdsong to digital text messaging.
Does it have a positive or negative colouring? For example, an advertising company selling a perfume would use the words: *fragrance; scent* and not the words: *smell, odour.* The first two words suggest a pleasant perfume, the latter two words unpleasant.
Research and find a 'new' noun which has been coined in English in the last two years. Try out these questions with your 'new' word.
These examples will be discussed later in this section.

Table 5.11   Noticing words: uncountable nouns and the plural form

Example	Questions and answers	Teaching ideas
hair or *hairs*?	**Question:** Is there a plural form of *hair*? Does the word change its meaning in the plural? **Answer:** Yes: hair is regular in FORM in the plural. It adds an -s ending: *hairs*. However, the plural has a different MEANING and CONNOTATION. This is because hair is **uncountable**. **Uncountable nouns** do not have a plural form, or when the plural is used, they change in meaning. **Examples:** *I like your new hair!* is a compliment – but *I like your new hairs* would not be! *You've lost a lot of weight!* would be quite different to *You've lost a lot of weights!*	Try writing paired sentences of your own using uncountable nouns. Other nouns which are uncountable in British English are: *cheese, wine, milk, water, accommodation, information* The first sentence uses the uncountable noun in its singular form. The second sentence tries out the uncountable noun in the plural. Is the plural form possible, and if so where, when and with what meaning?

Examples of transitive verbs are

> *I promise*   *you (a pronoun)*
> *offer*   *to tell your mother (a verb)*
> *threaten*

Table 5.12   Questions to ask about verbs

Teacher as linguist: questions to ask about verbs
Does the verb change its form with the different pronouns *I, you, he, she, we, they*?
Does the verb require other words to complete its meaning – a noun, a verb, a phrase?
Does the verb have forms to describe past and future time?
Does the verb have a progressive form?
Does the verb change its meaning when it changes its form?
Does the verb change its meaning when attached to a particle/preposition (as in group C below)?
Try and answer these questions for yourself with the verbs below. Each group shares similar characteristics. What are these?

Group A: *must, should, ought, may*	**Group B:** *promise, offer, threaten*
Group C: *see, think, understand, hear*	**Group D:** *get on with, fall for, fall out with, split up with, take in/on/out/over/up, get on with, fall out with, fall for, split up with*

The Group C verbs in Table 5.12 are all verbs of the five senses, which change their meaning in the present progressive form. *I see* is often used to mean 'I understand!' *I am seeing* has many different meanings, as the following examples show.

- 'Are you *seeing* anyone these days?' 'Yes, I've got a new boyfriend called Nazeen!'
- 'Are you free on Saturday?' 'Oh no sorry, I'm *seeing* a film that evening.'

Group D consists of verbs which change their meaning when attached to prepositions (or particles). They are called **phrasal verbs** because their meaning is conveyed through a complete phrase. Often this meaning is idiomatic, and cannot be guessed by understanding each part of the phrase. So for example:

- To *fall for* means to fall in love
- To *fall out with* means to have an argument

Knowing the meaning of words

There are many ways words can be grouped according to meaning. Table 5.13 gives an example of some of these groupings. They are useful categories for the teacher, as research into vocabulary acquisition suggests we tend to learn vocabulary more easily in connected clusters, and where we can make associations between words. A study by Durso and Coggins (1991) showed that children are more successful in comprehension tests when vocabulary is presented in related groups. However, their study and others such as Stahl et al. (1992) show that word groups in themselves are not enough. Essential to their usefulness is that learners are encouraged to articulate the themes and relationships between words, by activities such as drawing word stars, labelling groups of words and building patterns of their own. In Table 5.13, column A suggests word groups, column B suggests the connecting theme, topic or function, and column C suggests ways in which learners can be guided towards articulating these themes for themselves.

Table 5.13 Ways of grouping words

Column A: Word groups – examples	Column B: Ways of grouping words	Column C: Teaching tips and ideas
car, helicopter, ferry, tram	Words related by **topic area** or **lexical set**	Conduct a word race, where students write as many words as they can within one topic.
go to the travel agent's, look though a brochure, book a flight, get a visa.	Words and phrases describing a **process**	Put these process words and phrases in order and add the missing stages in the process.
garbage, trash, rubbish, refuse, waste, recycling	Words similar in meaning or **synonyms**. As discussed in the section above, very, very few words mean **exactly** the same thing. Here, *garbage* and *trash* are words used in the USA; *recycling* has acquired a positive connotation; *rubbish* is an expletive; *refuse* is a more formal and official word than the others.	Find as many differences as you can between 'synonym' sets. Use the questions about nouns above to help you. Synonym race: Choose an adjective: *friendly, sad, kind.* See who can write down the most synonyms in one minute. Draw up a collective pool of all the synonyms. See who can identify the most differences between the words in three minutes.
happy: sad good: bad true: false	These are **antonyms**, or opposites. The adjectives in this list are 'true' opposites, but many adjectives do not have exact opposites, and context may change the meaning – for example, the opposite of *dry weather* is *wet weather*, but the opposite of *dry wine* is not *wet wine*.	Draw up a list of adjectives. Which ones have 'true' opposites and which ones do not?
hot, cold, cool, warm, freezing, boiling	Words which can be graded along a **cline**, or **spectrum of meaning**	Compare different ideas about how these words on a cline might be organised. Are our idevas personal, cultural, or specific to our mother tongue?

however, nevertheless, even so, having said that	Words or phrases which divide up discourse (**discourse markers**)	Practise adding these words to the start of new sentences to extend an argument or discussion.
stubborn, strong-willed, determined, obstinate	Words with different **connotations**; *stubborn* and *obstinate* have negative overtones, *determined* is neutral, *strong-willed* implies admiration on the part of the speaker	Find words with the opposite connotation; for example, *clever* and *cunning*; *slender* and *scraggy*; *mature* and *old*
flower or *rose*?	A general, or generic word which describes a whole category of things is called a **superordinate**. Specific members of the category are called **hyponyms**. For example: *flower* is a superordinate. This is a list of wild flowers becoming extinct in England. These are hyponyms. Moonwort; moon daisy; southern marsh orchid; autumn hawkbit; sheep's sorrel; self-heal; eyebright; hay rattle.	Category race: Pick a category: • Animals • Birds • Countries • Languages • Food See who can write the most hyponyms in three minutes. Knowledge of hyponyms can suggest detailed specialist knowledge. It is an opportunity for students to share specific knowledge about their interests, culture and expertise.
kids, littlies, wee-ones, children	A difference in formality/informality is called **register**. For example, *kids* is a shared colloquialism which would only be used in an informal context: *littlies* and *wee-ones* are terms which might be used within the family, as families generate their own nicknames to describe family members. *Children* is a neutral term for all of these.	Share colloquial/local/family nicknames for the following: • Family members • Favourite and least favourite teachers

Table 5.14   Collocations with 'tea'

Column A	Column B
iced tea green tea to make tea to brew tea	frozen tea brown tea to cook tea

Knowing how words connect with one another

Words which connect together naturally are 'collocations'. For example, we do find the combinations in column A of Table 5.14, but not the combinations in column B, even though these are grammatically and semantically possible.

Sometimes words form pairs to create a 'set phrase', sometimes changing the meaning of the separate components to form an idiom.

Neither *here nor there*
He didn't know if he was *coming or going*.
I'm *sick and tired* of it all.
She was *all hot and bothered*.

Some words can combine with others to form a new, joint word called a compound. For example:

Arm can combine with *pit/chair/band* to form the words *armpit/armchair/armband*
Hair can combine with *brush/do* to form the words *hairbrush/hairdo*
Air can combine with *port/line* to form the words *airport/airline*

What is interesting about these combinations, however, is that they cannot be generalised to other combinations, even where these might make sense semantically.

We can have an *armchair* but not a *backchair*.
We can have a *hairdo* but not a *facedo*.
We can have an *airport* and a *carport*, but not a *boatport*.

Collocations can be practised and explored through matching activities such as the ones below. There are only limited matches between the words in column A and column B, although in terms of meaning, the others should linguistically be possible. However, collocations have some of the qualities of idioms, in that they cannot always be predicted and are best learnt through exposure and example.

Which words and phrases in Table 5.15, column A match with the words in column B?

What do you notice about the linguistic connections between time and money in Table 5.16 Are these the same in your language? Explore collocations at:

<http://www.englishclub.com/vocabulary/collocations-lists.htm>

Table 5.15   Collocations 1: classifiers

Column A	Column B
a ball of	cards
a bar of	string
a cube of	sugar
a bottle of	carrots
a bunch of	paper
a pack of	water
a pad of	chocolate

Table 5.16   Idioms of time and money

Column A	Column B
free	time
dead on	
right on	money
ready	
run out of	
save	
spend	
make	

Knowing the sound and spelling of words

Part of knowing a word is knowing how it sounds when spoken aloud, and how this relates to its spelling. Rhyme words are a revealing way of showing the various spellings possible for the same sound. Building up rhyming lists is a 'noticing' activity for learners and teachers which can lead to the building, too, of rhymes and jingles, mixing the rhymes into patterns such as these examples:

Rhyme lists

pear	hair	scare	their
thorn	warn	lawn	faun
bright	height	kite	

Rhyming/spelling jingles
My teacher told me I wasn't bright.
I thought that wasn't fair.
It's just I like to think at night,
and by day to plait my hair.

Pairing words highlights interesting features of the sound–spelling relationship. Table 5.17 shows ways in which words can be grouped together according to their spelling. Column C shows the way these spellings change meaning.

Table 5.17   Homographs, homophones and homonyms

Column A: category	Column B: example	Column C: link with meaning
Words which are spelt exactly the same but SOUND different (homographs)	*read* /riːd/ and *read* /rəd/	The difference between the simple present of the verb, and the simple past
Words which SOUND the same but are spelt differently (homophones)	*dear, deer* *red, read* *tail, tale* *which, witch*	The spelling changes the meaning and the function of the word in each case. What happens to meanings in each of these examples? *The cat with the long tail.* *The cat with the long tale.* *Dear Deer* *I saw you run through the woods. You were a beautiful red colour.* *Which witch flew on this broomstick last night?*
Words which are SPELT the same and SOUND the same but have different meanings (homonyms)	*bank* *crane* *bark* *kind* *trip* *fine*	Can you identify two different word functions for each of these words? For example: *bark* (verb: the sound a dog makes) *bark* (noun: the surface of a tree trunk) How does the change in function change the meaning?

Implications for the teacher

There are some helpful messages for teachers that emerge from our study of words. One key message is that both teachers and learners can become researchers of new language and share in the task of noticing how language is developing in the modern world. Below are some examples of 'noticing' activities in the language classroom.

Task 5.4 Learner and teacher research activities online 💻

Below are a series of search activities which teachers and learners might engage in together online, to discover words. Try these out for yourself and notice what you learn about words, and how you might include these activities into language teaching.

1. Teachers and learners might look at how a word is really used in everyday English by referring to a corpus website. They could compare this corpus information about the word with the information presented in the coursebook.

The link below gives you the opportunity to check corpus data for any word or phrase you would like to research for the classroom:
<http://www.lextutor.ca/concordancers/>

2. Teachers and learners could look at everyday language and 'notice' unusual, interesting or new examples of 'word-building'. What new words are being coined and why? How are word-building blocks being used to make these new words? The website below gives you multiple examples of new words being coined in English: <http://www.learn-english-today.com/new-words/new-words-in-english.html>

3. Teachers might invite learners to recognise 'morphemes' or the building blocks of words for themselves by: building word 'stars' and word families, sharing knowledge with their peers, or using sources of information such as dictionary or corpus websites. This link leads you to the Online Oxford Collocation Dictionary, which is a free and fully online resource: <http://oxforddictionary.so8848.com/>
Word-building activities could include:
- experimenting and making 'families' of their own, and researching which experimental words are and are not used in English
- inventing new words of their own using word-building blocks – for example, to describe a new product or invention, or give a name to a real-life object or activity not yet officially named
- classifying words in a family according to their meaning (abstract or concrete; animal, human or object); their word function (verb, noun, adjective, adverb); their connotation (positive or negative)

4. Teachers might invite learners to share and compare the different words used in their own cultures and contexts, to describe categories such as family members, colours or household items. These ideas can be compared with corpora such as <http://www.corpora4learning.net/resources/corpora.html>
This link gives you an overview of corpora worldwide of English and Englishes, including English from East Africa, New Zealand, India, the Philippines, Singapore and Europe. Each corpus draws on a million or more words of written data.

5. Teachers and learners might share collocations which do or do not occur in natural language, and look at those which are exchanged by other learners and teachers online, such as <http://www.englishclub.com/vocabulary/collocations-lists.htm> and <http://prowritingaid.com/Free-Online-Collocations-Dictionary.aspx#.UQFQWGdhL1U>

Task 5.5 Researching teaching
What should I do when students ask me the meaning of an unknown word?
This is an action research question derived from Grabe and Stoller (2002: 188),who evolved a selection of 'model action research questions' for teachers.

Imagine you are a teacher in a class of intermediate learners. The following words have emerged in a class discussion about inventions and discoveries. Review the 'ways of knowing a word' in this section, and think about how you might respond to your learners. What 'knowledge' about the words do you think would be useful?

How might you practise, explain or discuss these words and phrases with the class?

- *international*
- *innovation*
- *discovery*
- *experiment*
- *hypothesis*
- *in the same field*
- *on the same path*
- *to take up an idea*
- *to write up an experiment*
- *the idea took off*

Task 5.6 Research new words and collocations online 🖥

Act as a linguistic researcher for one week, and notice any 'newly created' words you might overhear – perhaps on the radio, in social settings or community settings such as on the bus. Note these down and think about how the word is structured and how it might have emerged. Then see if your 'new words' are listed in this corpus (Learn English Today, last accessed 17 January 2012): <http://www.learn-english-today.com/new-words/new-words-in-english.html>

Now do the same for interesting or unusual collocations. Note down examples you have noticed.

Then search for your examples and further examples in these collocation resources: Oxford Online Dictionary of Collocations <http://oxforddictionary.so8848.com/> and <http://prowritingaid.com/Free-Online-Collocations-Dictionary.aspx#.UQFQWGdhL1U>

5.3 DEVELOPING STRATEGIES FOR ACQUIRING VOCABULARY

Research into second-language vocabulary learning

Research into vocabulary learning is relatively recent compared to other aspects of language learning research. This is because vocabulary was regarded as an aspect of other skills, such as reading acquisition. However, since the 1990s researchers have asked detailed questions about vocabulary acquisition which are helpful for teachers. Some of these questions are summarised below.

How many words should a language learner know?

Nation (2006) suggested that 4,000 word families, or 10,000 individual word items, are needed for reading with the support of a teacher. For fluent reading, he suggested this figure rises to 9,000 word families. This compares to a 'threshold level' of 3,000 words identified as a 'common core', which gives a learner capacity to function effectively in the target language (Van Ek 1973). A study by Laufer (1992) showed that, where a learner had fewer than 3,000 vocabulary word families in the second language, they had low test scores in reading comprehension even if they had a high academic level. This was the threshold needed to transfer comprehension skills from one language into the other. We thus have a distinction between the desired vocabulary level for general and everyday effectiveness, and the desired vocabulary level for fluent reading moving towards academic proficiency in the target language.

Which words should be taught and learned?

Several researchers have answered this question by suggesting that frequency is a key criteria for selecting words to teach. One justification for this is that the most frequent words in English occupy a large percentage of the words we actually use in written texts and in spoken utterances. Nation (2001, 2004) found that 1,000 common English words occupy 71 per cent of written texts: so these words, in theory, have a high value and currency for second-language learners. However, when we look at these high-frequency words as teachers, it will be apparent that many have limited potential for meaningful learning activities. Many, for example, are function words such as *the, would, all, she, her, more, been, about, here, when, is* (Grabe 2010: 280).

We thus need to balance the criteria of frequency with other criteria which make sense for teachers and learners. These include:

- Choosing words which emerge naturally from classroom activities and learner interest
- Separating words which will be useful for everyday use and spoken contexts from words which are needed only in specific domains, such as reading technical writing or completing a specific task. The former can be taught and practised for active and productive use; the latter can be taught for use in the specific context, and given less emphasis in production and practice
- Identifying words which are specific and relevant for the learners' target context, such as the school-leaving exam, or an in-company conference

How can vocabulary acquisition be enhanced?

Researchers have answered this question in several ways which are interesting for the teacher. Nattinger and DeCarrico (1992) argued that native speakers develop fluency not by learning words as isolated units, but by learning them as unanalysed 'chunks' which have a communicative function. For example, a child learns the meaning of 'there's a good boy!' or 'go to sleep now' before being able to recognise the individual parts of the phrase. As native speakers, we recognise and memorise chunks which are useful for communicative purposes, and integrate vocabulary learning into our absorption of the whole message (DeCarrico 2001; Nattinger and DeCarrico 1992). For the teacher, this offers the message that we might identify 'chunks' and phrases which are useful in the learners' context, and practise these without isolating the individual parts. This idea led to the lexical approach, in which lexical 'chunks' formed the organising principle of the whole syllabus (Lewis 1993). Whilst the lexical approach as a single determining principle may be limiting, elements of the approach remain significant for the eclectic teacher and the eclectic syllabus.

Research by Nation (2008), Blachowicz et al. (2006), Nagy (2005) and others suggest that the following are strategies which can enhance effective vocabulary acquisition:

Table 5.18   International words used in English

Words used internationally	Loan words from other languages used in English
OK *taxi* *TV*	*judo, kimono, sumo, sushi, karaoke* (Japanese) *salami, spaghetti, pizza* (Italian) *sarong* (Malaysian) *kangaroo, koala, boomerang* (aboriginal Australian) *glasnost, perestroika* (Russian) *paprika, palinka, goulash* (Hungarian) *television, telephone, telepathy* (Greek)

- Noticing links and differences between mother tongue and second language vocabulary
- Developing memory, and memory-building activities
- 'Word-mapping', or building up word families and word associations
- Principled use of the dictionary, bilingual dictionaries and glossaries
- Deduction strategies for dealing with unknown and new vocabulary
- Frequent repetition and exposure to new vocabulary in different contexts

We will now look in more detail at these strategies, which teachers have found to be helpful and researchers have shown to enhance learning.

Strategy 1: Notice links between first and second language vocabulary
Languages tend to borrow words from one another, often adapting them to fit the new patterns and sound system. There are many words borrowed from other languages which are used in the English language, and this 'permeability' between languages is increasing as English becomes a world lingua franca. Table 5.18 illustrates some words used in English which have the same meaning in other languages, and words which are borrowed from other languages into English. This is a useful starting place for teachers working with beginner learners, since they will discover that they do, after all, know some words which are already used and useful in the English language.

However, there are many words which are very close in sound and form, but are different in meaning. These are 'false friends', and can cause confusion if the differences are not made explicit. Table 5.19 shows some of these false friends.

We have seen that it is helpful to encourage word associations and connections, as long as these do not induce confusion. Thus the examples above are helpful for awareness-raising with students at the appropriate level of proficiency; and with

Table 5.19   False friends

English	Other languages
gymnasium (means sports hall)	German, Hungarian *gimnázium* (means high school)
sympathetic (means understanding)	French *sympathique* (means kind)
affair (main meaning is love relationship)	Swedish *affär* (means shop)

learners at earlier stages, it is useful to make meanings and differences explicit when the word arises naturally within context.

Strategy 2: Develop memory for vocabulary development

The development of memory has been seen to contribute to the success of vocabulary learning. We all know tens of thousands of words in our own language, and can retrieve most of these in a fraction of a second. This suggests that the words are systematically stored in our mind, in our 'mental lexicon'. Research suggests that we may store a word in more than one place so that we can retrieve it when we want, and that these storage places are linked in a complex and constantly-changing kind of web (see for example Meara 1992, Gupta and MacWhinney 1997). The following are characteristics of the lexicon that researchers have so far identified:

- The main way we seem to store vocabulary is by grouping together words with similar meanings (e.g. *sad/unhappy*); or words which are co-ordinates, that is, items in a lexical set (e.g. *hand, arm, head*, or *yellow, red, purple*).
- We also seem to store items according to spelling rules, and the general phonological 'shape' of a word – e.g. trying to recall a word like 'rough', we might think of 'through'.
- We have a system for storing words according to their grammatical class (e.g. nouns, verbs).
- We store words as wholes, but also store 'bits' of words so that we can reassemble these (e.g. un + happy + ness).
- We store words not only singly, but also in chunks of words that often occur together (e.g. *'on the tip of my tongue'*).

It is clear that the more times we hear a word (some people believe that at least seven times are necessary), the easier it becomes to recall and use it. We also know from our own life experience that if we do not use and practice a word or phrase after our first meeting with it, we tend to forget it.

Teaching implications

- Revise and recycle words frequently that have been taught in class; at the end of the class, the next day, the next week, and then again at regular intervals.
- Keep a record of words that arise in class. This could be in a notebook, or on slips of paper that are put in a 'word box' and used in games of various kinds.
- Encourage your students to revise at home.
- Develop memory by using mnemonic strategies such as word cards, vocabulary memory games, colour coding (for example, with nouns, adjectives, adverbs in different colours), mind maps and word stars to activate visual memory, matching activities.
- Develop memory through patterns – for example, patterns of word groups, word forms, rhyme words.
- Recycle words so that they recur often and in different contexts and settings.
- Avoid interference between items – for example, where an item is a false friend, or where two items are confusing when connected (Nation 2002: 271).

- Engage all the five senses in learning a vocabulary item – touch, sight, smell, sound, taste. Edge and Garton give us this example: 'if you are told the name of a fruit in a foreign language just as you have bitten into it, and are holding and looking at it, tasting and smelling it, you have a very good chance of remembering its name' (Edge and Garton 2009: 34).

Strategy 3: Develop strategies for when students don't know a word
The teacher can help the student develop the following useful strategies for learning new vocabulary.

Know how to ask when a word is unclear:

- *What does --- mean?*
- *How do you say --- in English?*
- *What's the English for ---?*

Find an alternative way to say what you want, if you do not have the words. Here are some useful phrases to 'fill in the gap':

- *It's a thing you use for ---*
- *It's something to do with ---*
- *You use it when ---*

The skill of deducing the meaning of unknown words in reading texts has also been debated by researchers and practised by teachers. Some researchers have found this skill to be a significant one for word learning (Nassaji 2003; Nation 2001). Beck et al. (2002), however, suggest that not all words and contexts are amenable to guessing. Some contexts might lead learners to the wrong meanings; others might not yield enough information for any clear guess to be made. The characteristics found to be critical for helpful guessing are when the learner knows 'almost all the surrounding words' (Grabe 2010: 275), and when they can identify the meaning of the unknown word precisely. For this to happen, and for guessing to be most efficient, systematic training over a period of time is found to be helpful. This training would include ensuring that learners recognise the clues in the text, including the meanings within the immediate context of the new word. They might be encouraged to ask these questions about the meaning of the unknown word:

- Do I know from the surrounding sentence whether the word is a noun, verb, adjective or other?
- Can I deduce how the word relates to others in the sentence?
- If I were to replace the word with one I do know, what would that be in order to keep the sense and meaning of the sentence?
- Is it likely to refer to a human being, or something inanimate?
- Is it likely to be positive or negative in connotation?
- Is it likely to relate to another word in the text which I do understand?

When all the clues are used carefully and appropriately, students can start to make useful guesses that help them to learn vocabulary and understand its meaning in context.

Strategy 4: Develop dictionary skills

Nation (2001) and Schmitt (2000) report on research which shows that students find reading easier when they have access to glosses of unknown words. Knight (1994) showed that Spanish college learners achieved better results in comprehension when they were able to use a bilingual dictionary. This is not always the case, however. Other studies have shown that dictionaries have little effect on comprehension (Bensoussan, Sim and Weiss 1984), and that they are not necessarily useful to young readers. The message teachers can derive from this is that dictionary use is of value when it is used in a principled way, and can be counter-productive if used unhelpfully, as in Marina's case below:

> I didn't know about extensive reading, and I looked up every word that I couldn't understand. So I got through very few pages in two weeks' time and I had to return the books. (Marina, in Tsui 2009: 83)

What then, are the principles for using dictionaries effectively?

- Ensure that the overall context and message of the text – the 'gist' – is understood before detailed meaning of individual words is attended to.
- Select for dictionary reference only those words which cannot be deduced from context, using the questions suggested in Strategy 3 above.
- Select for the dictionary only those words which are critical for meaning.
- Practise the subskills of using a dictionary, such as alphabetical order, and searching for 'head words' such as verbs in the root form and nouns in the singular.

Strategy 5: Group words together for effective learning

We mentioned in Section 5.1 that studies by Stahl et al. (1992) and Durso et al. (1991) suggest that we learn words best when we can make connections and associations between them. Groups of random words are much harder to remember than a series of words which relate to the same situation or context. We also saw in Section 5.1 the multiple ways in which words can be grouped together. Teachers might plan their vocabulary lessons, not as isolated units, but according to a number of these groups, teaching words in clusters. Table 5.20 suggests ways of grouping words which are also windows into our perceptions of connections and classifications in the world – what is referred to as our 'schema'. It will be interesting to ask, in the classroom: how far are these groupings specific to our own culture and context? What other ways are there of combining and grouping words within each of these broad categories?

Teaching case study 12: Czech Republic

Nana Svecova is a teacher and teacher trainer in the Czech Republic. She describes her own approach to teaching (Lindsay and Knight 2006: 148):

Table 5.20   Grouping words (derived from Grabe 2010: 285)

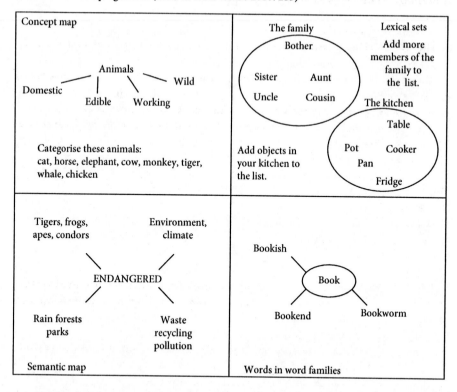

Reading exposes learners to vocabulary and language they are not familiar with. My students often worry about failing to understand everything and try to use the dictionary. Looking up all the unknown words from the text is very slow and boring. They often need a lot of time just to get past a few sentences. Sometimes even the dictionary does not help. My students sometimes tell me that they do understand the meaning of all the individual words in the sentence, but the overall meaning is still unclear. It discourages them from further reading because they feel the effort invested is not worth the outcome.

Task 5.7 You as teacher adviser
'*My students sometimes tell me that they do understand the meaning of all the individual words in the sentence, but the overall meaning is still unclear.*'

Have you encountered the problem Nina describes here, either as a teacher or as a learner?

Some students say they experience this even in their mother tongue, when the content of what they are reading is very new or difficult. Have you ever experienced this?

Do you have any strategies to help yourself or your learners understand whole meanings?

'My students often worry about failing to understand everything and try to use the dictionary. Looking up all the unknown words from the text is very slow and boring.'

When do you use a dictionary?

Do you use a dictionary in your mother tongue when you encounter a new word?

Do you use a dictionary in a second language in the same way as you use dictionaries in your L1?

What is the difference in the way you use the dictionary in each case?

Draw on your ideas from the two questions above to identify three pieces of advice for Nina and her students.

Task 5.8 Exploring learner strategies: research task

This activity is adapted from Wray, Trott and Bloomer (1998: 70).

Memory trial 1

- Draw up a set of eight to ten words chosen at random.
- Ask a class of language learners to memorise the words.
- Test them, and note down how many learners memorised more than five words.
- Ask the learners with the most memorised words to tell the class what techniques they used to help them.

Memory trial 2

- Now draw up a second set of eight to ten random words.
- Test the class again and suggest they try out the techniques suggested by the 'best' students in memory trial 1.
- Note how many learners memorised more than five words.
- Has the number improved?
- What successful vocabulary learning techniques emerge from this research task?

Task 5.9 Exploring vocabulary resources and the lexical approach 🖥️

Paul Nation at the University of Wellington, New Zealand has developed a series of resources for teaching vocabulary, and a battery of short tests for assessing the number of words learners have.

<http://www.victoria.ac.nz/lals/resources/vocrefs>

<http://www.victoria.ac.nz/lals/resources/vocrefs/vocab-tasks>

Explore these resources and note down:

- How would you share these resources with learners in a language teaching context you are familiar with?
- What would the teacher need to do to set this up and prepare learners to best use the resources?
- What would the learners need to do to benefit most from the resources?

5.4 FURTHER READING 🖥

Explore the following further readings in the online resource for this book.

Task 5.10 Blachowicz, C. L. Z., P. J. L. Fisher, D. Ogle and S. Watts-Taffe (2006), 'Vocabulary: questions from the classroom', *Reading Research Quarterly*, 41, 524–39.
Task 5.11 Nagy, W. E. (2005), 'Why vocabulary instruction needs to be long-term and comprehensive', in E. H. Hiebert and M. L. Kami (eds.), *Teaching and Learning Vocabulary: Bringing Research to Practice*, Mahwah, NJ: Erlbaum, pp. 27–44.

5.5 CONCLUSION

This chapter asked the questions:

What are the main influences on the teaching of vocabulary today?
We have seen that research builds on what has gone before, in that we are returning to earlier concepts of memorising, using dictionaries, and learning from written texts. But our understanding has progressed by looking at what really happens in the classroom. We have learnt from this, for example, that dictionaries only work if they are used effectively; that careful training needs to take place for guesswork of new words to be efficient; and that memorisation is best activated through motivating activities.

What does it mean to 'know' a word?
We have also discovered that 'knowing' a word involves a number of skills, which involve teacher and learner being linguists and collectors of words. There are multiple ways a teacher can respond to this invitation: by encouraging learners to collect, group and manipulate words; guess and hypothesise about new meanings; rhyme and build up words; invent words using word-building blocks.

What are useful strategies for acquiring vocabulary? What does this mean for the teaching of vocabulary?
The principle of 'noticing' is one which has high priority in all research studies. Grabe tells us that 'almost every current review of vocabulary now stresses the importance of making students aware of the new words they encounter' (Grabe 2010: 279). The contemporary teacher of vocabulary has much to notice, as words are invented and shaped daily and communicated rapidly via digital media.

5.6 GUIDED READING AND WEB BROWSING 🖥

Nation, I. S. P. (2008), *Teaching Vocabulary: Strategies and Techniques,* **Boston: Heinle Cengage**
Nation's book defines clear principles for teaching and learning vocabulary, based on large-scale and long-term research into vocabulary acquisition. He notes that teachers 'need to see the learning of any particular word as being a cumulative process where knowledge is built up over a series of varied meetings with the word' (Nation

2009: 97). These 'meetings' will include both deliberate learning, the kind of 'notic-ing' activities described in this chapter, and also fluency development, where known vocabulary is practised and experienced. Nation describes fluency development as taking place when 'learners bring a lot of knowledge and experience to the task so that the burden of the task is rather light and the chances of success are high' (Ibid. p. 93).

McCarten, J. (2007), *Teaching Vocabulary: Lessons from the Corpus, Lessons for the Classroom*, Cambridge: Cambridge University Press
Explore in more detail McCarten's analysis of the links between the corpus and vocabulary teaching, discussed in Section 5. 1 above:
<http://www.cambridge.org/other_files/downloads/esl/booklets/McCarten-Teach ing-Vocabulary.pdf>
The lexical approach takes the view that all aspects of language can be taught through the unit of the word, as this is the central building block of messages. Explore this view in more detail on the websites below:

<http://www.cal.org/resources/digest/0102lexical.html>
<http://www.teachingenglish.org.uk/activities/lexical-approach-classroom-
  activities>
<http://iteslj.org/Articles/Kavaliauskiene-LA.html>
<http://www.teachingenglish.org.uk/think/methodology/lexical_approach1.
  shtml>
<http://www.teachingenglish.org.uk/think/methodology/lexical_approach2.
  shtml>
<http://www.ericdigests.org/2002-2/lexical.htm>

6

TEACHER KNOWLEDGE AND THE FOUR LANGUAGE SKILLS: UNDERSTANDING WRITTEN AND SPOKEN LANGUAGE IN THE TWENTY-FIRST-CENTURY WORLD

INTRODUCTION

In 'real' language interaction, the four skills are rarely isolated. As readers, we talk about what we have read; as writers, we draw on knowledge gained through reading and listening. Increasingly, through digital modes of communication, the boundaries between speaking and writing are changing and the conventions that separated the written and spoken word are dissolving. We recognise as teachers, researchers and language users that language is a holistic activity involving the combination of multiple skills. If the classroom is to mirror and prepare for the real world, it is meaningful to understand and teach these skills in combination rather than as discrete units of study.

Yet it is also the case that there is much to learn and understand about the separate processes of learning to read, write, speak and listen in a second language. To integrate these skills successfully, we also need to understand the processes of each. Writing and reading involve engagement with the written word and its changing conventions, whilst speaking and listening involve appreciation of an evolving, various and changing spoken grammar. Another way of looking at the skills is that reading and listening involve receiving and interpreting messages generated by others, whilst speaking and writing involve generating our own messages. How can the teacher both integrate the four skills, and at the same time appreciate the specific characteristics needed to develop each? Chapters 6 and 7 respond to this question from two different angles. Chapter 6 considers what we need to know about the language itself in spoken and written modes. Chapter 7 considers what we need to know as teachers about the teaching and learning of the four skills. Chapter 6 asks the questions:

- How has our understanding of the spoken and written language changed in the twenty-first century? What does this mean for our approaches to teaching?
- What should teachers know about the reading and writing process?
- What should teachers know about the spoken word?
- What should teachers know about pronunciation?
- What are the implications of this knowledge for teaching and developing the language skills?

Chapter 7 will look in more detail at the final question, and consider the implications of this knowledge for the design and teaching of language lessons.

Changing language: changing pedagogies

Our understanding of language has been informed by important developments since the 1980s. This chapter and Chapter 7 explore the implications of these developments for teaching the four skills.

- We saw in Chapters 4 and 5 that we have a great deal of information about how people use language naturally in their everyday lives, as a result of **corpus linguistic** research. It is thus possible to determine not how people should speak and write, but how people actually speak and write, based on millions of words of actual naturally-occurring data. The Cambridge–Nottingham Corpus of Discourse in English (CANCODE), for example, provides a database of five million words 'constructed from spontaneous, everyday English speech in a variety of social contexts', and generated from speakers across the full social, cultural and regional spectrum of the UK (Carter and McCarthy 1997: 7). Chapter 4 showed us that corpus data raises questions such as: how does the corpus require us to rethink our notion of 'grammar'? How does this influence the way we teach accuracy or view 'correctness', or the examples we offer of appropriate spoken and written language? Pedagogic grammars such as the *Cambridge Grammar of Spoken and Written English* have been developed in answer to this question (Carter and McCarthy 2006). Tognini-Bonelli (2001) suggested that pedagogy should be not simply informed by corpus linguistics, but driven by it; in other words, that the corpus should not be used to illustrate categories, patterns and rules, but to rethink these completely.

- We thus need to consider what we regard as 'correct' or 'appropriate' by looking not just at the small units of language such as sound, words and syntax, but at the longer exchanges between speakers, and the qualities and characteristics of spoken and written interaction in different settings. This is a **discourse analysis** approach. McCarthy (1991) and Cook (1989) explore the ways in which this approach can significantly inform the way teachers approach writing and speaking skills. For example, instead of teaching each element in the structure 'Good to see you!', a discourse analysis approach would teach the whole chunk, look at the context in which such a phrase is typically used, and the kind of reply that would be expected, and look at the way the same sentiment might be reframed in a written context. This approach has led to a **genre analysis** approach.

- **Genre analysis** looks at text types, such as an email message compared to a dictionary entry, the abstract of an article compared to a textbook introduction, a diary entry compared to the blurb for a novel. It also looks at the domain, or context, within which something has been written: for example, the kind of texts a student might encounter when studying at a University, or when working in a bank, or when teaching a child to read. The generic characteristics of texts have been extensively analysed as a resource for teachers; for example, by Swales (1990), Bhatia (1993) and Hyland (2004). This has led to teaching resources such as Swales and Feak's *Academic Writing for Graduate Students* (2004), which organises writing activities according to genre or text type, and grammar books such as Biber (1999), which classifies structures according to four text types: conversation, fiction, news reportage and academic prose, and shows how these text types determine grammatical choices.

- **Conversation analysis** is also an analysis that takes us beyond the surface of the language, considering patterns and systems in longer sections of language. It goes even further than discourse analysis in exploring the social significance of these patterns, teasing out social structures, cultural norms and hidden systems in the way we use language to interact. So, for example, a conversation analysis might compare the different responses to the question 'Good to see you!' to see whether these are markers of age, gender, social status, region or power relationship. Wong and Waring (2010) show us how this approach can be translated into a second-language pedagogy. Walsh (2011) suggests that teachers can use this approach to understand their own processes and interactions in the classroom
- As we saw in Chapter 3, English has become a **lingua franca** worldwide, and is spoken by more second and foreign language speakers than by native speakers. As English is shared between speakers of multiple other languages, a third and new 'English' is evolving which remains mutually comprehensible to users of the language and yet is exclusively 'owned' by none of them. This 'interlanguage' has come to be known as ELF – or **English as a Lingua Franca**. It is developing its own systems and varieties, and is more widely used and powerful than native-speaker varieties of English, as Jenkins (2005, 2009) has found. Thus, when we teach conversational strategies, genres and text types, or approaches to grammar and pronunciation, we need to take account of the varieties of interpretations there are of appropriacy. Barron and Schneider (2008) use the term 'variational pragmatics' to highlight the fact that our understanding of conversational conventions varies from culture to culture, context to context; and that pedagogy needs to take account of this and not presume one standard or set of conventions.

6.1 TEACHER KNOWLEDGE OF THE WRITTEN WORD: WHAT SHOULD THE TEACHER KNOW?

As teachers, we need to take account of the natural ways in which our learners encounter written language. Table 6.1 gives some examples of the kind of texts we read and write 'naturally' in our daily interactions outside the classroom, and the reasons why we do so.

The 'text types' include many that would not have been available to the writer or reader fifty years ago, such as Wikis, emails, blogs and tweets. Written messages today travel much faster than fifty years ago, when we relied on printed books and the delivery of paper messages through the post. Messages now are instantaneous and can travel as fast as speech. They often need to be brief and have immediate visual impact so they can be understood at a glance. For these reasons, the written word in the twenty-first century has acquired many of the qualities and characteristics of spoken language. Below are some examples of these changes.

- Written language now includes short forms, abbreviations and recognised visual symbols (or *emoticons*) to replace words: for example, :-)

Table 6.1   What we read/write and why we read/write (derived from Emmitt et al. 2006: 32)

Reason for writing/reading: why read?	Type of text
To inform and advise	Wikipedia, reference books, dictionaries, catalogues, travel guides, websites, Wikis, notices, invitations, prospectuses
To follow instructions	instructions, guides, manuals, recipe books, rule books, stage directions
To amuse or entertain	poems, short stories, plays, reviews, graded readers, jokes, riddles, anecdotes
To keep in touch, to explore and maintain relationships	emails, Twitter, weblogs, blogs, postcards, notes, letters, memos, text messages, Facebook messages
To know what is happening in the world	newspapers, news reviews, online news
To find out when and where	maps, tour guides, announcements, TV and film schedules, railway timetables, school timetables, travel itineraries, programmes
To make contact, network, develop a career	application letters, curriculum vitae, websites, advertisements
To record feelings, observations	personal letters, poems, diaries, journals
To persuade	manifestos, campaigns, advertisements
To clarify thinking	note-taking, mind maps, diagrams, jottings
To predict or hypothesise	research abstracts, horoscopes

- Instant worldwide communication means that a new buzzword or idiom can become recognisable very quickly, so written language is constantly changing and we are constantly inventing new words, as we saw in Chapter 5.
- The rapid exchange of information and ideas through digital media also means some words/text types fall out of fashion very quickly, or change their meaning.
- It is no longer expected that written forms should use complete sentences: note form, bullet points and key words are used in most of the contemporary written texts listed above.
- The written forms also often echo spoken language: written forms can be informal, colloquial and with short 'utterances', rather than complete sentences as the norm.
- Spellings of words are being 'reinvented' as text messages and Twitter use the minimum number of characters to give their message. These short forms reflect a new notion of the links between sound and spelling; here are some examples: *gr8* (great); *4U* (for you); *2CU* (to see you)
- The digital medium has also given us closer links between written language in terms of synchronous and asynchronous writing: that is, writing 'live' as if you were having a conversation, with replies in real time: and writing with a time lapse.

Task 6.1 Responding to changes as a teacher

How do the developments described in the section above affect the way written language is taught? Look at the text types in Figure 6.1 and consider these questions:

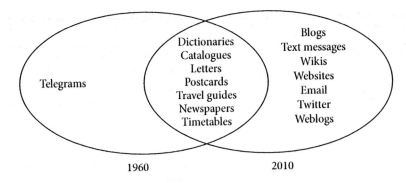

Figure 6.1   *Writing then and now*

Which of these texts would you take into the classroom? Why, or why not?

Which ones would you consider to be useful for language learning? Which ones would you consider not to be useful?

Below are some responses to these questions from three teachers. Which of them reflects your own view, or the situation in a teaching context you are familiar with?

> I am not happy to encourage students to use the language of text messages and Twitter: I think they need the old-fashioned skills of writing in complete sentences, and they need to know how to use the language formally. I personally only teach what I think is 'good' writing. I feel I need to stretch what they already know, and challenge their expectations of themselves.

> I accept that email, Twitter, Facebook really engage my students, and they get loads of practice with these in their own lives. They learn the language of these for themselves, so I don't need to teach it to them, but I do talk about it, how it differs from other kinds of writing – stories, letters, newspaper articles. I give them lots of practice in all of these.

> I don't think there is much need any longer for people to write formally. I give them a chance to read and understand different kinds of writing, but we only practice short writing pieces, and my students have never written more than 250 words for me because they simply don't need to in real life.

These three teachers represent a spectrum in their attitudes (Table 6.2). Where do you stand along this spectrum? Can you explain why?

6.1.1 WHAT SHOULD TEACHERS KNOW ABOUT THE READING PROCESS?

When we make sense of a text, we are deploying skills which go far beyond simply the recognition of letters and words on the page. The text below appears very simple to

Table 6.2   Teacher selection of text types: where do you stand?

Only texts which are familiar and used every day by students should be practiced in class	All text types, both formal and informal, should be introduced to give students maximum opportunities for reading and writing	Only texts which represent 'good' formal language should be actively taught in the classroom

read, but as you do so, you might identify what you know and what you do in order to interpret it. Then compare your list to the one below:

1. remove fire extinguisher from bracket
2. open valve
3. approach source of fire
4. extinguish fire
5. close valve
6. replace extinguisher on bracket

You are likely to have drawn, consciously or unconsciously, on the following in order to read this short text:

What you know when you read

- You know that the structures *open/approach/replace* are all verbs in a form which suggests a command or instruction. You can answer the question – is the sentence a question, a statement or a command? How do you know? This is **syntactic knowledge**.
- You may not know the word *fire extinguisher*, but you might know the word *extinguish* meaning to put out/turn off a light. You might understand that, whilst *extinguish* describes an action, the *-er* at the end turns this into an object – perhaps a mechanism for spraying water. In other words, the *-er* ending has changed this from a verb into a noun. You can answer the question – what information do the parts of words give me? This is **morphological knowledge**.
- You know that the words *fire extinguisher* and *source of fire* relate to the subject of putting out fires. You could also add words of your own to this topic, if required. You could answer the question – what is this text about and how do I know? This is **topic knowledge**.
- You know (at least at first glance) that this text includes instructions because of the numbered list, and is likely to be a formal notice, perhaps posted on a wall in a public building. You can also deduce that the numbered instructions are designed to be followed in chronological order. You can answer the questions – what type of text is this? Where would I see it and who is it written for? This is **genre knowledge**.
- However, if you look more closely at the text, you might notice the instructions are rather over-simplified, and if this were a real fire, would hardly be helpful at all. So

Table 6.3   Developing reading knowledge: what is it we know when we read?

Questions about reading: developing reading knowledge
Is the sentence a question, a statement, or a command? How do you know? *syntactic knowledge*
What information do the parts of words give me? *morphological knowledge*
What type of text is this? Where would I see it and who is it written for? *genre knowledge*
What is this text about and how do I know? *topic knowledge*
How does the text fit with what I know about the real world? How does the real world help me understand it? *general world knowledge*
How does the cultural and social context affect my understanding of the text? How is the text shaped by the context in which it was written? *sociocultural knowledge*

is this a real public notice or not? How does the text fit with what you know about the real world? How does the real world help you understand it? You are now using your **general world knowledge.**

- The text is in fact a 'one-minute story' written by the Hungarian writer Istvan Orkeny during the Russian occupation of Hungary. Its title is 'Life should be so simple'. You will probably now make links between the title and the text, and rethink whether the instructions are intended to be taken seriously, or if they are instead an example of the impossible and unrealistic. This would make the title and the text coherent, and would connect with what you know of the real world. In effect, you are reframing your reading to include what you know about stories, or about being 'occupied' by another country, or what writers of stories try to say as compared to writers of public notices. You are asking the question: how does the cultural and social context affect my understanding of the text? How is the text, indeed, shaped by the context in which it was written? This is **sociocultural knowledge.**

These knowledge areas, and the questions they answer, are a useful checklist for you as a teacher. They are questions which it is useful for you to encourage in your learners. Table 6.3 summarises the different types of knowledge we draw on when reading a text.

What you do when you read: reading strategies

We know that fluent readers use a number of strategies to help them access and activate this knowledge. Research has helped us to understand what these strategies are and make them explicit for teachers and learners. They are often divided into two broad types: 'bottom-up' strategies and 'top-down strategies', or what Grabe and Stoller (2002) call lower-level and higher-level processing.

Bottom-up strategies involve decoding surface features of the text, starting with the words on the page and what is visible in the language. Alderson (2000) described readers as 'passive decoders of sequential graphic-phonemic-syntactic-semantic systems, in that order' (Alderson 2000: 17). As 'decoders' of language, readers start by recognising how letters form themselves into words (graphic and phonemic decoding). Then they recognise the significance of word order within sentences, and the function of words within them (syntactic decoding). Then they understand how the connected words convey meaning (semantic decoding). Using bottom-up strategies, you might read a text with a dictionary beside you, looking up examples of unfamiliar words; or you might take note of the verb forms, noticing, for example, that they move from describing past time in one paragraph, to future time in the next.

In contrast, *top-down strategies* start with the meaning of the whole. They look at the overall 'gist' of the message – for example, whether the story ends happily; whether the experiment was successful in a piece of scientific writing; whether a film critic recommends the film or not. Using top-down strategies you might look quickly at the opening and the ending, moving your eye rapidly through the middle noticing the visual impact of the text. For example, you might notice that there is a lot of dialogue in the writing, or that there is a numbered list, or skim ahead and look at the pictures and captions. Higher-level processing carries you deeper into the message of the text. Our expectation is that reading makes sense and that sentences are coherent and connected; so where they appear not to be on the surface, we activate our shared knowledge to fill in the gaps, 'read between the lines', and recognise hidden connections. Part of our strategy will be to connect the words on the page with what we know, both in the real world and in the world of texts. This capacity to 'read between the lines' is known as 'inferencing' and is a skill of the fluent reader.

Both these approaches are useful ones which are used by competent and fluent readers, even though they are likely to be done without conscious decision-making. We also know that successful readers use both kinds of strategy, often simultaneously with one another, adapting them for different kinds of reading purposes and texts. This capacity to adapt is critical. Which strategies are used change with 'new task variations, new texts, new topics and new goals' (Grabe and Stoller 2002: 82). In second-language reading, research suggests that using strategies generically without adaptation to context does not help reading fluency. Anderson (1991) found that 'readers scoring high and those scoring low (in comprehension tests) appear to be using the same kinds of strategies' (Anderson 1991: 468–9). He goes on to suggest that 'it is not sufficient to know about strategies; a reader must also be able to apply them strategically' (Ibid.: 468–9). This means second-language readers need to become skilled at 'orchestrating' the strategies which are needed for each reading situation. What are the implications of this for the teacher?

Implications of strategy research for the teacher of reading

- Strategies are learnt slowly and need to be built up gradually over a long period of time.
- Reading needs to take place for enjoyment outside the classroom as well as inside,

Table 6.4   Students' accounts of reading strategies (Janzen 2002: 261)

Before reading	While reading	After reading
• Predict • Ask questions about the author • Skim: look at pictures and headings • See if I find the title interesting • Look at the questions	• Check predictions about the text • Underline • Use the dictionary • Guess • Translate • Connect reading with what I already know • Connect previous parts to what I'm reading	• Take notes • Reread • Think about text structure • Check for answers to questions • Evaluate whether I like/ agree with the text

so learners develop the 'habit' of reading; and so strategies are practised in non-instructed as well as instructed settings. See Task 6.2, which invites you to explore resources for learners which provide opportunities to read for pleasure.
• Students need practice in applying appropriate strategies to different texts and text types.
• Multiple strategies need to be developed and practised so that readers can draw on them spontaneously as appropriate.
• Strategies developed in first-language reading can be explicitly identified and carried over into second-language reading.
• Texts need to be monitored for level, so it is achievable for readers to transfer reading strategies into the second language.

Janzen (2002) conducted a study in which she asked students to describe the strategies they use when they read. Their responses represent strategies which students find helpful according to their own testimony. We are also able to see from this research the sequencing of strategies, from preparation for reading through to 'while reading' and 'after reading' (Table 6.4). These are useful for the teacher in suggesting a way of sequencing the reading lesson.

We will see in Chapter 7 how the research described in this section can be built on by the teacher in selecting reading texts, planning the reading curriculum and designing reading lessons and activities.

Task 6.2 Researching your reading processes
Some of the research into reading has entailed 'verbal protocols', which means that the reader comments on and records his or her processes and strategies aloud while these are happening. These kinds of protocols involve readers in noticing their own processes, and in so doing, recognising with more clarity what sustains and what blocks their reading fluency.

Self-observation entails participants reporting the specific, predetermined processes used in a particular reading task, either during or immediately after reading (Koda 2010: 214).

Self-revelation entails 'a stream of consciousness disclosure of thought processes' (Cohen 1987: 84).

Select one of the paragraphs in a later section of this book that you have not already read. Read the paragraph silently to yourself and record your thoughts, either as self-observation immediately after reading, or as self-revelation while you are reading. Verbal protocols involve recording yourself as you think aloud; but if this is not feasible, you might like to write notes straight after reading.

As you read, what strategies are/were you aware of using, to help you make sense of the paragraph?

How do your strategies compare with those of Janzen's informants listed in Table 6.4?

6.1.2 WHAT SHOULD TEACHERS KNOW ABOUT THE WRITING PROCESS?

What you do when you write: writing strategies

Many of the aspects of reading discussed in Section 6.1.1 above carry over to the process of writing. Reading well has been recognised as a crucial factor in writing well. We also emphasised, in the section on reading, the value of matching reading in the classroom with authentic reading in the world. This is equally important in the teaching of writing. When we write outside the classroom, we have a reason and purpose; we also have a clear sense of our audience, even if that audience is invisible, or inside our own minds. Sometimes what we write leads to an intended action: a diary note, for example, may lead to fulfilling an arrangement; a shopping list may lead to a shopping trip. Simulating these qualities in the classroom makes writing a meaningful and motivating process. We thus open this section by looking at these 'natural' writing processes, and considering the implications of these for the teacher.

Table 6.1 listed some reasons for the reading and writing we do in our daily lives. Returning to this list, we can see that some of these writing activities might be for private use only, such as personal diaries or reminder notes to yourself; others are intended for an audience or even a 'public', such as job applications, or letters of complaint. This distinction is important, because when we write for ourselves we can 'invent' our own rules and systems; but when we write with an audience in mind and for a specific purpose, we need to adapt our writing to meet the expectations of our audience. For example, a letter applying for a job will set out brief details of your background and an assessment of your own strengths and suitability for the job. This information would be entirely inappropriate if you were writing a letter of complaint about faulty goods bought in a shop, or a message inviting a friend to a party. Appreciating what to write, to whom, why and how are thus all aspects of effective writing.

The implications for the teacher are that the writing programme needs to include a wide range of text types, with attention drawn to the characteristics of each. The questions asked about reading in Section 6.1.1 above can equally be asked about writing: and the answers to reading questions be used to model writing. In Table 6.5 are some examples of text types a teacher can bring into the class.

Table 6.5   A writing programme – kinds of writing (Hedge 2000: 322)

Personal writing	Public writing	Creative writing
diaries	applications	poems
journals	forms	stories
shopping lists	letters of enquiry, complaint	autobiographies
reminders	websites	songs
Social writing	**Study writing**	**Institutional writing**
letters, email, blogs,	notes, summaries, synopses,	public notices, advertisements,
Twitter, text messages	essays,	timetables,
	bibliographies, abstracts	reports, instructions,
		speeches, CVs

Task 6.3 Reflecting on your writing processes

- Think about the kinds of writing (or text types) you have engaged in during the past month, and note down as many examples as you can.
- When you have finished your list, compare it to Table 6.5. Can you add any further text types to the boxes?
- Have you noticed which text types you tend to write most frequently and which least frequently?
- Can you identify for each of these text types your 'reasons for writing'? How do these 'reasons' compare to those listed in Table 6.1 on p.112? Are there any 'reasons' missing?
- Notice which are your most frequent 'reasons for writing', and which your least frequent reasons. Do you think learners in a context you are familiar with might have the same writing patterns and purposes? Why, or why not?

We also noted, in our discussion about reading, that questions can focus on detailed features of the text such as verb forms, vocabulary, syntax and structure; while a more general approach would focus on holistic aspects of the text, such as its overall meaning and purpose. When we apply this distinction to writing, we arrive at a number of useful strategies which are used in combination by fluent writers. Table 6.6 shows what discrete/detailed skills and holistic skills mean for writing.

It is interesting to note, from studies of learner writing strategies, that proficient writers start with some kind of plan for their writing and use form to serve this need, whilst less proficient writers focus on accuracy and surface aspects of language but tend to run out of ideas earlier on. Gebhard's research (1996) led to interesting insights into the strategies used by fluent writers, compared to those who were less proficient. He found that proficient writers spend some time planning and preparing before starting to write, and are prepared to reformulate and edit once the first draft is complete. Flower and Hayes, in an earlier study (1981), found that confident writers were constantly revising and editing as they went along. There are a number of useful implications for teachers from this research. These will be developed in more detail in the next chapter, in Section 7.2.

Table 6.6   A checklist of writing subskills

PART Discrete/surface writing skills	WHOLE Holistic writing skills

Appropriate choice of vocabulary
Correct spelling of vocabularvy
Correct syntax:
  correct sentence forms
  correct verb forms
  words used with correct function
Appropriate use of clauses and
  conjunctions between clauses
Grammatical use of punctuation
Appropriate use of discourse markers to
  connect sentences
Appropriate use of discourse markers to
  mark stages in the text
	Identifying the features of the text type:
	  text organisation
	  typical structures
	  appropriate register
	  appropriate vocabulary choices
	Identifying the purpose of the writing
	Identifying the target audience
	Identifying what information is shared
	  with the audience
	Identifying what information is 'new' and
	  what is 'given'
	Interest and force of content
	Development of ideas
	Sense of audience and style

Writing and the influence of technology

We saw in Section 6.1 above that the online and digital medium has generated language which lies midway between written and spoken forms. This means that traditional notions of correctness have given way to new rules of correctness and appropriacy. The notion that writing takes place with an invisible or distant audience is not the case when we send text messages, or write messages in 'live' contexts such as Twitter, Facebook or email. We are often engaging in simultaneous, 'real-time' written dialogue which is parallel to a spoken conversation. In addition, Stapleton and Radia (2010) remind us that technologies provide multiple resources for learners to develop and improve their writing, such as spell checks, grammar tools, word lists and plagiarism analysis. Their article is discussed in Section 6.5 below.

What do these developments mean for the teaching of writing? Think about the teaching implications below and notice how these affect your own approach to writing.

Teaching implications of online and digital writing

- Encourage responsible and critical use of online correction opportunities. For example, spell checks are able to identify whether words have a viable spelling, but not whether they are the right word in the context. A spell check, for example, will not recognise the difference between *their/there*; *it's/its*; *wear/where/we're/were*.
- Younger learners are likely to be more proficient than their teachers at online and digital use of abbreviations, emoticons and text message jargon. Rather than attempting to suppress this knowledge, a teacher might make a choice to bring it into the classroom in order to make explicit the writing conventions of different contexts.
- Learners are likely to be engaged naturally in a wide variety of online writing – blogging, wikis, Wikispaces, Twitter, Facebook, text messaging. These writing opportunities can be drawn into the classroom as natural practice opportunities if the technology is available. There is more discussion of these opportunities in Chapter 8.

- Consider the appropriate measures of 'correctness' within each writing medium. For example, a formal letter applying for a study programme is likely to need a high level of formal accuracy, even if sent through the email medium. Look at the text types in Table 6.5 and identify which of these are likely to require a high level of formal accuracy, and which of them are likely to have a high tolerance of grammatical and lexical variation from standard English.

Task 6.4 Evaluating online resources 🖥
Stapleton, P. and P. Radia (2010), 'Tech-era L2 writing: towards a new kind of process', in *English Language Teaching Journal* 6:2, 175–83

The authors explore the 'developments in software and online resources' which might help students in their writing. Below are some of their suggested resources. Explore these for yourself and then think about: how would you set up and encourage use of these resources in the classroom? How would you monitor their usefulness?

- Online concordancers as a pedagogical tool in writing classes
- Track change facility, which marks changes in colour and highlights marginal comments
- Electronic thesaurus (Shift + F7 in Word)
- Search engines (such as Google) for checking, for example, the frequency of collocations. The authors give the example of a Japanese student translating 'heavy illness' directly from the mother tongue; checking this in Google and finding the frequency of this collocation is very low compared to 'serious illness'.
- Search engines such as Check My Words: <http://mws.ust.hk/cmw/index.php>
- Specialised websites such as Google Scholar
- Online translators such as Bing Translator <http://www.bing.com/translator/>
- Plagiariasm analysis website Turnitin, which measures the amount of synergy between student text and other published texts available online: <http://turnitin.com/static/index.html>

This section has shown the close connections between reading and writing as complementary and mutually nurturing skills. We have implied that to read well leads to writing well, and that the teacher of reading and writing will model in the classroom the kind of processes that take place in real-world reading and writing. We have looked at some of the key influences in the teaching of reading and writing, including:

- a generic approach to text writing
- a process approach to writing which includes multiple drafts
- purposeful reading and writing
- integration between the skills
- responsible inclusion of current varieties in the written word
- taking account of the strategies of effective readers and writers

The next section will consider what knowledge is specific to the spoken word, and how this might be helpful to the language teacher.

6.2 TEACHER KNOWLEDGE OF THE SPOKEN WORD: WHAT SHOULD THE TEACHER KNOW?

Section 6.1 explored some of the influences on the English language which have changed the way we perceive correctness and appropriateness: corpus linguistics, discourse analysis, conversation analysis, English as a lingua franca and the notion of a 'variational pragmatics' that takes account of the different cultures and contexts in which language is spoken. Section 6.2 considers the implications of these changes for the spoken word, and for the teacher of the spoken word.

Task 6.5 Reflecting on spoken language
Reflect on the questions at the top of p. 123 and note down your responses.

When you have finished, compare your own responses to Table 6.7 and the commentary that follows.

Table 6.7   The differences between written and spoken language (Emmitt et al. 2006: 151; Jenkins 2009: 135)

Written language	Spoken language
Usually there is the opportunity to plan writing. There is also usually the opportunity to return to, correct and edit what has been written. The written word is harder to erase: it forms a more fixed and permanent mark, whether this be on the Internet, mobile phone, computer or paper. There is a time delay between writing, and a response to writing. Technologies such as texting and email have minimised this delay so that written response can be almost instantaneous. Information is made clear and explicit. The reader has no external clues, so the writer has to make clear what he/she is referring to. The beginning and ending of messages are usually made clear: for example, with sentence boundaries, or through layout and paragraphing. Writers might choose complex sentences, and more precise, formal or technical vocabulary (depending on context and writing type).	Spoken language is usually spontaneous and rapid. Once spoken it is very difficult to edit and change. The spoken word disappears instantly, unless it has been recorded. Speaking is instantly interactive, with speakers needing to rapidly recognise and respond to other speakers. Information is often implied through non-linguistic cues such as intonation, facial expression or body language. A great deal of information can be understood from external clues, so does not need to be made explicit. There are no clear sentence boundaries or visual/print clues in speech. The opening and closure of messages needs to be shown in other ways. There is a tendency to prefer simple, less formal structures and vocabulary.

- Compare writing an email to make an arrangement, and making the arrangement by phone. What are the key differences in the language you might use?
- Now think about making these arrangements in a second language. Which of these tasks would be easier for you and which more difficult? Can you explain why?
- From your notes above, list what you consider to be the specific challenges for the learner in using spoken language.

Speaking requires rapid production, with little time for planning and no time for editing what you have said. It is also a reciprocal process, requiring the speaker rapidly to process, understand, interpret and respond to the spoken language of others. This also involves picking up 'hidden' clues which are not on the surface of the language, such as the other speaker's attitude and mood, shared (or unshared) knowledge, or unspoken expectations. These characteristics raise important questions for the teacher: if spoken language involves being 'unplanned', speaking rapidly, and without the possibility of editing and correcting, how can we best help the student to achieve speaking fluency?

We can begin to address this question by looking in more detail at the differences between written and spoken language. When we write formally, the convention is to write complete sentences, and include sentences which are complex and varied. By contrast, when we speak, we rarely use completely formed sentences: we use fragments of sentences, run sentences together, convey our sense with single words, repeat parts of a sentence several times over, echo and overlap one another. Section 4.1 made the distinction between the two terms *sentence* and **utterance**: *sentence* is a term used only for written language, whilst *utterance* is the term used to describe units of speech.

Table 6.8 is the transcript of a conversation between two government ministers, A and B. On the left is their conversation: on the right are aspects of spoken English which the teacher might notice.

A typical extract of natural conversation such as this thus raises several questions and implications for the teacher, including those we asked at the start of this section. Should the teacher **teach** these examples of vague language, interruptions and repetition? Is being spontaneous and speaking rapidly actually more important than being accurate?

Below are some responses to these questions. You might like to consider your own position in relation to each of these:

- There are many ways in which the meaning of spoken language is conveyed – for example, through body language, intonation, gesture, the context. This means that 'correct' structures and explicit information are much less important than in writing. A priority in teaching spoken English might be: *can I be understood?* rather than *am I being accurate?*
- Being exposed to examples of real spoken English helps to prepare learners for real-world communication.
- Teachers and learners can also be researchers of spoken language, gathering examples of the way language is spoken in their real-world context.

Table 6.8   Analysing a conversation from <http://news.bbc.co.uk/1/hi/5188258.stm> (last accessed 24 January 2012)

Spoken English	What should the teacher notice?
A: I'm just . . . **B: You're leaving?** (1) A: No, no, no not yet. On **this trade thingy** (2) . . . (3) [indistinct] (4) B: Yeah, I told that (5) to the man. A: Are you planning to say that here (5) or not? B: If you want me to. **A: Well, it's just that if the discussion arises . . .** (6) **B: I just want some movement.** **A: Yeah.** (7) B: Yesterday we didn't see much movement . . . A: No, no, (7) **it may be that it's not, it may be that it's impossible.** (8) (9)	1. Speakers often guess what other speakers are about to say, and complete utterances for one another 2. Vague language like 'thingy' is typical of spoken language. 3. Fragments of a sentence are sufficient to convey meaning or start a new topic. 4. We also fill silences with *umms* and *ahhs*, sometimes to show we haven't finished our comment and are searching for the next few words. 5. Speakers use words like 'that' 'here', 'over there', 'this one', which are clear to other speakers because they refer to knowledge shared by both about previous conversations, and the real world. These words which 'point' to something are called **deictics**. 6. Speakers often interrupt one another so one utterance cuts into the middle of another, as Bush does here. 7. We tend to indicate that we are listening with encouraging interventions such as 'yeah'. 8. Repetition of words and phrases is also typical of speech. 9. Speakers often reformulate an utterance several times, as A does here: – it's not . . . then starts again . . . it may be that . . .

- All features of spoken language can be explicitly taught, to give learners the strategies and skills for speaking naturally and recognising natural speech.
- If teachers are aware of the characteristics of spoken English, they can recognise where the models in the coursebook are not realistic and adapt them to be more so, or choose coursebooks which are based on corpus data and research (e.g. *Touchstone* series from CUP).

As with reading, successful listening involves two parallel processes: **bottom-up processing**, which involves gathering information from the language itself, including its components such as stress, intonation, individual sounds, vocabulary, syntax; and **top-down processing**, which involves learning from knowledge which lies outside the spoken language and rather resides 'inside the head' – such as cultural expectations and norms, knowledge of the world, appreciation of social context and the hidden dynamics between speakers. These two processes often happen concurrently and in partnership with one another. To be a successful speaker/listener in any language, we are likely to be aware both of the language itself, and of the multiple factors surrounding the language which affect the way we speak – for example, how formal or informal we are, whether we use conventional formulaic language or break patterns, which topics we choose to talk about, and which vocabulary we choose for discussing this.

These two processes, working in partnership with one another, enable you to answer questions such as these by 'noticing' what is happening in language:

- When people say 'I'm sorry', do they mean: 'I feel sympathetic' or 'I apologise'?
- Why do waiters in a café look annoyed when I say 'I want a cup of coffee?' Which other structure should I use instead of 'I want'?

These processes are part of the learner's capacity to monitor precision, accuracy and detail in speaking. Exploring spoken language in these ways allows learners to develop an 'internal teacher' so they can ask and answer questions for themselves, just as the linguist might. Table 6.9 on page 126 is a list of the features we noticed in the conversation, with 'awareness-raising questions' the teacher might try in the classroom for developing speaking and listening.

However, if we were to master all the surface features described above, would we then be competent speakers? Our understanding of the spoken language shows there are deeper competences which make us able to interact with others appropriately and successfully. Dell Hymes, who opened the profession to the study of language as communication rather than grammatical system, said 'there are rules of use without which the rules of grammar would be useless' (1972: 278). We master these rules intuitively in our mother tongues, so have a repertoire of skills which can be made explicit and drawn upon in learning a second language. These are often categorised into four competences: linguistic, discourse, pragmatic and strategic, each of which will now be discussed in some detail.

Linguistic competence
Linguistic competence includes the following specific skills:

- Using the right grammatical form to convey your meaning.
  What are the differences between these utterances? They are all generated by native speakers, but are all of them equally acceptable to you as teacher? Can you imagine a 'story' for each of them?
  He shouldn't have done it, really.
  He should've done it, really.
  I wish he'd have done that.
- Using the right pronunciation of sounds within words, to make the meaning clear:
  A lady goes into a department store and asks a staff member: 'Do you sell clothiz?' (rhyming with moth-is). To her frustration, she is not understood. After three repetitions, the staff member says, 'Oh, you mean clothes!' (rhyming with loathes).
- Using the stress and intonation of words and sentences to convey precise meaning:
  A famous writer travelled all round the world talking about his books. English was

the language in common in these countries. In one city he visited he was introduced to a large gathering of people by the local mayor: 'We are proud to have such an IMpotent person with us today!' Was the writer pleased or offended? what did he mean to say?

• Choosing the vocabulary item that conveys your meaning, and using it in the

Table 6.9   Teaching spoken language: characteristics of conversation

Spoken language feature	Teaching listening	Teaching speaking
1. Interrupting and completing utterances	How do speakers respond when they are interrupted?	What do you do if you are not happy about being interrupted? When is it acceptable to interrupt and when is it not?
2. Vague language	What 'vague terms' do the speakers use? Make a list of useful ones: e.g. *thingamajig, watchamacallit, whats-her-name.*	Make a list of vague words you could use if you forget: – the name of a person – a place – the name of an object When is it acceptable to use these vague words? When is it not acceptable?
3. Fragments of a sentence are sufficient to convey meaning or start a new topic	How do speakers start a new topic? What key words do they use?	
4. Fillers	What do the noises/sounds made by the speakers mean: to show they are listening? to show they are thinking? Are these the same in your language?	Make a list of phrases which you can use in the following situations: When you are on the phone When you are in a hurry When you're going to be late Make a list of noises or sounds you might use: To show you're thinking To show you're listening To show you're searching for a word
5. Deictics: *over here, there*	What do you think the speakers are referring to when they say *here, this, that one*?	
6. Repetition of words	Notice words which speakers repeat: 'Yes, yes!' 'No, no!' 'Good, good!' What is the effect of this?	
7. Reformulating		If you find you cannot complete something you have started to say, start again using: A different word An easier verb form A short phrase

Table 6.10   Linguistic competence: 'noticing' ideas

Vocabulary choice	How would you respond to a speaker who said each of these utterances to you? Would you consider it necessary to check meaning, or suggest another word? *In my country is high productive tea.* *Can you French?* *Can you understand me this word?*

appropriate form and place in the utterance. Here are examples of utterances where the vocabulary item is either in the wrong form, or an inappropriate choice, making the meaning unclear:

She had beautiful long red hairs.
There became me a letter.
We went out for the day in the adventure vehicle.
I want to tell compliments to the cooker

As we have seen, even though these skills refer to surface features of the language, they can cause serious misunderstanding if they are not observed. What does this mean for the teacher? One strategy discussed in earlier chapters is that of 'noticing': teacher and learner both become researchers of the language, and gather information for themselves about its use in everyday life. These examples of natural language might be brought into the classroom by the teacher through recordings, Internet, authentic materials, published resources or those prepared locally by the teacher; or in contexts where English is a first language, second language or lingua franca, it might be available for the learner in the world outside the classroom. In either case, 'noticing' is a strategy that will help learner and teacher to make sense of spoken language and use it for themselves. Table 6.10 is an example of 'noticing' vocabulary choice.

Discourse competence

Discourse competence relates to longer chunks of conversation and the way we navigate through our interactions with others. You are deploying these skills when you take turns appropriately in a conversation, help someone else to come into a conversation, appropriately start a conversation, or show the conversation has ended (see Table 6.11). The situations below are those you could explore with students, discussing appropriate responses in each case, and comparing these with responses in the students' mother tongue.

You are with a group of friends planning where to go that evening and notice one of your friends has said nothing. What do you say/do?

Giving others the opportunity to take a 'turn' in a conversation could include: asking a direct question such as 'you haven't said anything, what do you think?' or 'Are you OK with that?' using their name, or simply pausing, nodding or making eye contact to indicate an opportunity.

Your friends have nearly come to an agreement and you haven't yet had a chance to put forward your opinion. What do you say/do?

Table 6.11   Discourse competence: 'noticing' ideas

Discourse competence	Teaching listening and speaking
Taking turns in a conversation	Listen and: • Notice how people 'invite' others to join the conversation. • Notice how and when people join the conversation. • Set up role plays for a group conversation. Try out these strategies for yourself.
Responding appropriately in fixed routines (adjacency pairs)	Notice what the replies are to each of these 'pairs' of exchanges. *How are you?* ------- *Thanks very much!* ------- *Can I speak to [x]?* (on the phone) ------- *Can I help you?* (in a shop) ------- Collect examples of 'pairs' from different settings: • a shop • reception of a hotel • in the marketplace • in a crowded bus or train • bumping into someone you know/don't know in the street Notice other such 'pairs' of exchanges in your own context and add these to the list.

You might wait for a gap or pause in the conversation, but if this does not happen, you might interrupt and flag this up with a phrase such as, 'Hold on! I haven't said my bit yet!' But is it appropriate in every culture to interrupt? Is it more appropriate in some situations rather than others – such as informal settings and between peers? What about in more formal situations? These questions take the discussion into a sociocultural arena.

You've spent several minutes at the end of the party saying goodbye to the host, and now you want to leave. What do you say?

Here you will be using 'closing' conventions to show the conversation is concluding. This is likely to include the convention of thanking – 'that was a great party, thanks so much'; explanation for leaving – 'so sorry to leave now but I don't like walking home in the dark'.

The closing 'turn' may also include the promise of a future meeting: 'you must come over to us next time'. What are the closing conventions for your learners in their mother tongue?

There is a knock at your door and when you open it, it is a relation who has been away for some months and just returned. What is the first thing you say?

There are likely to be a number of opening steps, starting with recognition and delight – 'Mansur! You're back!', a welcome, 'How great to see you!', and an invitation, 'Come in!' These stages act as ritual to mark the warmth of the relationship, and the shared knowledge between the two. What are the different opening rituals in your learners' home culture? How do these differ depending on the closeness of the speakers – relations, friends, acquaintances – or depending on the formality of the setting, from your own home to the street, an office, or a public event?

You are having a conversation with friends and you want to tell them a story to illustrate a point you are making. What do you do to signal this and to command and keep their attention?

You would need to signal that you are now taking a longer 'turn' in the conversation. You may do this by flagging up your intention – such as, 'there's this story I must tell you!' You will know if you are given permission to do so, through the body language of your friends such as eye contact, nods, encouraging smiles, their silence or confirming noises; and further 'listening' sounds or encouraging laughter to show they are continuing to listen.

Pragmatic competence - *hidden messages behind words*

Pragmatic competence looks beyond surface language features to the hidden messages behind words. We adapt our language behaviour in response to all the features of the situation: whether it is formal or informal, what the expectations and conventions are of the situation, whether the other speakers in the conversation have equal, less or more power than ourselves, and whether these power relations are foregrounded or not. We also convey our responses through subtle and multiple cues including eye contact, gesture, intonation, how near or far we stand to the other speakers, speed, pitch and tone of voice. In Section 9.2 we shall look in more detail at critical aspects of this competence, such as politeness strategies. Here are some scenarios:

You meet an acquaintance you haven't seen for some time in the street and stop to have a conversation. But it is soon clear to you she is in a hurry and would rather move on, so you close the conversation quickly. The acquaintance did not SAY anything to suggest she was in a hurry, so what do you think were the clues that helped you realise this?

You are chatting to friends in a café when your boss comes into the café and joins you. How and in what ways does the conversation around the table change?

A friend has expressed interest in a book which is very precious to you. You decide to lend this to him, but when you do so it is clear he thinks it is a gift, and thanks you profusely. What do you say/do?

The competence you use to decode each of these situations and respond to them appropriately is pragmatic competence. It may vary from setting to setting, language to language, culture to culture, and is an area that can generate rich opportunities for discussion and comparison in multilingual classrooms.

Strategic competence

You want to tell your friend in a second language that you have seen a dustcart (large lorry that collects domestic waste) blocking the road, and she should drive another way. But you don't know the word for 'dustcart' in her language. What do you say/do?

You may search for other words, draw the dustcart in the air with your hands, or use an alternative message such as 'you must go another way. This way is not good'. These are skills we use all the time both in our mother tongue and in a second language to find ways to fill gaps in knowledge, selecting the information that is or is not important for our message (see Table 6.12).

You have gone into a shop to buy a tin of beans, in a country where you have newly arrived. You had hoped to be able simply to pick up the tin of beans from the shelves: but

Table 6.12 Teaching strategic competence: 'noticing' ideas

Strategic competence	Teaching listening and speaking
Finding alternatives to unknown words or structures	Ask students to think of an object. They must describe the object to their neighbour without using the actual word. Can the neighbour guess what is being described? Then change places.
Repairing language which has been misunderstood	You have been talking to someone who is using a second language very fast and unclearly. Which of these do you do? – Ask them to repeat what they have said more slowly. – Pick key words you understood and connect them to give you an idea of what is being said. – Work out from the intonation if what is being said is a question, and if not, say nothing. – Ask them to explain what has been said more simply. – Pick up the general tone and expression of the speaker, make a guess on the meaning, and reply. What are the different things that could happen with each of these alternatives? How could they go wrong? What would you do if they did go wrong?

you see that all the food is behind the counter, and you have to ask the shopkeeper for it. However, you don't know the words. What do you say/do?

Here is the response of one language learner who found herself in this situation:

'At first I panicked, thinking – I'm going to starve in this country! Then I looked up and down the shelves and couldn't see what I wanted. But I did see bags of rice and I thought – well, that will have to do: so I pointed to them, made myself understood that way and vowed there and then to learn ten words for basic food before the day was out!' (Sally)

Task 6.6 Research task: comparing cultures

- Find two or three friends, relations or colleagues who have experience of another culture, country or language apart from your own.
- Interview your partner and find out their responses to the situations in Table 6.13 on p. 131. Compare these to your own responses.
- What do you notice about pragmatic and conversational similarities and differences?
- How might you 'teach' these to a learner arriving for the first time in one of these cultures?

Task 6.7 Analysing spoken language online 🖥

Explore for yourself examples of fluent, connected spoken English and analyse features you notice of spoken competences. Below are links to children talking, socialis-

Table 6.13   Comparing responses to situations

What do you do and say when . . .	Your context	Your learner's context
. . . you meet someone for the first time?		
. . . you visit someone's home for the first time?		
. . . you want to borrow something?		
. . . you have to refuse an invitation?		
. . . there is an empty seat at a table and you want to sit down?		
A situation of your own:		

ing, telling stories, speculating. The final clip is of a twelve-year old girl giving a short speech to the United Nations. In Chapter 7 we will consider how authentic talk of this kind can be used as part of a listening activity.

Using language to socialise
<http://www.youtube.com/watch?v=DIQcGjtl7d8&feature=related>
<http://www.youtube.com/watch?v=fwc2Gd2MjuI>
<*Using language to speculate*
<http://www.youtube.com/watch?v=FoJIvOQFgeU&feature=related>
Using language to tell stories
<http://www.youtube.com/watch?v=ZlqQtyXAa6s&feature=related>
The girl who silenced the world
<http://www.youtube.com/watch?v=TQmz6Rbpnu0>

6.3 TEACHER KNOWLEDGE OF PRONUNCIATION: WHAT SHOULD THE TEACHER KNOW?

This section offers the teacher a brief introduction to the sound systems of the English language. It is organised from the smallest unit, the single sound or phoneme, to the largest unit – the 'tunes' which combine to form fluent speech. For the teacher who wishes to pursue this section in more detail, Roach (2009) offers a helpful introduction.

The pronunciation of the language involves the ways in which sounds are combined and created to form meaning. It includes the following components:

- Phonology: studying the smallest building block of language, the *phoneme* or individual sound
- Stress: learning how these individual sounds behave and change in combination with one another
- Intonation: learning the 'tunes' of language and what they mean, for example, whether the voice goes up or down at the end of an utterance, and whether this denotes a question, surprise, or a statement
- Continuous speech: learning how words and sounds combine in fluent connected speech

We have seen in Chapter 4 that these features of the sound system do not stand in isolation. A change in the stress pattern of a word can significantly change its meaning; a change in intonation pattern can make a polite utterance sound rude. Given the importance, then, of pronunciation, should it be taught separately in a timed part of the lesson, or should it be integrated into other activities so pronunciation is integral to every aspect of language learning? If the latter, when should it be taught? When new words are learnt? During the listening lesson? Should every pronunciation error made by learners be corrected? If not, which errors should be corrected? Nation and Newton (2009) suggest that teachers might be selective about the pronunciation elements they choose to introduce in class, and the errors they choose to correct. A principled approach might include the following considerations: how far does the error hinder comprehension? What might be native speaker tolerance of the error? For example, we saw above that native speakers are less tolerant of intonation errors (because these might suggest a speaker is being rude) or errors in stress (because these might make a word incomprehensible or confusing).

Sound and spelling patterns

Sounds, or phonemes, are the smallest units of language. Sounds of the language are divided into two, depending on how they are articulated: vowels and consonants.

Task 6.8 Explore phonetic symbols online 💻

Explore the symbols used to denote sounds in the English language. These symbols are used throughout this chapter.

<http://phon.ucl.ac.uk/home/wells/phoneticsymbolsforenglish.htm

   Do you think these symbols would be useful to introduce to learners?

   What would be the advantages of doing so?

   What would be the disadvantages?

What are vowel sounds?

Here are three definitions derived from Celce-Murcia (1996: 93):

- Vowels allow poets to create assonance and rhyme.
- Vowels are the core or 'peak' of a syllable. A syllable is the smallest pronounceable unit of a word. Each syllable has a vowel at the centre of it. For example: *cut, rub, run* have one syllable. *Cutter, rubber, runner* have two syllables.
- Vowels involve 'a continual vibration of the vocal cords and the airstream is allowed to escape from the mouth in an unobstructed manner'.

The list in Table 6.14 represents the different vowel sounds in English. Can you find the common sound in each line? How many different spellings do you notice for each sound?

What are diphthongs?

Dipthongs involve the rapid combining of two vowels so that we hear them as one. Table 6.15 gives a list of diphthongs.

   Notice the number of ways in which each diphthong can be spelt.

Table 6.14   Phonetic symbols and spellings for vowels

Vowels	
ɪ	bit, marriage, women, village, wicked, business, pretty, hymn, build
e	dress, bed, head, many, said, friend
æ	bad, plait
ɒ	wash, hot, cough, knowledge, what, because
ʌ	mud, love, blood, cup, money, young, does
ʊ	foot, good, woman, put, could
iː	sea, machine, seen, machine, people, beat, receive, complete, piece, key
uː	goose, two, blue, group, do, true, food, through, rude
ɑː	car, heart, father, laugh
ɔː	thought, law, north, war, all, cord, pour, caught, saw
ɜː	nurse, stir, learn, fern, journey, bird, world, earth, turn
ə	about, common, standard
i	happy, radiate, glorious
u	thank you, influence, situation

Table 6.15   Phonetic symbols and spellings for diphthongs

eɪ	face, day, break, wait, ages, great, they, weight
aɪ	price, try, I, high, lie, aye, cry, find, eye, buy, hide
ɔɪ	choice, boy, buoy, coin
əʊ	goat, show, no, oh, toe, sew, low, home, though
aʊ	mouth, how, plough
ɪə	near, here, weary, ear, weir, here, beer, pier, idea
eə	square, various, there, air, wear, heir, fare
ʊə	poor, jury, who're, cure, tour

The teacher could turn these patterns into noticing games and activities in a number of ways:

- Jumble up the words and ask students to reorganise them into groups with the same sound
- Create rhyming pairs and patterns, as in the example in Section 5.2
- See how many words with the same sound each team can create in two minutes
- Find others in the class who share the same vowel sound in their name

What are consonant sounds?

Consonants are sounds created by blocking and releasing air, using the lips, teeth, nose, roof of the mouth and tongue as 'musical instruments' to create these blocks and passages of air. Some consonant sounds also involve vibration of the vocal cords (voiced sounds). A 'voiced' sound uses the vibration of the vocal chords to create it, and this

Table 6.16   Minimal pairs chart: phonetic symbols and spellings for consonants

Column A: Voiced sounds		Column B: Unvoiced sounds	
Symbol/sound	Spellings	Symbol/sound	Spellings
b	*ban* *bale*	p	*pan* *pale*
d	*din* *dial*	t	*tin* *tile*
θ	*thin* *thought*		*taut*
g	*gave* *gap*	k	*cave* *cap*
v	*veil, vale* *van* *view*	f	*fail* *fan* *few*
m n	*mail, nail*		
l r	*lane, rain*		
dʒ	*gaol, jail* *gin*	ʃ tʃ	*shale* *shin* (also compare with tʃ below) *chin*
z	*zeal* *zoo*	s	*seal* *sue*
w	*wail* *whack*	j	*yale* *yak*
		ð	*this, then, thus*
ʒ	*jejeune*		

vibration can be felt either by blocking your ears with your fingertips as you make the sound, or by placing the first three fingers of your right hand across your throat.

In Table 6.16 are twenty-two consonant sounds in English. Try saying these sounds aloud, noticing the positioning of each sound and the difference between those in which the vocal cords vibrate (column A) and those in which they do not (column B). Notice, too, how some of these sounds are placed in pairs. These are sounds which are articulated in the same place, but differ in just one feature: for example, /t/ and /d/ are both articulated by tapping the tongue on the 'alveolar ridge' at the top of the palate. However, /t/ is unvoiced and /d/ is voiced.

Pairs of words which differ in a single sound are very useful as a teaching tool to isolate and contrast individual sounds. They are known as ***minimal pairs***.

Silent letters

Most teachers, when they hear of 'silent letters', tend to think of particular letters like the silent 'h' or 'b'. However, there are many more silent letters in English, and they occur in initial, medial or final position in words.

Apart from a few letters (f, j, q, v, x, and z), most letters can be silent in some words. Notice the silent letter in each of these words, shown in brackets.

(a) pleasant; (b) subtle; (c) muscle; (d) budget; (e) preference; (g) foreign; (h) honest; (i) business; (k) knit; (l) chalk; (m) mnemonics; (n) condemn; (o) leopard; (p) psychology; (r) arm; (s) debris; (t) ballet; (u) biscuit; (w) answer

Cross out the silent letter in the following words:

yoghurt	exhibition	comb	hour
history	honour	hierarchy	heiress	guilty
mountain	secretary	vegetable	Britain	vehicle	lamb
palm	could	ferment		

Students and teachers can become researchers of the language by 'growing' this list and deducing from it patterns and generalisations about sounds/spellings such as these:

i)   'u' is often silent after a 'g', as in *guess, guest, guide, guitar*
ii) 'l' is often silent after a vowel, as in *balm, could, helm, film*
iii) 'ph' often sounds like 'f', as in *photograph, pharmacy, philosophy, physics*
iv) 'k' is always silent if the word begins with 'kn', as in *knave, knight, knife, know*
v)   'g' is often silent before an 'n', as in *sign, campaign, gnat, gnaw, reign*
vi) 'gh' is often silent as in *sigh, high, might, weigh, taught, though*

Sound contrasts

It is helpful as a teacher to notice sound contrasts, and their match or mismatch with the sound systems known by your learners.

For example, Spanish has a sound which lies in between the English /b/ and /v/.

A Mandarin speaker has a sound which lies between /l/ and /r/.

A German speaker has a sound which lies between /v/ and /w/.

Table 6.17 contains examples of teaching activities drawing on minimal pairs which isolate the sound contrasts /v/ and /b/ and /i/ /i:/.

Table 6.17   Noticing sound contrasts

Linguistic competence	Teaching listening and speaking
Pronunciation: /v/ and /b/ contrast	Which can you hear? Choose one and tell your partner. VEIL BALE VAT BAT VAIN BANE VAN BAN
/I/ /i/ contrast	How are the two sounds differently produced? Can you add any other examples to this list? Can you make lists of your own for the following minimal pairs? ship sheep /I/ /i;/ lane rain /l/ /r/ thin tin /θ/ /t/ Which particular sounds do your learners find difficult? Can you develop some minimal pairs for them to practice? Create tongue-twisters: try 'Gerry's Charming German Cherry Gin' (Kelly 2011: 63)

Table 6.18   Voiced and unvoiced -s/es endings

Column A	Column B	Column C
/s/	/z/	/iz/
ropes	stings	houses
lakes	bugs	palaces
socks	frogs	breezes
	bulbs	dances
	shoes	

You can search further examples of these contrasts in Swan and Smith (2001), which includes examples of typical errors that arise from a difference between first and second language. Their examples include contrasts between English and Portuguese, Arabic, Mandarin Chinese and Turkish, amongst other languages.

Sound and grammar

It is helpful as a teacher to notice the link between grammatical patterns and sound patterns.

When morphemes are added to words, not only does the grammatical form and meaning change, but so do individual sounds and the length and type of syllable.

Plural forms

The words in Table 6.18 are grouped according to the sound of the -s/es morpheme ending (on nouns and verbs): those that end in the /s/ sound and those that end in /z/ or /iz/.

Task 6.9 Noticing activity: verb endings and sound harmonies

Look at the different verbs in columns A, B and C of Table 6.18. Notice in particular the verb as it would be in its root, or unchanged form.

Try and identify any rule or pattern you notice for the words in each column. Then compare your ideas to the notes below.

The -s/es ending is determined by the final sound of the root form of the noun or verb: that is, what the word looks like before any endings, or morphemes, are added.

- Notice that in column A, /p/ and /k/ are unvoiced sounds and are paired with /s/, another unvoiced sound.
- Notice that in column B, /b/ and /g/ are voiced or vibrating and are paired with /z/, another voiced sound.
- Notice that in column C, verbs which end with a /s/ or /z/ sound need to have a vowel introduced before the morpheme -s is added. Two sibilants, or /s/ /s/ sounds together, would be unpronounceable.

Past tense verbs

Table 6.19 illustrates the ways in which the regular past tense ending -ed differs in pronunciation, depending on which sounds precede it. Before you read on, do you

Table 6.19   Voiced and unvoiced past tense endings

/t/	/d/	/id/
walked	banged	waited
locked	moved	shouted
hoped	rubbed	ended
thanked	grabbed	painted
stopped		

Table 6.20   Building consonant clusters

Column A: Cluster	Column B: Examples	Column C: Building clusters
Two-consonant clusters in initial position	black; please; prefer; bring; thrill; drum; thread; trunk; thrifty; dry; spin; scarf; steam	lack --- black ring --- bring
Three-consonant clusters in initial position	street; sprinkle; screw; square; splayed; straight; split; screen	laid --- played treat --- street rue --- crew --- screw
Consonant clusters in final position	contract; relax; facts; conflicts; whisks; sixths; oaths; against; months; respects; sulks; fifths; wisps; corrects	whis --- whisk --- whisks sick --- six --- sixth --- sixths

notice any principle emerging which explains what the verbs in each group have in common?

Notice how the verbs follow a parallel principle to -s/es endings above: the unvoiced verb endings /k/ and /p/ are paired with the unvoiced /t/, and the voiced sounds /g/ and /b/ are paired with the voiced /d/. A typical error might be to introduce the vowel sound in columns A and B above: /lʊked/ rather than /lʊkt/.

Another pattern we find in column C involves verbs which end in /t/ and /d/. These endings are articulated in the same place as the past tense morpheme -ed. This means that, in order to be pronounceable, we need to introduce another sound in between: the /i/ sound separates the two.

Consonant clusters

Some languages, such as Spanish and Japanese, separate consonants by placing a vowel in between. The clusters in Table 6.20 would thus have particular challenges for some students. Each part of the cluster can be practised sound by sound, starting with the final one and building backwards to include each, as the examples in column C show.

Table 6.21   Stress patterns and word meaning

reFUSE or *REfuse*	These words appear to be the same on paper, but they can be pronounced in two different ways with quite different meanings. These words are called **homonyms** – meaning literally 'the same word'. reFUSE: verb – meaning to reject REfuse: noun – meaning rubbish	What is the difference in meaning when the stress changes? *proDUCE PROduce* *esCORT EScort* *preSENT PREsent* Can you identify any other words in English which change their meaning in this way? *object, record, rebel*
vegetable, secretary, chocolate, interested	All of these words have a similar phonological pattern – a syllable which is written but not spoken – e.g. *veg/table*; *secret/ry*. They also all stress the first syllable of the word.	Spot the syllable in each word which is unsounded. Group the names of learners in the class according to: – number of syllables – stress pattern

Word stress

When a word has more than one syllable, it is critical for comprehensibility to know which syllable to emphasise and which is 'weak' or more lightly weighted. This knowledge is known as *stress*, and research suggests that it is even more critical to the meaning of a word than the pronunciation of individual sounds (Table 6.21).

What happens when you change the emphasis in an utterance?

Try saying the utterances in column A of Table 6.22 aloud, and notice the way the emphasis changes meaning.

Now experiment with other utterances in the same way to see how the stress pattern changes meaning. Below are some examples to start with.

Are you sure that happened?

We both know he is telling the truth.

Connected speech: changes in sounds

In fluent, connected speech, the ending and beginnings of words are often **assimilated** together, or lost altogether (elision).

Read these utterances aloud, using the phonemic symbols in this section and in Task 6.8 to help you.

Notice which sounds have been lost, changed or introduced.

ðerw ətemen (Therwetemen) There were ten men.

gʊbɔɪ! (Gooboy) Good boy!

hiːz ə r ɑːð ə f æ pɔɪ (He's a rather fapoy) He's rather a fat boy.

ð ə mi: dʒ ə r ə rt ə bl eɪm! (The meejerere to blame) The media are to blame.
itw ɒz ər iːl ɪg ʊk ɒns ə (It was a really gooconce) It was a really good concert.
huːj ə aːft ə (Hooyeafte) Who are you after?

Elided sounds: sounds such as /n/, /t/ and /d/ are often lost from the ends of words when they connect with another consonant: teN Men becomes /temen/; gooD Concert becomes /g ʊ k ɒ n s ə/.

Changed sounds: a single 'interim' sound often replaces two for ease of articulation: faT Boy becomes faPoy.

Introduced sounds: in some local varieties the /r/ sound is introduced to separate two vowel sounds: the mediA Are becomes meejerare.

Weak sounds: many vowel sounds become 'weak' in connected speech, so syllables appear to be lost. huːjə aːftə as an informal London greeting loses completely the verb 'are', making the phrase potentially incomprehensible.

Connected speech: intonation

Connected speech has a 'tune' which conveys meaning and mood, and which can be critical in the way we appear to others.

Task 6.10 Researching intonation patterns

In Table 6.23 are a number of utterances. Try saying these aloud to convey the moods suggested.

As you do so, try and identify the following variations you make for each mood/utterance:

- The speed of different parts of the utterance
- Which words you emphasise and which are weak
- Whether your voice is raised or lowered at different parts of the utterance
- The pitch of your voice at different parts of the utterance: loud or soft

Table 6.22   Changing emphasis, changing meaning

Column A	Column B
DO you really mean that?	– or do you actually mean something else?
Do YOU really mean that?	– or is that what he/she meant?
Do you REALLY mean that?	– or are you joking?
Do you really mean THAT?	– or have I misunderstood you?

Table 6.23   Conveying mood through intonation

Utterances	Try saying them in the following moods
• Are you planning to say that in public or not? • I suppose it's a long way for you to come? • Are you sure this is the right way?	• polite • worried • angry • surprised • pleased

Now ask two or three other English speakers to do the same: say the utterances showing the different moods.

- Were your variations and 'tunes' similar or different?
- Can you identify any rules, patterns or features for conveying each of the moods below?

Task 6.11 Establishing a standpoint as a teacher
Below are two teachers' responses to different questions about pronunciation.

What is your position in relation to each of these?
Can you explain the reasons for each of your choices?

- Should pronunciation be taught separately in an explicit 'pronunciation practice' part of the lesson, or should it be integrated into the teaching of grammar, vocabulary, speaking and listening?

I teach pronunciation as it arises in speaking practice – two minutes here and there like a 'drip, drip, drip'.	I set aside five minutes in every lesson and plan a particular sound or pronunciation I think will be interesting, important for the task, or particularly challenging.

- Should you correct every pronunciation error made by learners? If not, which errors should you correct?

I only correct pronunciation errors where it has made the student impossible to understand or could cause offence or misunderstanding.	I save up pronunciation errors as I hear them during the lesson, then have ten minutes at the end of the lesson to talk about them and see if students can correct them for themselves.

- Should learners know the symbols for the phonetic alphabet? Why, or why not?

I use phonetic symbols all the time – they are in the dictionary. Some students know them from the mother tongue and it's perfect for making comparisons.	I just use them with advanced learners as otherwise it's confusing, especially as they are learning the Roman alphabet too.

- How do you deal with the lack of straightforward rules and patterns?

Many languages, such as Spanish and Bahasa Malay, have a direct connection between the spelling of a word and the sound. In English, however, most sounds have a number of different spellings, and conversely, a spelling can have a number of different possible pronunciations. One way to deal with this in English is to suggest not that there are spelling 'rules', but rather spelling/sound patterns.

- How do you decide what is acceptable or 'right' pronunciation, when there are so many accents and forms of English pronunciation even within the realm of 'native speaker'?

My students are taking a public international test, so I think they should learn the same pronunciation as their examiners!	I think the pronunciation which is used locally is the most useful one, but I also make sure students know the difference between different possible pronunciations and when to use them.

6.4 FURTHER READING 💻

Explore the following further readings in the online resource for this book.

Task 6.11 Ferris, D. (2010), 'Does error feedback help student writers? New evidence on the short- and long-term effects of written error correction', in K. Hyland and F. Hyland, *Feedback in Second Language Writing: contexts and issues*, Cambridge: Cambridge University Press, pp. 81–104.

Task 6.12 Jenkins, J. (2007), *English as a Lingua Franca: Attitude and Identity*, Oxford: Oxford University Press.

6.5 CONCLUSION

We asked at the start of this chapter:

How has our understanding of the spoken and written language changed in the twenty-first century? What does this mean for our approaches to teaching?
We have seen that rapid and global access to English is shaping 'new' worldwide Englishes. Conventions and standards are no longer 'owned' by one language community, but are shaped and adopted in different ways to reflect different communities and contexts. We have also seen that this has led to a 'hybrid' language that lies somewhere between written and spoken language. All this opens many questions for the language teacher: which 'English' should we teach, and why? What is our notion and standard of 'correctness'?

   In answer to these questions, we have suggested teachers and learners become observers of the language, noticing it at every level – from the way sounds and spellings are linked, to patterns of behavior and language in conversations. We have also suggested teachers question their own beliefs and establish their own answers regarding which language to teach, which texts to select, which behaviours and competences to prioritise, based on learner needs and contexts. We have also noted that the four skills are closely intertwined in our everyday interactions, so the teacher needs to consider not only the characteristics of each skill independently, but also how they integrate with one another. The strategies of fluent readers, speakers and writers are useful ones for us to understand how success is reached; but what is also evident is that there are multiple ways in which this occurs, and one strategy for the teacher is to mirror 'real-world' activities and incentives in the classroom. Chapter 7 explores what this really means in practice, for planning the lesson and designing language activities and materials.

6.6 GUIDED READING

Hyland, K. (2009a), *Teaching and Researching Writing*, **Harlow: Pearson Education**
Hyland brings together insights from research into the practice and teaching of writing.

> From research on writers we are familiar with the idea that composing is non-linear and goal-driven, and that students can benefit from having a range of writing and revising strategies on which to draw. Equally, research on texts themselves shows the value of formal knowledge and the positive effects of language proficiency (Hyland 2009: 77).

He discusses several examples of writing courses which draw on these research insights. For example, one writing course for New Zealand undergraduates 'resists a narrow focus on form and disciplinary genres to develop techniques for generating, drafting, revising and responding to a variety of texts' (Hyland 2009: 79).
How might you take account of the finding that proficient writers are 'goal-driven' and 'non-linear' in their approach – in your own writing? or in your teaching of writing to a group you are familiar with?

Koda, K. (2010), *Insights into Second Language Reading*, **Cambridge: Cambridge University Press**
This book explores the complexity of negotiating reading skills in two or more languages, moving from micro-skills, such as the visual recognition of words and the role of vocabulary knowledge in comprehension, to whole-text skills, such as understanding the coherence of texts and exploring the nature of narrative and expository texts. The approach throughout considers what can be learnt by developing these skills across more than one language, and the potential for exploring contrasts, influences and variations between languages. It opens contrasts such as the following:

> In some cultures the primary function of writing is basically referential, whereas in others it seems both cognitive and expressive. Consequently, the relative emphasis placed on a particular function within a cultural group shapes perceptions of both text content and form appropriateness. [---]? Given that these perceptions strongly influence writers in shaping and organizing their ideas, it is hardly surprising that basic discourse patterns – content, organization

and explicit organization cues – vary across languages and cultures (Koda 2010: 168).

Roach, P. (2009), *English Phonetics and Phonology* **(4th edn), Cambridge: Cambridge University Press**
Roach provides a practical and comprehensive overview of the sound system and its connections with meaning and messages, from the individual sound to stretches of discourse. This is an invaluable resource for teachers, leading them systematically from phoneme to intonation, with practical resources and activities and a 'noticing' approach that models how teachers might share this knowledge in the classroom. Explore the website, which gives you further resources, including a podcast of Roach talking about the book: <http://www.cambridge.org/gb/elt/catalogue/subject/project/item5629545/English-Phonetics-and-Phonology/?site_locale=en_GB&currentSubjectID=382387>

McCarthy, M. (1991), *Discourse Analysis for Language Teachers,* **Cambridge: Cambridge University Press**
This book remains a classic in explaining how every level of language contributes to overall message, with rich examples from natural language. The book offers the teacher a solid foundation for the understanding of discourse. It is structured with chapters dealing in turn with grammar, vocabulary, phonology, the spoken language and the written language, and the way whole messages and meanings are structured and built.

Wong, J. and H. Z. Waring (2010), *Conversation Analysis and Second Language Pedagogy,* **Abingdon: Routledge**
This book 'increases teachers' awareness about spoken language and suggests ways of applying that knowledge to teaching second-language interaction skills based on insights from Conversation Analysis (CA)' (Routledge 2010). Its content is divided into sections related to turn-taking, the sequencing of conversations, including the way we tell stories or manage topics, and the structuring of talk, such as openings and closures. The book includes many transcripts of natural conversation, showing the way talk really takes place It also includes practical tasks which both explore and develop understanding, and which are designed for the language classroom.

7

METHODS AND PRINCIPLES FOR INTEGRATING THE FOUR SKILLS: READING, WRITING, SPEAKING AND LISTENING

INTRODUCTION

We saw in Chapter 6 that in natural settings there is a constant integration of the four skills when we interact with one another; and that at the same time each of the skills offer specific challenges for the learner. This chapter will consider the implications of these findings for the teacher. It will ask:

- What should the teacher know about designing the language lesson so that the four skills are integrated and developed?
- What does our understanding of the written and spoken language really mean in practice, for planning and designing language lessons?
- How can research into reading, writing, speaking and listening processes translate into effective language teaching?

7.1 DESIGN PRINCIPLES FOR INTEGRATING THE SKILLS

In Chapter 6, we looked at the characteristics of the spoken and the written word; and also at research that helped us understand reading, writing, speaking and listening processes. In the section that follows we will look at the implications of this research for the teacher, and for the design of principled language teaching activities.

Principle 1: the four strands
Nation and Newton (2009) suggest that the principled language course will balance four strands:

- **Meaning-focused input** groups together listening and reading, both skills which involve receiving, interpreting and processing language generated by others.
- **Meaning-focused output** is the capacity to convey messages and ideas oneself, and communicate these effectively to others. Speaking and writing both entail language output.
- Nation and Newton point to the importance of 'noticing' strategies. This strand in their balanced syllabus entails attention to '**deliberate learning**', detail and precision in understanding how language is built and operates (Nation and Newton 2009: 1).

- The fourth strand in the balanced syllabus is the **development of fluency**. We first met Nation's notion of fluency in relation to vocabulary in Chapter 5, which was 'the best possible use of what is already known' (Nation and Newton 2009: 151). Fluency also entails focus on meaning, rather than the detailed building blocks of meaning; and is processed in real time rather than recycled and slowly deliberated.

As we explore the principles of integrated skills teaching, and the characteristics of each skill in turn, we might draw on these four strands to ask the questions:

Is attention to input (written and spoken texts) balanced with attention to output (speaking and writing)?

Is attention to detailed and conscious learning balanced with attention to real-time and fluent language use?

Principle 2: introduce information transfer

We have seen that the four language skills are rarely isolated from one another in authentic settings. For example, we might read a film review and discuss it with a friend, or check a train timetable and make a note in our diary. Reading leads to, and is often, at some point in the reading cycle, integrated with, discussion, note-taking, listening or action of some kind. Similarly, listening might lead to making a note in a diary, marking a place on a map, or choosing an item from a list. This process of transferring information so it changes into another form is called *information transfer*. This cycle can be achieved in the classroom by replicating these real-world connections between skills. The learner starts with a stimulus such as a set of instructions or a map, and changes the information, presenting it in another form or ***doing*** something with it that reveals understanding of its message. Table 7.1 offers a number of information transfer examples. Column A suggests the starting point – a visual, written or spoken stimulus. Column B suggests the real-world changes we might make with this information, and in so doing, we transfer the information from one medium (written or spoken) into another. Each of these real-world changes could also be translated into teaching activities.

Task 7.1 Planning information transfer activities

Think of as many examples as you can remember of texts you have read or listened to naturally in the past month. Note these down in Table 7.1, column A.

Think about what you naturally did with this information and note this down in column B. The verbs in column B offer possible activity ideas.

Use these natural 'information transfer' processes to plan five ideas for information transfer activities in class.

For example:

- You play a voicemail message to your learners in which the speaker confirms an arrangement.
- Learners check the arrangement and record it in their diary.
- The learners share electronically photographs of their friends and families.
- They work in pairs to give each photograph a caption.

Table 7.1   Information transfer framework

Column A	Column B
Start with	**and transfer**
An itinerary of a journey	Plot journey on map
Written or spoken instructions for making origami	Give a partner verbal instructions
Factsheet on global warming	Compare with partner's factsheet and make a note of new information
News story on the radio or in the paper	Summarise story to a partner
Recipe	Make a shopping list of ingredients
Advertisement	Role-play buying/selling the item
Job description	Make enquiries about the job
Biography of a famous person	Plan interview questions for the person
A song where we know only some of the words	Guess the missing words, listen for them and note them down
Film reviews	Discuss films with a partner, choose one
Episodes in a story (oral or written)	Organise the episodes into a sequence
Letter to an agony aunt column	Reply to the letter offering advice
A horoscope	Tell your partner's future
A photo or a picture	Write captions
Your own suggested starting points	**Your own suggested activities** compare; summarise; correct; reorganize; dictate; note; match; combine; fill in gaps; list; guess; share information; write captions; label; mark; record order; organise

Principle 3: classify information with text organisers

One very useful way of developing fluency in reading and listening is to organise information visually. Flow charts, Venn diagrams, cycles, onions, pyramids, mind maps and 'radial diagrams' all help us to visualise the relationships within a text, to explore ideas and to make sense of them. For example, in earlier chapters of the book we have:

- considered learner contexts as an 'onion' (Fig. 3.1)
- looked at word families as a 'spidergram' or 'radial' diagram (Figure 5.1)
- compared written forms in 1960 and in 2010 as a Venn diagram (Figure 6.1)
- filled out grids comparing cultural responses to situations (Table 6.13)
- classified opinions along a spectrum (Tables 2.3 and 6.2)

Figures 7.1, 7.2 and 7.3 show information about the building blocks of reading and writing in three different ways.

Figure 7.1 shows the different levels of language, from the smallest to the largest building blocks of messages, as a pyramid.

Figure 7.2 shows the same information as an 'onion', with the smallest unit of a text, a word, at the centre of the onion, radiating outwards to the whole text.

Figure 7.3 shows the process of writing as a cycle, moving from first thoughts and key words to whole text.

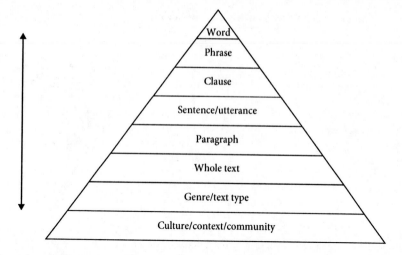

Figure 7.1   *The different levels of language as a pyramid*

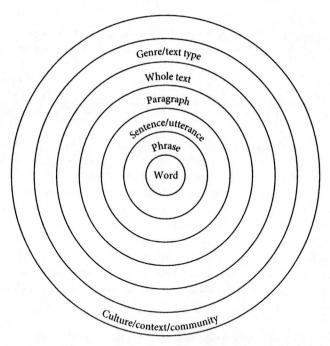

Figure 7.2   *The different levels of language as an onion*

Task 7.2 Exploring text organisers for integrated skills practice 💻

What is the difference in the kind of information suggested by Figures 7.1, 7.2 and 7.3?

Explore this book and find further examples of text organisers: 'onion', Venn

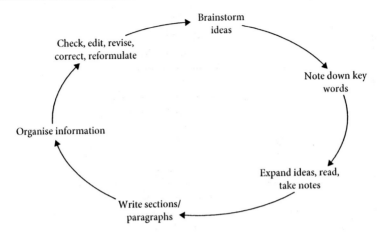

Figure 7.3   The process of writing as a cycle

diagram, spidergram, grids, pyramid, cycle, opinions classified along a spectrum. Principle 3 on p. 147 guides you to these in earlier chapters of the book.

Why do you think these text organisers were chosen? In what ways do they help to make the information or activity clearer?

Listen to one of the talks in the links below. You met these talks earlier in this book in other contexts.

A ten-minute lecture on the history of the English language, with visuals: <https:// www.youtube.com/watch?v=rexKqvgPVuA>

The Hole in the Wall Project: <www.ted.com/speakers/**sugata_mitra**.html> (Chapter 2)

The girl who silenced the world:
<http://www.youtube.com/watch?v=TQmz6Rbpnu0> (Chapter 6)

Experiment with different visual ways of representing the information in the text. Try at least two different methods of text organisation, as represented in Figures 7.1 to 7.3.

Which text organisation suits your listening best? Why?

In what ways does it help to make meaning clear? In what ways does it hinder?

Can you suggest other helpful ways of note-taking, recording or classifying the information you hear?

Principle 4: introduce an information gap

One of the reasons why classroom language can be artificial is that teachers often ask questions when they know the answer. In settings outside the classroom, when we ask a question we usually do not know the answer, and are making a genuine enquiry. This need to exchange information gives us a reason to communicate with one another. The gap between what you and I separately know, experience and understand is known as an 'information gap'. When teachers introduce an 'information gap' into an activity, they are mirroring our real need to exchange messages in the outside

Table 7.2   Introducing 'gaps' into activities

Memories of my first day at school	Experience gap	Memories of your first day at school
Should learning a foreign language in school be compulsory? My view	Opinion gap	Should learning a foreign language in school be compulsory? Your view

world. An information gap can turn a mechanical practice of form into a genuine conversation.

In the examples below, student A and student B have different sets of information. In order to solve a problem and complete the task, they need to exchange information.

Student A has unlabelled photographs of people.
Student B has written descriptions of people with their names.
Together they match the photographs with the correct names.

Student A has a street map of a town centre with no buildings shown.
Student B has a written set of instructions showing where key buildings are (the railway station, the bank, the high school).
Together they mark the buildings on the street map.

Student A has an incomplete set of instructions for the Japanese tea ceremony.
Student B has a set of pictures showing the stages of the Japanese tea ceremony.
Together they write down the missing stages in the instructions.

From the examples above, we can see that information gap activities often involve all four language skills; students need to talk and listen to one another in order to solve a problem. They also need to share resources such as pictures, maps, photos, sets of instructions. As they do so, they need to read and write purposefully, in order to exchange information and resolve problems together. A reading or listening activity can become an information gap activity by introducing the idea of *jigsaw*: student A has half the text, student B the other half. The information they exchange may be factual as in the examples above, but there might also be gaps in experience, opinion or ways of reasoning (Table 7.2):

Principle 5: introduce game-like activities
Principles 1, 2 and 3 reflect the need to make classroom activities as lifelike as possible, mirroring the ways we 'really' use language outside the classroom. Another way in which classrooms can helpfully mirror non-instructed settings is to look at the way we 'play', and replicate these qualities through learning. Jackson (2009) voices many a teacher's wish when she states: 'Most teachers only dream of their students spending the amount of motivation, attention, passion, and critical thinking on their classes that some students do playing videogames' (Jackson 2009: 291). Thus we can ask:

what are the characteristics of games, and how can we replicate these characteristics in the lesson?

Some teachers may find it surprising that many of the pedagogical methods that games use are based on well-established language learning theories. These include Vygotsky's notion of the 'zone of proximal development' described in Section 2.1 (1978); Savery and Duffy's (1996) three main constructivist tenets; Willis's (2001) Task-Based Learning; Prensky's (2006) 'inductive discovery', where learners take multiple risks and learn from their mistakes; Csikszentmihalyi's (1990) 'flow theory', which describes the total engagement of a learner/doer in a task and Gee's 'opportunities for reflection and learning', where learners become active problem-solvers, again taking risks and learning new ways to learn (Gee 2003: 44). In studying and comparing games, we can identify the following useful characteristics which teachers can apply to their lessons:

- Competition – a race provides incentive, whether it is to compete with one's own best, or to represent a team to achieve a collective best. Competitions offer instant 'measures' of success which can be motivating if the goal is within one's grasp – or could be, with effort. These characteristics are highly adaptable to classrooms. An activity can be turned into a game by introducing a 'race' element: who finishes first? Who has the most number of ideas/correct answers? Which team can solve the problem first?
- Constraint – another characteristic of games is that they often have a constraint built in, such as a limited amount of time, or number of guesses, or a word or phrase disallowed. A preposition practice activity can become a game by introducing the constraint; guess where I've hidden the prize. Ask me questions and I can only give yes or no answers: e.g. *Is it under/over/under/behind ---?*
- Incentive – many games too have a specific goal such as a prize or reward. A writing activity can become a game by introducing a 'reward' for the winners: the winning poem by popular vote will go into the school magazine/will go on the wall as a poster/will be read aloud at a festival or event.
- Team spirit – competitions, games and sports are some of the best ways to create a sense of team cohesion and responsibility. A shy learner may be energised by being the one who runs fastest for her team. In a team competition, each member of the group has a role and significance, and their successes become visible. A class test can be transformed by dividing the class into two or three teams and inviting them to ask and answer quiz questions in competition with one another.

Task 7.3 Reflecting on games
Think about the party games you played as a child and note these down.
   Notice what the characteristics and qualities were of each of these games.
   Compare your analysis to the games in Table 7.3 and draw up your own table.
   How could these games be adapted for the language classroom?
   What language would they practice?
   What changes might you need to make to take account of a class-size of learners?
   What guidance or information would you need to give as teacher?

Table 7.3   Game principles and game activities

Game	Constraints
Word association race	What animals would you see on a farm in your country? Write down as many as you can in two minutes.
Memory game	There are twenty items on a tray. Look at them for two minutes, memorise them, and write down as many as you can remember.
Memory game	Run to the other side of the room, memorise the sentence on the wall, run back and tell your team. The first team to read all the sentences wins.
Guessing game	I am a famous person. Guess who I am, but you only have twenty questions.
Rhyming game	Describe a favourite pet in five sentences – but the sentences must all rhyme! We will vote on the best poem.

Computers have generated entire digital parallel universes in which either self, or an 'avatar' of self, can 'play' or simulate play. Section 8.3 will explore the role of computers in game activities and their potential for language development.

7.2 DESIGNING THE WRITTEN WORD INTO THE LESSON: READING AND WRITING

Whilst the principles above are generic to all four skills, and in fact lead to the natural integration of these four skills, Section 7.2 will look at the specific challenges for the teaching of written language, and ways in which the teacher might respond to these challenges.

Principle 1: prepare for reading and writing

In our everyday lives we rarely read or write something without preparation, purpose and even intent. When we turn to a text, we are able to make informed predictions about what we are reading on the basis of the choices we have made. These predictions also activate the knowledge we have of texts and the world outside texts. For example, if we turn to a recipe with the intent of baking a cake, we are prepared for its specific layout, vocabulary and text structure. When we read a newspaper, we know we may find news stories, classified ads or letters to the editor. We also know that each of these text types will take a different approach to news and information, and may be able to make predictions about the kind of language used. This is often called *prior knowledge*, and is thought to be an important component of our reading knowledge. We have seen that learners find texts easier to understand when this prior knowledge is activated. Preparation activities before reading can help to alert students to these connections between the text and what they already know. They involve the teacher asking about every reading task: what do my learners already know about the language, structure, genre or content? How does it connect with their knowledge of the world or of texts? Below are some examples of preparation activities.

Warm-up and pre-reading activities

- Predict content from the title
- Predict from the title where, when and why you might read the text
- Predict content and purpose from the layout of words on the page
- Prepare for the topic with an object/piece of clothing/song/picture
- Prepare for the topic with a mystery object to guess
- Write up words from the text and guess which kind of text it comes from
- Set up the situation in which the text would be found/read
- Play a piece of music to prepare for the mood of the text
- Discuss the topic of the text: if it was you/what do you think?

We have seen that proficient writers also prepare and plan in advance of writing. They are also more likely than less proficient writers to draw on other resources to inform them (Hyland 2009: 86). This has a number of valuable implications for the teacher. Firstly, it is a reminder of the importance of connecting the skills, and joining the writing task with reading, thinking, discussing, collating or brainstorming. Secondly, fluent writers show us that writing is part of a process with multiple 'iterative' cycles: rewriting, editing, revising and reformulating. The teacher can model these processes in the classroom by allowing time and opportunity for each of these stages.

Task 7.4 Reflecting on your writing processes

Think about a more extended piece of writing you have been engaged in during the past year: for example, a report, an essay, a newspaper article, a story, a long email or a letter.

Note down the processes you went through:

- to prepare for your writing;
- to support you while you were writing;
- when you had finished the first draft.

What do you notice about your own writing stages?
What helps you to write, and what blocks your writing?
How might these insights help you as a teacher of writing?
When you have finished, compare your notes to the lists below and add your ideas to the three different stages of writing.

Writing preparation activities

- Brainstorm topics in class
- Predict and practise key structures needed: for example, verb forms
- Predict key vocabulary needed
- Draw up synonym lists of words which will occur often in the text, using a dictionary

- Read examples of similar text types and identify key features
- Read examples of similar/the same task written by other students
- Draw a mind map of ideas for the topic
- Research the topic in advance
- Collate facts, ideas, information and images about the topic to inform planning
- Set up interviews or debates to generate views of the topic before writing

During and after writing: an ongoing cycle

- Develop the skills of editing for detail. This includes returning to the text and reviewing surface features such as spelling, verb form, vocabulary choice, the way paragraphs and sentences are connected. It is helpful to develop an editing check-list which focuses on specific accuracy aspects learners find difficult.
- Develop the habit of reformulation and redrafting of writing. This might mean expressing ideas more clearly, or in a different order; adding information that is missing; deleting information that is not needed.
- Develop the habit of peer reading and evaluation of writing. It is helpful to have writing reviewed by a 'critical friend' who can answer questions such as: does this make sense? Have I conveyed the message I intended? It is also useful to develop the 'critical friend' skill as a reader/evaluator of the writing of others. This transfers into sharpened judgement about one's own writing.

Principle 2: provide opportunities for free and extensive reading outside class
We suggested in Chapter 6 that fluent natural readers read for pleasure rather than in response to demands. A fluent reader will enjoy reading independently and will develop the capacity to read swiftly, grasping the overall story or message without being blocked by surface features. We also suggested that reading acts as a model for writing, and a learner's fluency in reading is often correlated to his or her fluency in writing. The teacher can take account of these findings by creating opportunities for extensive reading in and beyond the classroom.

Creating extensive reading opportunities

- Create an extensive reading space in the classroom. This can be developed with authentic reading materials such as magazines, newspapers, postcards, books exchanged or brought in by learners or colleagues.
- Create opportunities in class time for free and unmediated reading. Quiet reading time may be difficult for some learners outside the walls of the classroom, and to bring this into the classroom generates a culture and habit of reading.
- Provide incentives to read for pleasure outside class by, for example: encouraging learners to recommend books to one another; write reviews of books they have enjoyed; exchange books with one another; run their own reading circle.

As a teacher, be a model of someone who reads for enjoyment by bringing in books you have read and talking about your reading enthusiasms.

Task 7.5 Evaluating online reading resources 💻

The Extensive Reading Foundation was created in response to the recognition that second-language reading is best developed when it is pursued outside the classroom and motivated by delight in the reading process. In response to this, the Extensive Reading Foundation has developed a rich resource for learners to explore beyond the classroom and direct their own reading choices.

Explore the resource in this link, and notice the opportunities it provides learners to choose what they read: <http://www.erfoundation.org/erf/>

Notice:

- the different kinds of reading they can engage in: 'genres' or text types such as romance, detective, adventure, mystery
- the different languages levels and how these are explained so they are clear to learners

Evaluating the reading website

- What is your experience of directed reading controlled by the teacher, and in what ways is this website offering different opportunities for the learner?
- What is your own view of this? Could it work with learners that you are familiar with? Would it work for you, reading in a second language?

Principle 3: raise awareness of the generic features of text types

We have seen that appreciating the generic features of a text can make reading easier, and models the writing process too. These features can be made explicit by grouping texts of the same type together and setting up a process of discovery about shared features.

Task 7.6 Researching generic features of texts

Select a text that you have encountered in your own reading in the past month.

Explore the text by asking the questions below.

Use your response to these questions to draw up a list of features that are typical of the text type you have chosen. How might this list be useful when teaching learners to read and write?

Discovery questions about genre

- How is the text laid out on the page? – in paragraphs, bullet points, short lines?
- What words would you expect to find in the text?
- What verb forms would you expect to find in the text – referring to past time, present time, future time? Using the passive voice?
- What are typical sentence types in the text – questions, commands, statements, exclamations, all of these?
- What typically comes at the beginning of the text? In the middle? At the end?
- How are the stages of the text flagged up – for example, are there typical introductory phrases or words, or is there a specific layout or format on the page to show this?

Table 7.4   Learning from text types: recipes

	Stage one: notice generic features – appreciative reading	Stage two: brainstorm ideas for writing
Text organisation	Notice the recipe starts with a list of ingredients. Then it progresses to a set of instructions. The instructions are sequenced. It is important they are followed in the right order.	Brainstorm ingredients: *eggs, butter, sugar, cocoa* Brainstorm verbs used in cooking instructions: *mix, grind, blend, season* Brainstorm sequencing words: *first, then, next, while, after, finally*
Language features	The instructions are all in the imperative mood. Quantities are all described precisely, even for uncountable nouns like *butter, salt, cheese.*	List imperatives for cooking: *chop, stir, boil* Brainstorm ways of describing quantities for uncountable nouns: *a teaspoon of, a cup of, a knob of, a pan of*

- Draw on what you have discovered about your chosen text type to devise a table similar to Table 7.4 that you might use with language learners.

What kind of research and follow-up do you think would be useful to do with text types such as a recipe or set of instructions? Do you think this kind of research and follow-up would be useful for all levels of learners?

We have suggested that understanding the features of a text type can help learners create texts for themselves. Table 7.4 is an example of how you might make a bridge between appreciating the features of a text, to providing the 'scaffold' for learners to write their own examples.

Principle 4: move from development of surface skills to higher-level skills

We saw in our discussion of strategies in Chapter 6 that higher-level skills lead readers deeper into the text, to look at both what is and is not made explicit in language. Ideally, reading well goes beyond the reading skill itself into critical awareness, development of ideas and assimilation of knowledge. The teacher can encourage this kind of deeper encounter with the message of texts by phasing questions from surface to higher level. A core teaching skill is to develop the capacity for questioning that challenges learners at the appropriate level, and leads from text into understanding. However, these questions can be generated by moving from the question words *what? where? when?*, which yield factual answers that can be found from the surface of the text, to *how? why? why not? what if?*, which entail hypothesising, analysing, connecting and looking beyond the surface.

Questions about reading can also be classified into those which focus on detailed information, and those which focus on general message and ideas. Detailed searching of the text is often called *scanning*: general overview of the text, looking at overall

Table 7.5   Skimming and scanning questions

Skimming for gist (reading rapidly)	Scanning for detail (reading intensively)
What is the main message of the text?	What time do the verbs refer to – past, present or future?
From the 'look' of the text on the page, what kind of text is it – story, recipe, advertisement, letter, poem, instructions?	Read through the text and note down five features which are typical of the text type.
Look through the text quickly and pick out all the proper nouns – names of people or places.	When the pronoun he/she is used, who is being referred to?
Look through quickly and pick out all the dates.	Choose a date in the text and search the text for information about what happened then.
Does the author feel positively or negatively about the topic?	Pick out all the words or phrases which tell you what the author feels about the topic.

message, is often called *skimming*. The skimming questions can often lead naturally to the scanning questions, as in the examples in Table 7.5.

Task 7.7 Exploring teaching resources

Choose a coursebook you have used, or could use, in a learning context you are familiar with. Review the questions asked about the reading texts and classify them into two groups, as in Table 7.5 above:

- Questions about detail (scanning)
- Questions about overall message (skimming)

Does your coursebook tend to prioritise one kind of reading rather than another?
Do you feel there are any question types or reading skills which are missed out in your chosen coursebook?
Write questions of your own to fill any areas you feel are missing.

Principle 5: provide 'scaffolds' for reading and writing

The writing lesson, like the reading lesson, is best informed by the processes of 'real-life' writing. However, for many learners writing is the most difficult of the four skills, since some written genres entail a high level of formal accuracy. Although we have seen that fluent readers and writers tend to focus on meaning and message rather than form, this might not be a feasible option for learners still at the early stages of learning a language, or struggling with the formal properties of language. The teacher, however, can support the writing process by providing incentives to write (such as a 'real' audience, or communicative purpose), models of the kind of writing expected, and stepping stones for producing this. These stepping stones – often described as a 'scaffold' – might be examples of key structures, or key vocabulary, or a list of the generic features of the text type.

Table 7.6   Controlled writing: praise song similes (Spiro 2004: 50)

Column A		Column B
My mother/father		mountain
My brother/sister		rock
My boyfriend/girlfriend	*is like a*	flower: rose, daisy, hibiscus
My friend		fruit: mango, cherry
My husband/wife		tree: oak, willow, banyan
My son/daughter		

We saw in Chapter 6 that effective writing strategies include both holistic approaches to the whole message (mood, tone and meaning) and discrete approaches that focus on accuracy and surface features. Writers need to move between these two modes, sometimes adopting a free writing identity, and at other times a strict editor identity; but at some stages in the writing process, they do need to move between these two. The activities and principles discussed in this section will help the teacher to prepare for this in the writing classroom.

In addition, the teacher might want to 'phase' the writing from supported and guided stages to free stages, in any order or combination. Controlled activities are those in which a structure or support is provided by the teacher, giving students minimum opportunity for error. This kind of activity is valuable where accuracy is being practised, and when learners are at earlier stages of learning or writing. It ensures they are able to achieve the writing task, and that the product at the end is accurate and complete. Highly controlled tasks means that all the students in the class will produce work which is similar or even identical; but even so, it is possible and desirable to generate writing that is 'truthful', personalised and even creative. Below are examples of controlled and guided activities for elementary learners which lead to the writing of stories and poems while still offering learners detailed support for their writing. Depending on the level of the students, the teacher can give more or less help, and can allow more or less room for student choice.

Writing praise poems
Choose a person you want to write about in column A of Table 7.6 above.
    Choose a word in column B.
    Join the two words with the phrase *is like*.
    Write a sentence to say WHY. Here are some examples:

- My mother is like a lake. I can see my face in her.
- My father is like a rock. He is always there.

Examples of controlled writing tasks

- Match halves of a sentence that belong together
- Join two sentences with the relevant discourse marker: *because, although, while*
- Fill in missing words in a text

- Put sentences in the correct order
- Provide charts such as Table 7.6 above, where students make selections from a series of options, and are guided to correct forms

Writing a pattern story: The disappearing pot of gold
Ask learners to sit in a circle. Read paragraphs 1 and 2 of the story aloud to the class. Then dictate paragraph 3 and ask students to write this down and fill in the gaps for themselves.

Paragraph 1: A man one day found a pot of gold. 'I must hide it or someone will steal it from me,' he thought. So he hid the pot of gold under a tree. He hid it so well he forgot where it was.

Paragraph 2: Then one day an old lady was sitting under the tree and saw the pot of gold. 'I must hide it or someone will steal it from me,' she thought. So she hid the pot of gold _____ (where?). She hid it so well she forgot where it was.

Paragraph 3: Then one day ___ (who?) was sitting under the tree and saw the pot of gold. 'I must hide it or someone will steal it from me,' ___ (he, she, it or they) thought. So ___ (he, she, it or they) hid the pot of gold ____ (where?).

Paragraph 4: Then one day ___ (who?) was sitting under the tree and saw the pot of gold. 'I must hide it or someone will steal it from me,' ___ (he, she, it or they) thought. So ___ (he, she, it or they) hid the pot of gold ____ (where?).

Now pass your story to your neighbour on the right-hand side and write paragraph 4, filling in the gaps. Keep doing this until there are three new paragraphs, or until the class is ready to finish. Then write a final sentence to finish the story (Spiro 2007: 94–5).

While free activities give learners scope to 'spring out' in their own way, this does not mean no support is needed. The writing preparation stages suggested in principle 1 are equally, if not more, important where learners are writing for themselves and need to plan and structure their own ideas. We have also seen in the examples above that controlled and guided activities can gradually become free by stripping away the different 'scaffolds' so learners can complete these for themselves.

Principle 6: include a sense of audience that simulates real-world writing activities
We have seen that in real-world writing we are addressing someone, even if this someone is ourselves, or our older/younger self. In becoming conscious of our addressee, we become conscious of the register, style and form appropriate for our audience. You would choose different information, and frame it differently, if you were sending a birthday card or thank-you note to a great-aunt, a best friend, or a teacher.

Below are some ideas for connecting text type with 'real' people in the learners' environment. Review these ideas and adapt them so they match a context you are familiar with.

Who can learners write for?

- Themselves – diaries, poems, class notes
- Other students– autobiographies, book reviews, film reviews, stories, poems, class newspaper

- Friends and relations – party invitation, birthday card, thank-you note, love letter
- A newspaper editor – letter to the editor, news story, features story, interviews
- Visitors – travel guide, labelled town/city map, tourist information, travel tips

Principle 7: integrate feedback into the writing cycle

Student and teacher testimonies suggest that feedback is most helpful when it is seen as part of a learning cycle, rather than for the purposes of assessment. Ferris's research showed that learners were less responsive to feedback on final drafts of their work than on early and interim drafts, where there was opportunity to make changes and revisions as a result (Ferris 1995). Teachers also suggest that their intention is often to give feedback on meaning and content, but their actual practice often focuses instead on grammar and surface features (Lee 2009; Randall and Mirador 2003). This is likely to give learners the message that content is less important than accuracy, and that the writing process is mechanical rather than genuinely connected with the development of thought and ideas.

Teaching implications of research into feedback

- Vary feedback so it is appropriate for the level of the students, the goals of the writing task, and the type of text being written. For example, if the task is to write a recipe, the teacher might focus on the use of the command or imperative form (*cut, grind, blend, mix*) or the sequencing of ideas. If the task is to write a formal letter, the teacher might focus on formal modes of address, conventions for opening and closing letters, or the layout of information on the page.
- Allow opportunities for learners to respond to feedback by drafting and redrafting as a result.
- Vary feedback so it includes reference to content, message and meaning, as well as surface detail and accuracy.

Teaching case study 13: from one-way to process writing – Ching, Hong Kong (Tsui 2009: 239–40)

Ching is a teacher in a secondary school in Hong Kong who adapted her teaching of writing from a one-task activity to a process with multiple draftings. Below are some snapshots of what she did before, during and after this change in her teaching.

Before the process writing approach

Ching's approach to the teaching of writing was very much a one-way process. She gave students a topic and told them what they could write about. When she marked their writings, she focused mainly on grammatical accuracy.

Changes Ching made

- In order to involve students more, she changed from teacher-directed brainstorming to brainstorming in groups.
- She tried writing stories in pairs or groups of three and her students loved it.

- The students had opportunities to read and rework their compositions.
- She helped students to write freely by allowing them to draw pictures or to put down words in Chinese.
- She encouraged students to focus on content.

Positive outcomes

- The way the students responded to her comments improved.
- The students liked having the opportunity to read and rework their compositions.
- In the writing task they were able to go beyond answering questions and elaborated the content more.

Limitations

- Ching had a heavier marking load than before
- She never introduced peer feedback because of her doubts about the students' abilities.
- She wanted to remain in control by, for example, putting a word restriction on their stories and restricting which characters could appear in the stories.

Task 7.8 You as teacher observer

Can you explain the principles behind the changes Ching made, drawing on the ideas and research findings explored in this chapter?

What is your view of the limitations Ching experienced? Can you explain her concerns?

Can you suggest solutions to some of these?

What is your own practice as a learner/student/teacher/writer?

Do you tend to have a 'one-shot' writing approach or a multiple draft approach in your own writing practice/teaching practice?

7.3 DESIGNING TALK INTO THE LESSON: SPEAKING AND LISTENING

In Chapter 6 we looked at the many ways in which the spoken word has changed in the twenty-first century, due to the speed and availability of digital communication. We also saw in Chapter 6 that our notions of which spoken English to teach have radically changed as we gather increasing data about the everyday usage of the language and its multiple varieties in a world of globalised English. We noted that the teacher can approach the spoken word by developing and connecting linguistic, strategic, discourse and pragmatic competences. Section 7.3 considers those principles which are specific to the spoken word and the challenges it presents to teachers and learners.

In Chapter 3 we noted that a starting point for designing a programme is ideally an evaluation of needs, and this is particularly the case in the teaching of talking. What are the aspects of speaking/listening which are *needs* in the classroom, required by

Table 7.7   A sample curriculum for listening and speaking (based on Nation and Newton 2009: 17–18)

The sounds of the language Sound contrasts or clusters which are challenging or different between the L1 and L2	**Phrases for talking about yourself** *My name is ---* *I'd like ---* *I am --- years old* *I am married/single* *I have --- children*	**Phrases for everyday life** Shopping Travelling Meeting people Finding a job Using the telephone
Sight vocabulary Street signs, tickets, labels, bus signs	**Phrases for checking meaning** *Say that again, please?* *How do I say this?* *Please speak more slowly.* *What does this mean?*	**High-frequency words** Forms of transport Family members Telling the time and dates Numbers Colours
Classroom language Work in pairs/threes/fours Sit in groups Talk to your neighbours Underline	**Speculating, guessing and explaining** *It's a kind of ---* *It's something that ---*	**Supportive listening** *mmm; oh!;* *great!; uh-huh; ah* **Collect examples from your students in L1 and L2 contexts.**

the syllabus, the coursebook or the test? What are the actual *wants* of the learners, in contrast to these requirements? For example, the test may give learners opportunities only for controlled and mechanical practice of accurate speech; whilst in their own lives, learners would prefer opportunities to use it as a 'lingua franca' with other speakers and communicate in wider and non-instructed contexts. What are the gaps between these wants and needs, and where the learners are currently? The teacher might negotiate a pathway between these different variations to draw up a 'menu' of possibilities for teaching talk in the classroom.

A crucial aspect of this menu, however, is that it reflects the range of ways in which listening and speaking really happen. Table 7.7 is one way of categorising these.

Task 7.9 Drawing up a spoken language curriculum

Consider a learner or group of learners familiar to you.

Brainstorm and note down as many examples as you can in which your learner will need to use spoken English: listening or speaking.

How far are the categories in Table 7.7 useful for classifying these examples?

Add your own examples to the table above, and add further categories that you have identified as relevant to your learner.

Principles of lesson design for speaking and listening

Balance different kinds of listening and listening skill

We listen in many different ways, to match our purpose for listening. We may, for example, listen at the railway station for specific information about the train platform and departure time; or we may listen to a longer chunk such as a news bulletin, radio interview or telling of a story. In the first example, we would listen selectively just for the information that concerns us: in the second example, we may listen for the overall flow of the message without worrying if individual words are unclear. These listening skills have often been divided into two broad types: listening for detail in short intensive 'chunks', and listening more extensively to longer stretches of text. Rost (2011) fine-tunes these listening strategies and suggests, instead, six types of practice to develop the skilled listener. Table 7.8 on p. 164 connects these six listening types with activities the teacher can do in the classroom.

Develop skills and strategies to deal with misunderstandings
Many listening and speaking activities focus on what learners can hear and understand. However, in real-life settings, solving gaps in understanding and repairing misunderstanding is equally important. Field identifies the strategies of achievement, avoidance and repair used by learners in response to gaps and misunderstandings (Field 2010). These strategies are useful ones for the teacher to develop explicitly in class, thus giving learners a repertoire of informed responses to help them 'repair' communication gaps. Notice these strategies in Table 7.9 and consider where and how you might include them in the language lesson.

Prepare for listening by activating interest and prior knowledge about the topic. This matches the preparation for reading suggested in 7.1 above: predicting the topic from key words, pictures, music, the title; setting up the situation or context and planning or predicting how speakers might react or what they might say.

Provide a reason for listening, such as matching speaker reactions beside those already predicted; listen to fill in gaps in knowledge, gather information, solve a problem or complete a task. There is a place for listening for pleasure, as there is with reading for pleasure: for example, listening to music, a song, a story or a play without teacher intervention or instructed follow-up; but listening is a challenging skill, and needs to be balanced with supported listening, in which listening strategies are explicitly developed and trained.

Recycle listening so there are several opportunities to hear. Even fluent and proficient listeners need to listen several times in order to glean all the information they want, and even then, we miss or forget much that we actually hear. There are several different ways of listening, such as listening for detail, for tone and mood, for overall message, for specific information. It is difficult at one hearing to do all of these things. Ideally, give learners the opportunity to listen several times, with a different and explicit reason to do so each time.

Issues and challenges in planning for talk
For many teachers, teaching 'talk' is one of the most challenging aspects of classroom activity to manage. How much 'talk' is appropriate in the class? For example, learners and school leaders might have an expectation that learning takes place in silence, and 'talk' is a sign of disrespect. Other teachers might feel that too much talk is a sign of loss of control; talk might give learners an invitation to move away from the task at hand, or to use their mother tongue. There may also be practical

Table 7.8   Types of listening practice (Rost 2011: 183)

Listening type	Learning focus	Activity examples
Intensive	A focus on detail and accuracy at the level of sounds, words and structures	Listen for specific sounds: how is the name of a place or person pronounced? Guess the meaning of new words from the context or situation. Spot the language/factual errors in a listening passage. Fill in gaps in the words of a song.
Selective	Extract key information	Listen for names of places or people, numbers, dates and times.
Interactive	Interact with others to solve problems, gather information	Notice which phrases the speakers use to introduce or develop the topic/to express different responses. Count how many times the speakers interrupt one another. Encourage speakers to listen to and use strategies to deal with misunderstandings. (See Table 7.10)
Extensive	Manage larger chunks of listening, longer extracts	Listen to a story, radio broadcast, news bulletin. Identify how many speakers there are. Guess from background noise where the speakers are. Identify what the mood is of each speaker: are they angry, shy, in a hurry, anxious, helpful? Identify where the speakers might come from/if they have a regional accent.
Responsive	Respond to the listening; become involved as a speaker	Finish the story. Respond to the debate with your own viewpoint. Listen to a political speech. Would you vote for the politican? What questions would you like to ask him/her?
Autonomous	Develop independent listening without a teacher	Choose a song in English that you like. Share the words with others. Choose a nursery tale, folk tale or story you enjoyed as a child. Share it with others in your group.

Table 7.9   What do you do when you don't understand? Listening strategies as teaching ideas (based on Field 2010: 300)

Achievement strategies	Repair strategies
Use key words to guess meaning Focus on words given stress in the sentence Find analogy with other words in the L2 Find cognates with L1 words Accept a general/broad understanding of the word (lavender = a colour?)	Ask for help directly: What does *x* mean? Show need for help indirectly: for example by shrugging Ask for repetition: Could you say that again? Check your understanding: *Do you mean x?* Summarise your understanding: *So what you are saying is . . .*

difficulties in generating talk. In very large classes, this might create too much noise, so it is hard for the teacher to hear the students and the students to hear one another. Furniture might be fixed, making group work difficult to manage and 'mingling' activities impossible. What about learners who are shy and reticent, and may feel exposed by speaking activities? How can the teacher in a large class take account of the different pace of learning, and have the opportunity to hear and monitor every learner?

In Table 7.10 on p. 166 are some possible solutions. As you look at these, you might consider which of these strategies would be useful and effective in your own classes.

Teaching case study 14: 'Crazy English' – Li Yang in China

In China a new language learning method has become very popular. It was developed by a teacher called Li Yang, who was concerned that

> While huge numbers of Chinese learn English in school, only a handful are able to translate their skill at reading and writing, earned through hours of staring at books, into spoken English.

> Crazy English, or Fengkuang Yingyu, is Li Yang's attempt to break that oral barrier. Instead of writing sentences, students stand on the roof and scream them. One Chinese newspaper described the course as 'English as a Shouted Language.' While Crazy English still involves rote-learning, it has excited students with its mass rallies, during which everyone chants together, without embarrassment.

> Mr Li outlined his ambitious plans to the *New Yorker* magazine in 2008, saying that he wanted a retail chain of Crazy English schools that would be like Starbucks (Moore 2011).

Task 7.10 English as a shouted language 🖥

Find out what different learners you know think about this method by showing the online clip: <http://www.telegraph.co.uk/news/worldnews/asia/china/8757375/What-is-Crazy-English-and-who-is-Li-Yang.html>

Table 7.10   Tips and solutions for teaching talk

Teaching 'talk': tips and solutions	
What can the teachers do?	**What can the students do?**
Create strategies for learning and using students' names – such as name labels, naming games, or activities in which students introduce themselves or one another by name	Make name labels to help the teacher learn their names
Move around the room so learners at the back of the room become learners at the front	Change where they sit so the same learners are not always sitting at the back
Project your voice to speak to learners at the far corners of the room	Perform short sketches, model dialogues, speeches and talks in spaces in the room
Use activities which maximise class size, such as 'orchestrated' drills and repetitions, jazz chants and songs	Learn and practise ways of asking if they have not understood or need extra help with a task
Use non-verbal ways of checking understanding, such as: put up your hand if the answer is YES; stand up if the answer is NO	Learn and practise ways of reformulating ideas if they have not been understood or are not sure of the exact right word to use
Have teaching material such as posters, pictures, notices and information all around the room rather than just at the front	Work in pairs, groups and teams
Make instructions clear and simple, and invite learners to repeat these back to you in their own words	
Make it clear when it is acceptable to use the mother tongue, and when the task requires use of the target language only. Accept that the mother tongue may help the learning process, and build this into the lesson explicitly	

What does this tell you about which kind of learners might like this method and which would reject it?

7.4 FURTHER READING 💻

Explore the following further readings in the online resource for this book.

Task 7.11 Cheng, W. and A. B. M. Tsui [2009] (2011), 'Hong Kong Chinese and English native speaker ways of disagreeing', in R. Hughes, *Teaching and Researching Speaking*, Harlow: Pearson Educational, p. 168.

Task 7.12 Cullen, R. and I.-C. Kuo (2007), 'Spoken Grammar and ELT Course Materials: A Missing Link?', *TESOL Quarterly*, 41:2, 361–86.

7.5 CONCLUSION

This chapter began with the following questions:

What should the teacher know about designing the language lesson so that the four skills are integrated and developed?
We have noticed that design principles are those that replicate natural and everyday interaction. For example, in authentic interaction we exchange questions with a genuine 'gap' in knowledge; we transfer ideas and information from one setting to another. We have also learnt about good classroom activities by looking at the qualities of engagement and enjoyment in activities outside the classroom, such as games.

What does our understanding of the written and spoken language really mean in practice, for planning and designing language lessons?
We have suggested that the classroom needs to reflect the variety of texts, written and spoken, encountered outside the classroom. For the speaking context, this involves developing not only language for understanding and interacting in all the contexts useful for the learner, but also the language for repairing misunderstanding and dealing with 'not knowing' as well as knowing the language. This can offer the learner a repertoire of useful strategies with which they can continue to learn without the intervention of the teacher.

How can research into reading, writing, speaking and listening processes translate into effective language teaching?
By identifying the strategies used by fluent speakers, writers and readers, we have been able to suggest a repertoire of activities the teacher might use in the classroom too. For example, we know that when we read, write, listen and speak in authentic contexts we have a reason for doing so. In addition, we engage in most interactions with some prior knowledge of our audience, purpose and context. We have suggested that the teacher replicate these conditions for the learner too, by thinking about each skill as a cycle, involving preparation, activity, and some kind of outcome. We are all multi-skilled language strategists in our mother tongue, and one aim for the language teacher is to provide the opportunity for these skills to be developed, made explicit and explored so they are deployed in the second language too.

7.6 GUIDED READING

Reading and browsing about the written word: reading and writing
Grabe, W. (2009), *Reading in a Second Language: Moving from Theory to Practice*, Cambridge: Cambridge University Press
This book explores developments in our understanding of reading processes and practices, and shows how these connect with the teaching of reading, the development of reading comprehension, the reading curriculum and reading assessment. It defines and deconstructs important concepts such as reading fluency, the links between L1 and L2 reading proficiency, and the strategies used by fluent readers.

Myskow, G. and K. Gordon (2010), 'A focus on purpose: using a genre approach in an EFL writing class', *English Language Teaching Journal*, 64, 283–91

The authors look at the use of genre for the teaching of writing. Their specific example is a university application letter practised in a high school setting. They warn the reader that genre can sometimes be used as a mechanical and oversimplified way of developing writing, unless there is follow-up, research and focus on specific variations and audience.

Reading about the spoken word: listening and speaking

Thornbury, S. (2005), *How to Teach Speaking*, Harlow: Pearson

This book starts with a practical overview of 'what speakers do' and 'what speakers know'. Thus starting with the learner, and with the skills they transfer from the mother tongue into the second language, it provides teachers with rich opportunities for classroom 'noticing' activities, from the individual sound to pragmatic and genre knowledge. The book also ends with a useful exploration of how speaking might be assessed in the classroom, and the kind of criteria the teacher might apply.

Field, J. (2010), *Listening in the Language Classroom*, Cambridge: Cambridge University Press

This book questions the 'comprehension' approach to the teaching of listening, and advocates instead the teaching of listening as process. Field bases this position on a detailed study of the psychology of listening, including the way listeners decode sounds, syllables and words and handle information. He identifies four kinds of listening strategy: avoidance, achievement, repair and proactive strategies, which he sees as central to the way language users respond to communication challenges. Repair and achievement strategies are explored in Table 7.9.

Online teaching resources for teaching integrated skills

<http://iteslj.org> is the Internet TESL Journal, which is a multi-skill resource for both teachers and learners.

<http://www.bbc.co.uk/languages/> This BBC website is very popular and may be used by language learners of all ages and abilities. It offers many multimedia resources for teachers and learners alike.

<http://esl.about.com/> For several years, Kenneth Beare has hosted this extensive ESL site at About.com. Lessons are categorised according to skill level and special pages have been developed for ESL teachers.

Reinders, H. (ed.) (2012), *Digital games in language learning and teaching*, Basingstoke: Palgrave Macmillan

This book offers a starting point for exploring games online as part of the language learning classroom.

SECTION THREE: THE WORLD IN THE CLASSROOM

8

MULTIPLE LITERACIES: PROFESSIONAL, ACADEMIC AND WEB LITERACIES IN METHODS

INTRODUCTION

In the first section of this book, we considered language learning and language teaching methodology from the focus of learner needs in context. In the second section, we considered the link between the learning of language form, and learners' communicative needs in fulfilling real-world purposes, tasks and genres. In this respect, the English language profession has shifted from an open-ended view of language learning merely as targeted towards native-like proficiency, towards learners acquiring the levels of language accuracy and fluency appropriate for performing the tasks most relevant to the contexts in which they need to function. In this section, we will carry this concept of context-specific learning into pedagogic support of individuals engaged in the acquisition of multiple literacies in multiple contexts.

This chapter will ask the following questions:

- What are multiple literacies, and in what ways do they form part of the competences of the language learner?
- What does this mean for language learners who need English for specific professional or academic purposes?
- How can digital developments in the language help us as teachers and learners? What skills and competences do we need to take full advantage of these?

8.1 WHAT ARE MULTIPLE LITERACIES?
with Lynn Errey

Although in recent years English language teaching (ELT) has been influenced by research into learner motivation and the perception of contextualised interactive tasks relevant to learner needs, the idea of working with context-specific English language goals has been well developed for decades, in what became known as English for Specific Purposes (ESP). While ESP has developed in parallel with mainstream ELT, it started as far back as the 1940s, when the British government identified an urgent need to help Polish pilots entering the Royal Air Force to acquire English language competence in doing their very specific professional tasks. Given the very restricted time frame and resources, this called for a unique approach to syllabus design, materials development and teaching methods not yet reflected in general language pedagogy. Over the ensuing decades there has been a huge proliferation in specialist areas of ESP, such as English for Occupational Purposes (EOP) and English for Academic Purposes (EAP), working from very particular ESP premises.

ESP teachers and course designers are concerned with analysing and delivering programmes which enable learners to acquire task and discourse competence in specific tasks for specific contexts in restricted time frames. Although the task types and end goals may be very different in different professional and academic domains, reflected in distinct research trajectories and publications such as the *English for Specific Purposes Journal* and the *Journal of English for Academic Purposes*, most ESP provision is underpinned by a common approach to language learning, syllabus design and materials development reflecting real-world and context-specific 'wishes, needs and demands of people other than that of language teachers' (Hutchinson and Waters 1987: 7).

The ESP practical position on achieving context-specific rather than absolute proficiency as a language reality is theoretically underpinned by a sociolinguistic debate starting in the 1960s, when Dell Hymes took issue with Noam Chomsky's view of language as having 'universal' laws. Hymes (1966) argued that no one individual could or would need to be proficient in all aspects of a language, but rather would develop communicative competence within those life-domains or language communities unique to their experience. As we saw in Chapter 6, we adapt to the conventions and patterns of language behaviour that are acceptable in our language communities. In analysing language for specific purposes, these communities are perceived as occupational and professional ones, with their own purposes, cultures and identities. Just as with a regional community, so the language user needs to become competent in the discourse specific to those socio-cultural contexts.

Task 8.1 Reflecting on your language communities

List the different social groups you have interacted with in the last week. These may range from the intimately domestic, where your language may be used to negotiate family concerns, to professional and academic contexts, where you may have engaged in spoken and written texts related to language teaching and learning. It may also include contexts such as friendship and hobby groups, or service areas such as banks, libraries, shops.

How did you interact differently in each of these social groups?

Do you notice any strategies or language formulae which are unique to each group – for example, nicknames, acronyms and abbreviations, forms of greeting and closure, ways of marking stages in the conversation?

Without thinking about it, you are probably highly competent in all of these contexts. As an 'expert' in communicating in these contexts, you have membership in co-owning and contributing to their evolving discourse, or implicit behaviour rules as expressed in language. In turn, through ongoing membership, you will evolve different language identities in these different contexts.

But what happens if you are an 'outsider' to the discourse, where you find yourself without discourse competence? For instance, how competent would you feel today if obliged to apply for a job in say, particle physics, or investment banking? You would be engaging with speakers highly fluent in those discourses, but your unfamiliarity with the 'rules' of language behaviour in such cultures might give you away as an outsider, even if you all share English as a first language.

How do multiple literacies apply in TESOL?

The interesting question for ESP teachers of non-native speakers who wish to acquire competence in such target language domains is 'What would it take to help the learner acquire full competence in that discourse domain? And what would that competence look like?' This is a subtle consideration. Not only would such a learner need specific language typical amongst users of a specific domain, but also to be 'literate' in understanding and producing many different kinds of spoken and written texts; for instance, to know what to say and how to behave at meetings, when to speak and when to be silent, how to produce reports and data analyses. The complexities of competence extend from actual language knowledge to the strategies needed in order to learn quickly in restricted time, and in managing motivation within the uncertainties of the new target situation.

To encompass such complexities, the term 'literacy' has evolved in a special way to describe competence not only of the content of language proficiency, or the ability to perform tasks, but also the skills and autonomous strategies needed to understand one's learning processes and keep going. Johns (1997: 2) defines this as context 'literacy', in which we learn 'ways of knowing particular content, languages and practices' for discussing and producing texts, as well as familiarity with the social context of the discourse. It also includes understanding the roles and purposes of the target discourse community at social and cultural as well as cognitive levels.

Candlin and Gotti (2007) bring together a number of researchers working pedagogically in different professional discourse communities: business, legal, medical and political. But let us consider one example here of how ESP teachers might pedagogically respond to the real-world literacy needs of a specific group researched by Candlin and Candlin (2002). They researched the complexity of needs of non-native speaker doctors working in an English language context. On the academic level, such a group of doctors might need to know and use the English appropriate to reading and writing specialist medical research literature, and to speaking in conference with other doctors. On the non-academic but just as professionally important level, they might have engaged in language and language behaviours appropriate to communicating with patients and their families in personal everyday language of illness, with cultural awareness of how empathy could be conveyed.

Added to these linguistic and cultural literacies, such doctors might also belong to virtual communities to exchange information with trainers and peers. If so, then computer literacy would also be engaged. In this respect, we could pluralise their 'literacies' to describe the many contexts in which they would need to function, each with its own discourse and rules.

In Section 8.2 below, we look at two kinds of literacy which fall under the broad category of English for Specific Purposes: these are English for Occupational Purposes (EOP) and English for Academic purposes (EAP).

Task 8.2 Research task

Conduct your own research as an 'ethnographer' into a language setting or domain familiar to you: for example, a bookshop, the reception of a language school, doctor, or dentist; a bank, shop, department store; a café or restaurant.

Act as a silent observer and note down:

- Specific phrases or formulae which you notice repeated or typical of the setting
- Ways people greet, continue and close conversations
- Whether there are any patterns of behaving as people arrive, leave, or interact with one another

Which of these features you have noticed would you choose to teach/explain/make explicit to a language learner arriving in this setting for the first time?

Task 8.3 Web-based task: English language villages 🖥

ABC villages are total-immersion English language villages where children simulate the activities and competences of the outside world through the medium of English. Explore the ABC villages by starting with the link below, to the English village in Taiwan. In the link the children are simulating a TV news broadcast: <http://www.youtube.com/watch?v=hrbra3-siik>

What skills and competences are they practising and demonstrating?

How might these skills transfer into the world of work?

What preparations and guidance might have been put in place to make this 'TV broadcast' possible?

8.2 TEACHING FOR ACADEMIC AND PROFESSIONAL LITERACIES

In Chapter 3 we introduced the notion of needs analysis as a starting point for planning teaching and learning choices. Needs analysis is a central driver in the planning of programmes for specific academic and professional literacies. Hutchinson and Waters describe this as 'an approach to language teaching in which all decisions as to content and method are based on the learner's reason for learning' (Hutchinson and Waters 1987: 19). What kind of questions do we need to ask to establish these reasons, and where can the teacher and learner find the answers? Below are some possible answers to this question.

Task 8.4 Reflecting on your professional/academic context

In Task 8.1 above you considered your own language use in different social contexts and communities. You are now invited to focus on just one of these, and think about the language demands in more detail: for example, as a student in my subject discipline; as a teacher in my school; as a member of my local community.

Table 8.1 gives some ways in which we might explore the language needs of this context.

How would you answer these questions in your chosen context?

Are there any other questions which would be useful to ask?

Table 8.1   Target situation analysis for professional and academic purposes

Needs analysis	Example questions
How do people *interact* in this situation?	What are the rules of politeness and rules for addressing one another? How do people agree or disagree with one another? How do people conduct meetings? Who talks when? How much and which kind of information is exchanged and needed?
What kind of *text types* will I encounter in this situation? What kind of spoken contexts and situations will I encounter?	How do these texts structure information? What kind of vocabulary is expected – specialist or general? Where should I position myself as author – should I mention myself, or 'hide' my own role in the writing? How much should we refer to the ideas, research and writing of others, and how much to our own ideas? What are the disciplinary conventions for referencing and acknowledging these ideas?
How am I expected to *behave* in the target situation?	For example, am I expected to work independently or work collaboratively with others (or both?); share my ideas and knowledge or hide them?; share my opinions or reach a consensus?; socialise with colleagues or keep working and social life separate?
What am I expected to *know* in the target situation?	What assumptions are made about what I know and do not know? Am I expected to share new knowledge and/or acquire it from others? acquire it for myself? display it or hide it?

Murray (2010) and others (such as Bardovi-Harlig 1996) advocate that students should 'become their own ethnographers' (Murray 2010: 295), researching for themselves the answers to the questions above. Such knowledge can be gathered from multiple sources: from peers and fellow professionals, professional journals and papers, observations of typical and successful behaviour in the professional context. Table 8.2 presents an example of a trainee doctor's analysis of his own needs. Trainee doctor Nazeem 'shadowed' an experienced colleague for a summer, gathering the following specific examples of the literacies he observed amongst experienced colleagues.

Below is a case study of an 'academic literacies' student which illustrates the kind of issues involved in making a transition from one academic culture to another. In reading this case study you might notice the way in which the questions suggested in the needs analysis in Table 8.1 had, or had not, been addressed by both Olivia and her academic teachers.

Teaching case study 15: an EAP (English for Academic Purposes) student: Olivia in England, UK

Olivia before arriving at a UK University

Olivia has recently arrived from China to study Psychology and Business Studies at a British university. At her high school in China she was a high-achieving student who had achieved excellent marks in the school leaving exams and a high English language test score. She had focused on reading and writing skills which matched the

Table 8.2   Mapping professional contexts – trainee doctor observations

Social functions	Genres or text types
Offering reassurance Advising and recommending Explaining medical information Describing medical results Dealing with anger, disappointment, anxiety or pain	Prescriptions Information about drugs and medicines – (components, counter-indicators and side effects) Instructions; new research; research reports; medical results; websites; professional journals; databases
Strategies and skills	**Specialist vocabulary**
Making connections between symptoms Seeing connections and contra-indications between medicines Knowing where and how to gather information rapidly, both online and in hard copy Interpreting visual clues for medical information, such as X-rays Handling numerical and statistical information confidently Recording information clearly for use by others	Names of drugs and medicines Names of medical conditions in both specialist and lay terms Both medical and 'lay' descriptions of parts of the body and body mechanisms

expectations and conventions of her study context at school. She was accustomed to studying in large classes, following the procedures of the teacher carefully and spending time at home reading widely and taking notes. Before travelling to the British university she read all the books on the pre-university book list, and she felt confident, well-prepared and excited on arriving.

Olivia at her first class in the UK University

To her surprise, at the first class the teacher did not seem to expect the students to have done the pre-course reading: and in fact most of the other students had not. Also to her disappointment, the teacher did not spend much of the class time talking, but put the students in groups to discuss questions they had about the course. Olivia was too shy to mention that she had done all the pre-course reading and felt she did not have many questions about the course. She also felt frustrated because the students did not seem to have any particular knowledge that was useful, and because she did not receive this knowledge from the teacher. She was also confused as to what she was meant to learn by talking in groups in this way.

In analysing Olivia's situation, a number of issues emerge. Olivia had spent some time focusing on the content of her course, and was expecting this to entail a furthering of knowledge and information, carried over from the teacher and the coursebooks to herself. She had no particular interest in fellow students, as she did not expect to learn from them or with them. In contrast, what the teacher chose to emphasise at the first meeting was not the content of the course, but the importance of class cohesion and student dialogue. The teacher was also hoping to gather some ideas of the students' needs and expectations, and to give students practice in exchanging information, solving problems and coming to team decisions. All of these skills, she felt, modelled those expected of Psychology students.

An EAP teacher would consider ways of bridging the gap between Olivia's expectations and the teacher's. This would include making these mutual expectations transparent, and asking questions about the exact skills and literacies, conventions and behaviours expected. What constitutes 'good' learning in the target environment? How does this match, or mismatch, the EAP student's perception of good learning, and what would help him or her make the transition from one to the other? In this case, for example, Olivia needs to practise being confident amongst her peers, sharing her reading and knowledge with others, and using class discussion for developing ideas.

Task 8.5 The reflective teacher

In the first piece of writing for the class, Olivia was asked to write a 'reflective piece' explaining her view of business ethics. She spent many hours reading multiple books on the subject, and wrote a detailed account of three businesses which made claims to being ethical. When she received feedback from the teacher, she was given a low mark for not 'reflecting her own position clearly'.

What went wrong? What should the EAP teacher do about this?

Again, there had been a mismatch between the EAP student's former experience of academic writing, and what was expected in this new situation. Importantly, the teacher had not explained exactly what was expected from this piece of writing. Some pieces of academic writing will require you to write impersonally, describing research, or the writings of others, without mention of you as author. Other pieces of academic writing will expect you to place your own views, experiences or feelings at the centre. These may well be described as 'reflective' pieces, and the *I* personal pronoun will be expected of the writer; but academic tutors may not make these differences explicit.

Two key responses to the needs of the academic and professional learner have been highlighted: firstly, to generate programmes which are content-rich, and secondly, to adopt a genre and text-type approach to the teaching of texts. Content-rich classes might place at the centre the subject disciplinary knowledge of the language learners; or choose content areas of general interest which offer an appropriate level of intellectual engagement but do not require specialist knowledge; or alternatively make the language itself the 'content' area, as it was in Chapters 4, 5 and 6 of this book. In contexts where the medium of instruction is the target or second language, the language will be modelled and learnt through the subject discipline. This approach is known as CLIL, or 'content and language integrated learning', and for many teachers and learners is an expectation of their study in higher education. For example, Sweden, Kuwait and Hong Kong all include higher education study through the medium of English, irrespective of the students' mother tongue.

The second approach to the needs of professional and academic learners has been to adopt a text-type approach to teaching. We looked in Chapter 6 at the value of genre analysis for knowledge of reading. This is particularly useful in professional contexts in clarifying the conventions of the profession. Swales (1990) outlines the way in which texts are structured as a sequence of *moves* which are flagged up by

Table 8.3   Moves in a research article abstract (Swales 1990: 141; Wharton 2011: 223)

Text organisation of a research article	Examples from a research article abstract (Wharton 2011: 221)
Move 1: establish the territory *Make a generalisation*	Many UK universities offer degree programmes in English language specifically for non-native speakers of English. **Such programmes typically** include not only language development but also development in various areas of content knowledge.
Move 2: indicate a gap *Establish a niche*	**A challenge that arises is** to design courses in different areas that mutually support each other, thus providing students with a coherent degree programme.
Move 3: occupy the niche *Indicate structure of the article* *Outline purposes*	**In this article I will** discuss a BA programme involving Cultural Studies and Translation as well as English Language and Linguistics. **I will offer** a rationale for a course in critical text analysis. **It is intended to** promote language development and cultural awareness as well as skills of linguistic analysis and critical thinking.

key words or discourse markers. Table 8.3 presents an example of these moves in a research article abstract by Wharton (2011) about teaching EAP at a UK university. Wharton suggests in this article that cultural studies are a content-rich area for EAP students from multiple disciplines, combining the joint goals of developing language and academic literacy skills. The moves in her research article abstract, however, are typical of research articles in other fields too, and can be used as a framework for reading, understanding and writing in other disciplines and professions. What they reveal that is of practical value is that the abstract of an article contains the key 'moves' of the article as a whole and can be used as a research strategy to gather information rapidly from a wide reading base, without the need to read each article in detail. Table 8.3 shows in bold which key words and phrases mark the 'move'. These key words and phrases can be adapted to 'scaffold' the student's own writing, irrespective of subject discipline.

Learners can arrive for themselves at an understanding of the moves in any text type, by collecting multiple examples and placing them side by side. Task 8.6 uses questions suggested in Chapter 6 that help to elicit the characteristics of a text type.

Task 8.6 Teacher as text analyst

Select two examples of a text type that you use in your regular study or professional practice. Place the examples side by side and answer the following questions about each text, which derive from Chapter 6 of this book. Are the answers similar for both texts? Can you identify typical characteristics of the text type? Are there further questions which you think would be useful to ask?

- How is the text laid out on the page – in paragraphs, bullet points, short lines?
- What words would you expect to find in the text?
- What verb forms would you expect to find in the text – referring to past time, present time, future time? Using the passive voice?
- What are typical sentence types in the text – questions, commands, statements, exclamations, all of these?
- What typically comes at the beginning of the text? In the middle? At the end?
- How are the stages of the text flagged up? For example, are there typical introductory phrases or words? Or is there a specific layout or format on the page to show this?

Task 8.7 Academic phrasebank and corpus of academic writing 💻

The University of Manchester has developed a phrasebank that reflects the typical phrases used in academic writing at different stages of the discourse, such as in the opening sections and conclusions: <http://www.phrasebank.manchester.ac.uk/>

The phrases are also classified for different kinds of writing, such as critical reviews and reflective writing.

Explore the website and notice:

- how specific phrases help to mark stages in a piece of academic writing
- how specific phrases indicate the kind of writing that is being prepared: for example, critical, reflective, analytical or descriptive

The corpus of British Academic Writing, mentioned in Chapter 6, offers 3,000 examples of undergraduate academic writing assessed at merit or distinction standard in three UK universities across arts, sciences, humanities and social sciences.

Explore the website within one subject discipline that interests you, and notice the kinds of phrases and structures typical of successful essays: <http://www2.warwick.ac.uk/fac/soc/al/research/collect/bawe/>

Monash University has developed resources to support academic literacies for international students. Review these resources and notice the academic text types they have selected, and the specific language relevant to each text type: <http://www.education.monash.edu.au/students/current/study-resources/>

8.3 TEACHING FOR WEB LITERACIES
Liam Murray with John Eyles

Web and digital literacy is integral to being a professional in the modern world. Few of us would survive in work and professional contexts without the skills of information gathering and sharing, record-keeping, dissemination and communication of ideas through digital and online media. This not only gives language teachers access to multiple language and teaching resources online; it also provides opportunities to learn in a way that mirrors 'play' and communication in uninstructed contexts outside the classroom. Murray and Barnes (1998) asked language teachers to evaluate educational software by going beyond their initial 'wow' factor reaction (negative and/or positive). They argued that teachers needed to acquire evaluative competencies in order to accept or reject ICT (information communication technology) integration into their classroom, based on systematic and pedagogic judgements.

Since then, not only has the traditional perception of a 'classroom' changed, becoming a 'learner-facilitated pedagogical environment', but ICT integration has already occurred through mobile (or ubiquitous) learning. Such learning dictates that teachers and learners alike acquire multiple literacies (Warschauer & Shetzer, 2000) and through this *intermediality*: 'The pedagogy of telling and teaching to simplify complex concepts is being replaced with methods that engage future teachers in active and generative learning [and] learning is viewed as multidimensional and enhanced by students' own enquiry, problem-solving, and critical thinking' (Risko 2001: 91).

In this section, we shall discuss a number of the more effective types. One important point to bear in mind concerns the radical changes in the learners themselves. According to Prensky, 'today's students are no longer the people our educational system was designed to teach' (2001: 1). He goes on to emphasise a dichotomy between 'Digital Natives' (young learners, or 'native speakers of the digital language of computers, video games and the Internet') and Digital Immigrants (all those others who retain a 'digital accent'). Maclean and Elwood (2009) remind us that Prensky's formulation is very similar to the SLA process, where the L2 learner who makes use of ICT tools in their SLA will always carry a 'digital accent much as geographical immigrants do when learning a second language and culture' (Maclean and Elwood 2009: 157).

Electronic Tools

Language teaching practitioners have always been at the forefront in adopting and adapting new materials, strategies (Oxford 2011) and tools (Godwin-Jones 2003). Let us explore a number of the more prominent electronic tools that are currently being utilised in language teaching situations.

Blogs

We noted in Chapter 6 that there are many writing practices emerging from the digital medium which are changing the boundaries between the written and the spoken word. If blogs are changing our culture (Rodzvilla 2002), then they must carry some impact into our teaching culture. Researchers have shown how single-author and collaborative blogs may successfully promote self-expression (Rourke and Coleman 2009) and language learning strategies (Murray and Hourigan 2008). In the process of writing, bloggers 'become part of a discourse community in a complex multimodal setting' (Raith 2009: 276) where they may learn cooperatively in 'spaces where people negotiate and construct meaning and texts' (Richardson 2006: 74). The task of writing a blog in the target language obviously elaborates the writing skills of L2 learners, but also their ability to reflect upon and analyse the task. However, Myers (2010: 162) warns that L2 bloggers may encounter some difficulty in achieving the correct style and tone for their posts as they attempt a balance between the intellectual and personal voice when aiming to successfully complete a writing task.

Task 8.8 For whom does the L2 blogger write?

Ozkan (2011: 655) relates the use of blogging on a teaching skills course for preservice language teachers and reports that blogging is an important facility and a successful platform which allows a learning environment to grow and flourish because it may contain the following characteristics: *concrete experience* (or 'DO'), *reflective observation* (or 'OBSERVE'), *abstract conceptualisation* (or 'THINK'), and *active experimentation* (or 'PLAN').

Complete Table 8.4 by defining and offering possible examples of these characteristics in an integrated blog environment such as <wordpress.com>, where the blogging tool has been incorporated into a curriculum or module:

With rapid and easy access to blogging and social media sites such as Blogger, Wordpress, Facebook or its extension Ourspot, learners can connect and share their information and their learning through multiple media documents. Richardson (2006) has argued that this type of social interaction matches the world in which we live due to the collaborative construction of content. This is a continuing echo of Spolsky's (1999) and others' findings that because language is a social mechanism, the social context is a major influence on the learning process.

Table 8.4   Blogging stages

Concrete experience	**Do** This first stage involves listing activities that some learners/ pre-service teachers perform in class under peer observation. The roles are then reversed so that the observers can become the 'doers'. List such activities.
Reflective observation	**Observe** Now that all the learners/pre-service teachers have been active and been observed, the writing task is to reflect upon their learning experiences. List possible headings to follow in the task.
Abstract conceptualisation	**Think** This third stage is where the learner/pre-service teacher is asked to imagine a possible model or theory of what they have been observing. List possible starting points, e.g. scaffolding.
Active experimentation	**Plan** The final stage is where the learner/pre-service teacher aims at testing the model or concept from the previous stage. They may draw heavily upon the blog-posted comments of their peers from the earlier stages in order to plan for their future classes and teaching activities.

Suggested blogging task
A simple and straightforward task for L2 learners at intermediate level and above would be to evaluate a number of pertinent blogs, supplied by the teacher, and to compose their own critical summaries of these blogs within their own blog.

From chat to Twitter

Twitter is a micro-blogging service, and it cannot be ignored. With several key differences from a typical blog, this worldwide phenomenon offers its users (tweeters) text-based postings (tweets) which are limited to 140 characters, all answering the question: 'What's happening?' The modes of communication may be: one-to-one (a private exchange); one-to-many (a typical tweet, sent to all of a user's followers); or many-to-many (an 'RT' – ReTweet or text, broadcast simultaneously to many tweeters). As the convergence of media happens, so Twitter – like Facebook and blogging services – now allows users to embed videos into their tweets. Further convergence of usage is seen where Twitter is used by specialised groups for single-topic discussions, thus replicating the functions of online chatrooms. An example of this can be found by following the link <https://twitter.com/> and, in Twitter's search option, typing: '#ELTChat'. ELT Chat is an excellent example of user-driven content. The users offer up ideas for the weekly live discussion covering many of the most salient topics related to ELT and research. There are many online chatrooms available for both public and private English language interactions, such as <englishclub.com/esl-chat/> – again, users can join established chatrooms or organise their own with learners or other teachers.

In promoting the use of Twitter, Borau et al. (2009) emphasise the need for language production amongst learners, echoing Risko's (2000) demand for teaching methods that encourage 'active' learning with learners writing and interacting in the L2. Perifanou (2009) adopts a slightly different approach in taking Vygotsky's *Zone of Proximal Development* – where the learner moves from imitation to constructing their own learning paths – into the Twitter domain, to create informal play-based language learning activities. Antenos-Conforti (2009) has perhaps produced the most comprehensive study on Twitter and language acquisition, where she explored the tweeting habits of her students with regards to frequency, content topics, pedagogical evaluations, engagement and raising socio-cultural awareness. The latter proved to be the most elevated phenomenon in her findings, although at times during her use of Twitter, students did have a tendency to tweet extremely frequently on certain topics. Students did appear to be highly engaged with the Twitter tool throughout the study.

YouTube

Anecdotal evidence from students suggests that they are making greater use of video postings on YouTube in their learning. Documented evidence from Davies (2011) and from Watkins and Wilkins (2011) reveal how YouTube can be used to practise a wide variety of language skills, again within and outside of the classroom setting. From the obvious listening and pronunciation skills to reading and writing exercises and raising awareness of world Englishes, this vast video resource remains free for learners. Furthermore, students can create their own task-based videos and post them on public or private forums for peer and teacher critique. Watkins and Wilkins observed that the main two advantages are 'the exposure to authentic English as well as the promotion of a learning style that is more autonomous and student-centered' (Watkins and Wilkins 2001: 113–14). As with other user-driven content services such as Twitter, there is even a dedicated channel for teachers: <youtube.com\teachers>. A quick search on *EFL Teaching* within this channel reveals over 1,500 related videos.

Emerging area of games-based language learning

Section 7.1 above opened a discussion of games as part of language learning activity and showed how these drew on our understanding of learning processes and theory. Vygotsky (1978) has argued that learners would progress better in situations where they could avail themselves of the assistance of their peers. This is a cornerstone of the extensive amount of learning that is required to play games such as *World of Warcraft, Rift* or *Quest Atlantis* (known as Massively Multiplayer Online Role-Playing Games – MMORPGs), but it is also a general operating principle in most digital games. Cognition is not a phenomenon that occurs in isolation, but is socially distributed (Gee 2003), and MMORPGs certainly encourage engagement in 'collaborative social interaction' (Peterson, 2012: 89). Thus Thomas (2012: 25) concludes a succinct summary of previous research in this area with the positive statement: 'MMORPGs are identified with target language discourse management as well as with risk-taking and are amenable to a task-based approach.'

Another positive example comes from Anderson et al. (2008), who investigated the potential of the electronic game *America's Army* for improving the listening skills of Taiwanese language learners of English. This is one of many Commercial Off-The- Shelf (COTS) games that have been 'repurposed' for language acquisition opportunities. The repurposing or convergence of non-dedicated software for Computer-Assisted Language Learning (CALL) has a long and mostly successful history. The main reason for this has been the prohibitive financial cost involved in producing dedicated CALL software. It is a somewhat obvious prediction that this will continue in the future.

Podcasting

Chapter 6 noted the way the spoken word is evolving as communication becomes faster, more global and more accessible. Our notions of who 'owns' the English language, and what are its appropriate forms, are constantly evolving as a response. Listening and speaking as explored in Chapters 6 and 7 are acquiring multiple new resources to support and direct their development. Moving from video to audio production and distribution, podcasting has a short yet distinguished history in SLA. Thorne and Payne (2005) recognised the early potential of podcasting and listening to authentic materials. Travis (2007) added other exercises to enhance listening skills, such as dictation and project work. In spite of the origins of the term 'podcast', podcasts can be produced and listened to on any number of devices and not simply on the iPod. Travis and Joseph (2009) discuss the successful development of their popular podcasting site, Splendid Speaking (<splendid-speaking.

com>), using authentic conversations recorded via Skype. Whilst Ducate and Lomicka (2009) are more guarded in their evaluation of podcasts in their study, they do testify to the positive reception and enjoyment of this approach amongst the student body. In a highly pertinent and qualitative study, Deoksoon and King (2011: 5) show how podcasting practices carry 'transformative changes in ESOL teacher candidates' attitudes and perceptions, developing teacher professional identity while practicing innovative instructional technology'. Once again, there are many specialised podcasting sites aimed at EFL teachers, as a quick search on Google illustrates. However, for a more comprehensive introduction to education technology in general, we can recommend King and Gura's Teachers' Podcast site: <http://teacherspodcast.org/>

We must remember that none of these generic tools above was originally designed as a dedicated LT or LL tool. Conole (2011: 17) describes the need for 'mediating [these] artefacts' as the convergence of technologies takes place, and teachers must be able to assess the possible pedagogical repurposing of these tools.

Task 8.9 Integrating the skills with the mobile phone

The mobile phone is a modern digital Swiss Army knife in our pockets. It comes with audio recording, video recording, camera, text, spreadsheets, editing, and unending and more specialised apps. It can be used as a tool both to consume and to create digital content. Using Table 8.5, create four engaging and innovative pairwork or groupwork activities for the mobile phone that practise each of the four intralingual skills of speaking, listening, reading and writing.

Automated systems to teach and grade writing are becoming more common and accurate. They enable students to practice as often as they wish and to be provided with immediate feedback, along with tutorials that target identified areas of weakness.

Table 8.5   The mobile phone and the four skills

Skills to practise	Pairwork or groupwork activities
Speaking	1. 2. 3. 4.
Listening	1. 2. 3. 4.
Reading	1. 2. 3. 4.
Writing	1. 2. 3. 4.

They can support a busy teacher or be used stand-alone for self-study. Such systems provide a scalable mass adoption solution to teaching English language writing skills, particularly in developing countries where the scale is large, the need is great and the number of available and qualified teachers small. As result, they will undoubtedly become a standard part of the ESL landscape.

Task 8.10 Artificial intelligence writing tutors 💻

Review, compare and contrast three online artificial intelligence writing programmes. Determine what you like about them and any concerns you may have.

'My Access' School by Vantage Learning: <http://www.vantagelearning.com/products/my-access-school-edition/>

'Writing Planet' by Measurement Planet: <http://www.writingplanet.net>

'WriteToLearn' by Pearson: <http://www.writetolearn.net/>

Finding the right tool for the right job 💻

Complete Table 8.6a, ranking in order of appropriateness and effectiveness these tools in teaching the four intralingual skills, giving reasons for your ranking:

There exists an additional number of tools of peripheral but growing importance in this area. It would be beneficial to repeat the ranking exercise above; this time, in Table 8.6b, you will be given the name of the tool and a starting reference to begin your search and evaluation.

Finally in this section, let us not forget actual websites designed for ELT. One such site will suffice as a starting point: <http://iteslj.org/links/>, which is maintained by the Internet TESL Journal and contains over ten thousand links to a multifarious range of ELT topics, material and issues. Russell Stannard also runs a popular website <www.teachertrainingvideos.com> which collates and reviews by video many up-to-date tools from many sources which may be used in ELT. It is also worth mentioning ELT websites that provide localised ELT; for example, <www.

Table 8.6a   Evaluating web tools for learning and teaching

Tool	Appropriate for	Most effective for
Blogs	1. 2. 3. 4.	E.g. where would you rank 'summary writing' and 'descriptive reflection'? 1. 2. 3. 4.
Twitter	1. 2 . . .	1. 2 . . .
YouTube		
Podcasting		
Facebook		

Table 8.6b   Further web tools for learning and teaching

Tool	Appropriate for	Most effective for
Wikis	1. 2. 3. 4.	1. 2. 3. 4.
Second Life	1. 2 . . .	1. 2 . . .
Skype Digital games-based learning Digital Storytelling (Elwood, 2010) Also see: <voicethread.com> Apps		

bbcjanala.com> is the BBC's course for students in Bangladesh. It is the first ELT web-based course designed expressly for the language and culture of those living in Bangladesh. The English is spoken with a Bangla accent and the course is integrated with Facebook and Youtube, with the program as a whole using multiple platforms for achieving a greater audience reach including TV, mobile, CD, English clubs and newspapers.

Explore further links suggested in the online resource for this book.

Teaching case study 16: an online learner in Jakarta, Indonesia

This case study predominantly looks at the use of mobile phones as a new platform for online learning. The mobile phone is becoming increasingly relevant as a tool for individual and collective learning due to its ubiquitous nature and its accessibility. With over five billion mobile phone accounts worldwide in 2011, mobile technology allows for 'anytime, anywhere' learning.

Jakarta, Indonesia: A taxi driver is sitting outside the airport, not knowing how long he might be waiting until his next customer; he downloads a ringtone on his phone. This ringtone provides a three-minute English lesson which he can replay and practise as many times as he likes, and allows him to learn at his own pace. Within one month of downloading the daily ringtones, this taxi driver has added at least thirty new English phrases to his vocabulary. He is able to do his job better and earn more money as he is better able to communicate to international clients, and he becomes more economically viable as a result, all at a very reasonable cost.

The mobile phone content that the taxi driver accesses is produced by an American company, <www.urbanplanetmobile.com>, and is part of a Basic Taxi Driver English course. The content is delivered by the local mobile operator, who also takes care of the billing.

Task 8.11 What are the implications for teachers in this learning from an uninstructed context? What does it suggest about the importance (or otherwise) of structured teaching?

We have seen from several examples in this book that learners with incentive and resources can learn without the intervention of a teacher at all. Some of the qualities of this unmediated learning can be carried over by the teacher into the classroom.

What does it suggest about the importance of student motivation and incentive?
This learner had high incentive for learning the language. He deals with foreign clients on a daily basis and has the prospect of higher earnings through tips and ongoing business from foreign customers.

Can you suggest any problems or issues with learning online or through mobile phone in this way?
It depends on a high level of learner self-discipline and motivation, as there is the danger of isolation and a lack of opportunity for checking, feedback and self-evaluation.

8.4 FURTHER READING 🖥

Explore the following further readings in the online resource for this book.

Task 8.12 Prensky, M. (2001), 'Digital Natives, Digital Immigrants', *On the Horizon,* 9:5. Retrieved from <http://pre2005.flexiblelearning.net.au/projects/resources/Digital_Natives_Digital_Immigrants.pdf>http://pre2005.flexiblelearning.net.au/projects/resources/Digital_Natives_Digital_Immigrants.pdf
Task 8.13 Warschauer, M. and M. Liaw (2011), 'Emerging technologies for autonomous language learning', *Studies in Self-Access Learning Journal,* 2:3, 107–18. Retrieved from <http://sisaljournal.org/archives/sep11/warschauer_liaw/> http://sisaljournal.org/archives/sep11/warschauer_liaw/

8.5 CONCLUSION

This chapter asked the questions:

What are multiple literacies, and in what ways do they form part of the competences of the language learner?
We have explored the fact that a second language might be the means by which our learners can progress within their chosen study or career, or move between them more freely. Thus, in analysing language needs, we also need to analyse context and purpose well beyond the classroom itself. For example, a medical student using English for study will have needs that are both similar to, and different from, those of a taxi driver who needs English for his work. For teachers to take account of these differences, they have to become cultural analysts, and share this task with

their students. Becoming a teacher of multiple literacies involves listening to and learning from the contexts in which our learners function, gathering information about how language is used and which skills are needed. It also entails balancing language and skills which are generic to all learners, and those which are specific to their context.

How can digital developments in the language help us as teachers and learners? What skills and competences do we need to take full advantage of these?
The digital convergence of technologies has been a theme of this chapter. Throughout the history of ICT development, the various media have been and will continue to converge and offer similar facilities; for example, with Facebook incorporating messaging (one-to-one and one-to-many), texting, discussion fora, blogs, embedded video, news feeds; a whole electronic CV portfolio. However, at the same time we witness again a divergence of interests, as specialised groups emerge to make greater use of the tools for their own specific purposes. Historically, this happened just before the emergence of the World Wide Web, with Usenet newsgroups (see <livinginternet.com/u/ui.htm>) becoming more and more driven by the particular issues and interests of their users. From ELT websites to Twitter groups (#ELTChat) and teachers 'broadcasting' channels on YouTube, the personalisation pattern is easily discernible. The literacies may be changing, but many of the older practices are not. Yet the ongoing impact of ubiquitous and multifaceted technologies on teachers and learners alike cannot be discounted as they converge upon the latter.

8.6 GUIDED READING

For professional literacies
Basturkmen, H. (2010), *Developing Courses in English for Specific Purposes*, Basingstoke: Palgrave Macmillan
Basturkmen structures the designing of an ESP course into three, 'analysing needs, investigating specialist discourse and determining the curriculum' (Basturkmen 2010: p. x). The book leads the teacher of professional literacies through these three key stages of planning, showing how this planning would be realised in practice in case study examples for the police, medical doctors, and students writing academic theses.
Nesi, H. (2012), *Genre Across the Disciplines*, Cambridge: Cambridge University Press
This book draws on the British Academic Written English (BAWE) corpus of student writing, to explore the characteristics of writing across subject disciplines and within academic writing genres such as essays, critiques, research reports and reflective narratives. The book shows the ways in which students evolve 'creativity and the use of metaphor' as they work towards becoming 'experts in the genres of their discipline'. We see from Nesi's multiple authentic examples of writing in academic contexts, the way in which conventions are developed, and the way in which these differ from subject to subject, and text type to text type (Nesi 2012).

For digital literacies

Andrews, R. and A. Smith (2011), *Developing Writers: teaching and learning in the digital age*, **Maidenhead: Open University Press**

This book explores the skills of the writer in a multimodal age and traces the development of changes in the three decades before and after the millennium, in order to arrive at 'a new theory and model' for 'composing with multiple modes'. The authors identify the changes as a 'constantly widening range of text types', new formats, and new ways of composing socially and interactively. They explore the 'constant innovation, creativity and hybridity' needed to communicate via the multiple opportunities of the digital age (Andrews and Smith 2011: 146). The book guides the teacher and student through the literacy and skills required for these innovations, arriving at a 'new theory and model of writing development' which includes 'transduction – engaging in decisive changes from one mode to another', and 'remixing – such as using an image within a film or a section of a speech in a song' (Ibid. p. 146).

Starting points on the web:

- <www.ict4lt.org> is a collection of training modules for novices in ICT aimed at language teachers
- <http://www.eurocall-languages.org> is the European Association for CALL with a dedicated refereed research journal, *ReCALL*, and a large amount of on-line resources
- <https://calico.org/> Computer-Assisted Language Instruction Consortium is the US-based equivalent to EuroCALL, offering similar services as well as book publications
- <http://llt.msu.edu> is a web-based research journal, publishing refereed articles on aspects of SLA related to the use and implementation of technologies

9

CULTURAL COMPETENCES IN METHODS

INTRODUCTION

Both teachers and researchers suggest that the discrete parts of the language might not add up to the whole. Hymes (1972) identified an additional competence over and above the capacity to create grammatical sentences, 'communicative competence', from which emanated the communicative approach to language learning discussed in Chapters 1 and 2. In recent years, this has been subdivided into other competences;

- **Cultural competence:** Byram describes two approaches to the idea of cultural competence. The first approaches cultural competence as a 'sum of knowledge', such as understanding the festivals, customs, religion and folk traditions of a culture. This has sometimes been called the 'big C' approach. A 'big C' approach to the teaching of literature, for example, would include the 'sacred canon' of established and famous writers, and teach knowledge 'about' them and the culture they represent. The second model, and the one preferred in twenty-first-century approaches, involves the capacity to interpret a culture and appreciate the parallels between one's own culture and a new or foreign one (Byram 1994; 12). In this approach to culture, literature might be taught not as a body of knowledge, but as a humanising force that offers insights into the human condition. These differences will be explored in more detail in Section 9.1 below.
- **Social and pragmatic competence:** in Chapter 6 we saw the ways in which spoken interaction was not only about surface linguistic formulae and correctness, but entailed sensitivity to the conventions of conversations: how we open and close conversations, take turns, invite others into the interaction. These skills are all significant aspects of our cultural competence, and involve understanding of social conventions, the relationships between people, settings and situations and how these impact on the language we choose. These competences are both universal to the human condition, and specific to the language and culture within which we interact. Section 9.2 considers how to develop these competences within a context of cultural awareness.
- **Intercultural competence.** The capacity to interpret other cultures is taken one step further in the notion of intercultural competence. This is the capacity to move sensitively and intelligently from one cultural context to another, interpreting clues in order to act appropriately within the new culture. Some teachers and

researchers describe this as preparing learners to be **global citizens,** able not only to use other languages competently, but to live and work confidently beyond the comfort zone of the familiar.

This chapter will explore these broader social, cultural and intercultural competences embedded in the learning of a language and the way these impact on methods and methodologies. It will ask the following questions:

- What is the interface between learning a language and learning 'culture'? What does *culture* actually mean, and how far should this be part of the language teacher's role?
- What is social, cultural and pragmatic knowledge, and why is this so important for the language learner?
- How can teachers develop their own and their learners' social, pragmatic and cultural knowledge in the language classroom?
- What skills does the learner need to communicate between and across different cultures, and how can the language teacher help to develop these skills?

9.1 THE INTERFACE BETWEEN TEACHING LANGUAGE AND TEACHING CULTURE

This section considers the interface between learning a language and learning cultural knowledge in and about that language. This interface is a complex one, and starts with the much broader question: what is culture, and should this be part of the language teacher's role?

Task 9.1 What is culture?
What is your own definition of 'culture'? Below are several definitions. What is your view of each of these? Formulate your own working definition to add to these.
   'the common values and beliefs of a people and the behaviours that reflect them' (Gebhard 1996: 113)
   'the knowledge and practices of people belonging to particular social groups, for example national groups' (Byram 1994: vii)
   'linguistically mediated membership into a discourse community' (Kramsch 1995: 85)
   'the ways of a people' (Lado 1957: 110)
   Your definition: _____

_____

Before reading further, you might like to consider your own answer to the questions below.

- Do you think the English language teacher should teach 'culture' as well?
- If so, which culture: the English-speaking world? the places where English is a lingua franca? the interface between language and what it reveals about cultural norms and attitudes?

- Do you take the view that culture is a body of knowledge or information to be conveyed? Or do you take the view that it is a competence, entailing skills of analysis and interpretation? How would you teach for each of these approaches?
- Do you believe 'culture' includes what is everyday, commonplace and popular, or what is unique, exceptional and a product of unique genius, or both? How would you teach for each of these approaches?
- What skills do you think are involved in being successful within the target culture? What should the language user be aware of and sensitive to? How would you teach these skills?

This section aims to offer ideas and resources to help you answer these questions for your own purposes.

Since language pedagogy formalised as a profession, approaches to these questions have changed as radically as has our approach to language itself. These approaches can be broadly represented as a shift from 'knowledge about' to 'experience of' culture. Table 9.1 below maps these approaches, showing what they really mean for the language lesson and for the role of literature in the language lesson.

The 'big C' approach

Byram describes this as 'transmissable facts about other cultures', including examples of the 'exceptional or stereotypical' (Byram 1994). The 'exceptional' frequently included literary texts, chosen not only for literary merit and intellectual challenge, but as examples of mainstream culture. Learning tended to affirm what learners already believed about the culture of the target language. The notion of culture would often be monolithic, focusing on broad generalisations rather than fine-grained differences and nuances; for example, the English fondness for drinking tea, the Scottish habit of wearing kilts, or the American fondness for burgers. The grammar-translation approach adopted this view of culture, drawing on mainstream literary texts for translation, and often privileging the target culture above any other. Coursebooks would show us how 'typical' English or American families conducted their daily lives, generally sanitised from any difficulty or diversity. Table 9.1 gives examples of 'facts' about cultures which are easily transmissible and often isolated by coursebooks.

Table 9.1   Examples of 'transmissable facts about other cultures'

The British Royal family and the story of kings, queens, princes and princesses
The Welsh love of song in the Eisteddfod
The Hungarian making of home-made fruit liqueurs (*palinka*)
The Japanese tea-making ceremony
The talking drums in Burundi
The Chinese symbol of the dragon
The Hindu notion of *izzat* or honour
The Iranian notion of *taarof* (saying what you don't mean in order to be polite: see Task 9.8 below)

The strength is that this approach is easy to teach, as it tends to reinforce rather than to challenge and critique cultural stereotypes. But there are serious limitations in doing so. Valdes (2001) suggests that 'most people – see themselves and their compatriots not as a culture but as "standard" or "right" and the rest of the world as made up of cultures which are conglomerates of strange behaviour' (Valdes 2001: vii).

> In the bias of our own culture-bound worldview, we too often picture other cultures in an oversimplified manner, lumping cultural differences into exaggerated categories and then view every person in a culture as possessing stereotypical traits (Brown 2007: 190).

To stay inside this comfort zone limits a learner's participation in the 'exciting adventure' of linguistic and cultural travel, so many teachers have adopted more inclusive and more critical approaches to the language/culture interface.

The contrastive approach

A more inclusive approach is to see language not as representative of an indicative culture, but a lingua franca through which cultures can be compared and contrasted. In this approach, no one culture is privileged above another, and classroom activity might involve comparing experiences, responses and cultural events. In Table 9.2 is an example of a contrastive exercise about food developed by Corbett (2003: 109), and which could be replicated with other topics.

The ethnographic approach

In Section 8.2 we saw that Murray (2010) suggested giving learners the tools and metalanguage for analysing speech events for themselves; and in Chapter 8 we looked at how learners can arrive at an analysis of their own learner needs by behaving as ethnographers of their target situation. Taking this approach into the study of culture, how can learners be given the tools and metalanguage for analysing culture? One useful framework is provided by Hofstede (1997), who suggested a number of categories which can help us to analyse and compare different cultures. Look at these categories

Table 9.2   Contrastive approach to culture: foods of cultural significance (in Corbett 2003: 109)

	Brazil	Scotland	USA
Food	*Feljoada*	*Haggis*	*Hot dogs*
Ingredients	Salt port, pork sausage, ham, salted tongue, pig's knuckle	Sheep's stomach, heart, liver, lungs and windpipe; onions, suet, oatmeal, salt, herbs	Beef or pork frankfurter sausages, oval bun, optional mustard, ketchup, pickle
When eaten?	Wednesdays and Saturdays	Burns Night (25th January)	Sports events

Table 9.3 Becoming an ethnographer (Hofstede 1997, based on O'Neill and Gish 2008: 21)

Hofstede's dimensions	Questions for the teacher/learner
The masculinity/femininity dimension	Compare how men and women are expected to behave: – in the workplace – in educational settings – school/university – at home/with the family
Collectivist/individualist Do you perceive yourself as a member of a group acting responsibly within that group; or as an individual with free will to act as you wish?	What is the attitude in your culture towards: – disagreeing with friends/colleagues – doing something a parent disapproves of – leaving the family to live or be alone – spending money on yourself rather than your family
Uncertainty/avoidance	What do you do in your culture if: – you are asked something you don't know – you are given something to eat you have never seen before – you have to travel to somewhere you have never been before – someone you have never met comes to stay with you
Power/distance	What is the attitude in your culture to: – an older relation or person – a parent – your school and college teachers How do you address them? Who in your culture do you address with great respect? Who in your culture addresses you with great respect?

in Table 9.3 and think about these questions: how far do you think these categories may be useful and interesting to develop with language learners? What are the strengths and limitations of this approach? Are there other questions you think might be interesting?

Task 9.2 Research task
Below are two case studies of language/culture misunderstandings. What do they reveal about misunderstandings between cultures?

Teaching case study 17: a Japanese student in the USA
When Natiko, a newly-arrived second year undergraduate exchange student from Japan, was invited to a party, she was asked to bring a plate. Although this is an everyday, well-understood phrase, it was difficult for Natiko to understand its meaning in this context, and she was too polite to ask. It was only when she accepted a lift to the party that she realised others had food.

Teaching case study 18: a Native Australian rural child in a city school
Ronald, an aboriginal child in year 2 (aged 8), had moved from his rural community to an urban school. He appeared to leave his homework folder at home most days

even though his teacher had emphasised to always put it back in his bag after doing homework. Fortunately, the teacher realised that in his non-standard English there were fine differences when making reference to time and frequency. For Ronald, the term 'always' actually meant 'often'.

Examples from O'Neill and Gish (2008: 10)

The language:culture approach

In Section 8.2 we looked at a brief description of Wharton's project (2010) in which pre-university students were taught cultural studies combined with English language as a combined programme to prepare them for university study. This represents a 'blended' approach to culture and language as inseparable elements to be taught and developed together.

Teaching case study 19: Durham, UK and Paris, France – a language:culture blend

Below is a case study example of another such programme jointly run by the School of Education, University of Durham, and the Institut National de Recherche Pedagogique in Paris.

The fundamental principles Byram defined were as follows:

- The study of language is inseparable from the study of culture, 'by which we mean the way of thinking and acting in a social group' (Byram et al. 1994: 94)
- 'by culture we refer to what a person needs to know in order to be part of a social group – ways of thinking and valuing, ways of behaving, shared knowledge of the world'
- The acquisition of a foreign language involves acquiring some of the culture it embodies
- The course of study should be structured by principles of progression – in the nature of the content, difficulty of conceptual learning, techniques of teaching and learning
- Study of one language and culture shall prepare students for the study of others, and thus include acquisition of study techniques for other languages and cultures (Byram et al. 1994: 95)

Task 9.3 Teaching culture

The joint project leaders chose five topics around which to organise the language syllabus. These were:

Family
Education
Work
Regional identity
Politics

- These are broad topics which would be unworkable in themselves as a language syllabus. How would you subdivide each topic into issues and debates?

Table 9.4 Blending culture and language: an example

Topic/unit	Chosen issues	Links with language

Family	Name-giving
	Ceremonies
	Meal times
	Addressing relatives
		How names are pronounced + use of
		  prenominals (e.g. Mr, Dr, Ms)
		Forms of address (sir, Miss)
		Addressing relatives: (Aunty, Gran)
		Social language at meal-times (do we
		  really say 'pass the salt?')

Education	Education system
	Historical, political and
	  social contexts of
	  education
	Pupil dissatisfaction with
	  school
		Comparing key terms in education
		  across cultures: e.g. college, High
		  School, academy – how are they used?
		Classroom language and protocol: how
		  do you ask a question, reply to the
		  teacher?
		Feelings about school – language to
		  express feelings

Work	Patterns of employment Prestige of jobs Mobility Nature of work v. leisure Remuneration	Names of jobs: job titles in different cultures
Regional identity	Climate	
Politics	Power structure in social groups	Recognising status and relationships through language:

- How would you select components of the language syllabus to teach through these cultural topics?
- How far could you/would you use these topics and sub-topics in a learning and teaching context with which you are familiar? How would you adapt, refine or change the list you have drawn up for your own purposes?

When you have made your own notes in response to these questions, compare your ideas to those drawn up by the project leaders in Table 9.4.

Task 9.4 Bengali English Online: language and culture 🖥️

Explore <www.bbcjanala.com>, the BBC's course for students in Bangladesh. It is the first ELT web-based course designed expressly for the language and culture of those living in Bangladesh.

What topics, issues and questions are dealt with?

How do these topics, issues and questions introduce and develop specific aspects of language?

How would you evaluate the success of this project in developing an interface between the teaching of English and the culture familiar and meaningful to its learners?

9.2 TEACHING FOR SOCIAL AND PRAGMATIC COMPETENCE

In Chapter 6 we saw that spoken language entails competences much broader than simply the surface organisation of language. In interacting with others we also deploy many other competences, such as understanding how to take turns in a conversation, when it is appropriate to tell a long story or a joke, which register to use, and how to adapt this to the other speakers or the setting. We carry over these understandings intuitively from the mother tongue into the second language, but there may or may not be exact matches in these conversational strategies between the two language contexts. For example, in some settings it may be correct practice to approach someone and introduce yourself with your name and a handshake; in another culture (such as in the UK), you may conduct a whole conversation with someone before exchanging names. In some cultures you may be expected to tell personal details such as your income to someone you do not know well; in other cultures this would be entirely inappropriate.

Social and pragmatic competence entails these deeper understandings of what lies behind interaction, for example, the unspoken rules of politeness, or the conventions of how a conversation develops in different settings and with different speakers. This competence is important because 'interviews have been failed, fortunes ruined, relationships irretrievably damaged and, as Widdowson (1990: 95) illustrates, major battles such as the Charge of the Light Brigade lost due to pragmatic failure' (Murray 2010: 293).

In Table 9.5 are a number of situations in which social and pragmatic competence is critical. Consider how you might respond in your own mother tongue setting. How would you explain the social 'rules' to someone who did not share your intuitive and 'insider' knowledge?

For the English language teacher, we might ask: how far can we prepare language learners for situations such as these? What competences are needed, and should they be taught, or are they competences which any speaker will naturally transfer from the mother tongue to the second language? Richards (1990) suggested two possible approaches to this question. As teachers we might approach the competences indirectly, by leading students to their own understanding through role-plays, problem-solving activities and simulations. Alternatively, we might adopt a direct approach which involves explicit awareness-raising and 'noticing' activities.

Direct approaches to social and pragmatic competence

There are a number of ways in which the teacher might approach these competences directly and explicitly:

Table 9.5   Social competence in an L2: some questions

How do you summon a waiter in a restaurant?
How do you address an older person in a senior position to yourself – while in a professional context? in a social context?
When is it appropriate to tell a (fairly long) joke?
When is it appropriate to tell a personal story about something that happened to you?
When, and how, is it appropriate to greet someone you have never met before?
What topics of conversation are acceptable between strangers?

Table 9.6   Conversational gambits

| Have you heard the one about . . .? |
| Excuse me – we're ready to order now. |
| Do you work here? |
| Is this your first time here? |
| Have you been here before? |
| The same thing happened to me. |
| Yes, I've got the same sort of story. |

- provide examples of conversation openings or 'gambits' for different settings and situations
- provide examples of a 'spectrum' of responses to situations, depending on levels of politeness or informality
- provide frameworks for 'noticing' the rules and conventions of social interaction
- explore online resources as opportunities for hearing and communicating in authentic Englishes in multiple settings and contexts: for example, YouTube clips, online chatrooms, BBC iPlayer, online English language clubs such as <www.eng lishclub.com/esl-chat> and the resources in the online tasks for Chapters 7 and 8.

The tasks below invite you to explore conversation gambits as awareness-raising and teaching activities.

Task 9.5 Teaching conversation gambits
Can you identify the situation in which each of the 'conversation gambits' in Table 9.6 might be used?

Add your own conversation gambits for each of these conversational settings.

When would each of these be appropriate? When would they not be appropriate?

Conversation spectrum
What is the difference between the responses in Table 9.7 on p. 200?

Would any of them cause offence? Why?

A number of frameworks might help the teacher with 'noticing' activities, whether we critique the framework itself or use it as a guideline for our analysis of social inter-action. We will consider two of these, and ask how they can help form a structure for the teaching of social and pragmatic competence.

Noticing framework 1: Grice's co-operative principle
Grice suggested that conversations have an assumption of co-operation between speakers and that in order for this co-operation to work, there are certain 'unspoken' conventions which speakers share as a 'common frame of reference' (Murray 2010: 296). Although these conventions are as often broken as followed, speakers usually break them for a reason; for example, to save face, to be polite, to make a point, to make a joke, for sarcasm, self-protection or irony. These latter responses are easier to

Table 9.7   Politeness spectrum

Situation 1: in a restaurant
I want a veggie burger with chips.
Can I have the burger with chips?
Yes please, I'd like the burger with chips.
I'm gonna have the burger with chips.
Situation 2: request
Could I borrow a pen?
Do you have a pen I could borrow?
May I use your pen for a moment?
Would it be OK if I just borrowed that for a moment?
Can I have that, do you think?

Table 9.8   Conversational maxims (Grice 1975)

Maxim	Explanation	Example
Quantity	Provide as much information as the exchange requires. Don't provide more than is required.	You are asked for directions to the post office. In your explanation you choose the important landmarks on the route and purposely leave out details such as the names of every shop en route.
Relation	Be relevant.	'I was amazed walking into Broadlands School how it had changed.' The interlocutors are expected to pick up this theme and ask about it, or expand it. It would not be good conversational etiquette to reply, 'Must get my hair cut'. (Carter and McCarthy 1996; 78)
Quality	Try to say what is true. Don't say what you believe to be false. Don't say what you do not have evidence for.	If someone asks you your name you tend to reply truthfully with the answer (unless you have a reason to hide the truth). If someone asks you for directions to a landmark, you would be unlikely to send them in the opposite direction deliberately.
Manner	Be clear. Avoid obscurity. Avoid ambiguity. Be brief. Be orderly.	Again drawing on the example of asking directions, you would be unlikely to give directions that entailed taking a detour in the wrong direction, doubling back, retracing the route, and ending with a philosophical lecture on destinations.

understand and explain in the context of the conventions (known as maxims) they are flouting. These maxims, as defined by Grice, are presented in Table 9.8.

These maxims are interesting because they give us a measure by which we can understand what is happening when rules are broken. They provide a framework for 'noticing' what we are doing with language and open up underlying 'stories' or subtext.

Below are some examples which could be tried out with students:

An older relative gives you a book as a birthday present which you have not had time to read. When next you meet, he asks you if you had enjoyed the book.

Would you tell the truth? **(flouting the maxim of quality)**

You are showing a visitor you want very much to impress around your home town when he asks you the history of an interesting monument. You have no idea about the answer. What would you say? **(flouting the maxim of quantity)**

You ask someone the time and they reply, 'The evening prayers are just beginning.' In what circumstances would this answer your question? Does this give you an answer or not? **(does it flout the maxim of relevance?)**

Someone asks you the way to a restaurant in a town you know well. There are two routes: a very direct one and a very roundabout one which is three times longer. You know that the direct route is unlit and dangerous, so suggest the longer route. **(does this flout the maxim of manner?)**

Noticing framework 2: Lakoff's rules of politeness

Lakoff (1973) explored a different aspect of conversation which she felt cemented social understanding. These were the underlying conventions of politeness, which she felt were sometimes in conflict with the conversational maxims described by Grice. These conventions were:

- don't impose
- give options
- make your receiver feel good

They form a useful checklist for the teacher in developing conversational gambits or a spectrum of responses, or in analysing language when it does or does not appear polite (Table 9.9).

However, conversational rules are even more fluid in actual practice than grammatical rules, and because we are continually inventive in conversations, we tend to systematically break these maxims. We might break these rules in a way which is not evident to other speakers, in order to protect ourselves or the truth. For example:

A friend has recently become engaged to a man you know to be dishonest and unpleasant: what do you say to her? Do you follow Grice's maxim of quality, or Lakoff's convention of 'making your receiver feel good'?

Compare your reactions to the two situations below. When is it appropriate to violate the politeness rule of 'don't impose'? What are the experiences of your learners in their own contexts?

A thief is running away with a stolen wallet. A policeman running after him pushes through the crowds in the street and shouts, 'Get out of the way!'

A crowd of people are climbing onto a crowded bus. Someone at the back of the crowd pushes in front shouting 'get out of the way!'

Table 9.9   Lakoff's politeness maxims

Politeness rule	Conversational gambits
Don't impose	We tend to 'hedge' a request or demand with phrases like these: I'm sorry to bother you but--- Would you mind --------- I hate to interrupt you but------
Give options	When you offer food or drink you usually suggest options: *Do you want tea or coffee?* When you make arrangements you usually suggest alternative dates: *Are you free on Thursday evening? or Saturday?*
Make your receiver feel good	When you refuse an invitation you usually provide a good reason that allows the inviter to save face: *I'm so sorry but I'm studying for exams all this week.* When someone introduces you to someone/something they value, you tend to say something positive.

How would you respond in these situations?

Someone you do not know very well asks if you could lend her a substantial amount of money. How can you respond without flouting the politeness convention of 'make your receiver feel good'?

Whilst there is evidence that all cultures have conventions such as these that bind together communities, the boundaries of what is and is not conventional or acceptable are often very different. Below is a 'noticing' checklist for learners to bring to consciousness their own conventions and the ways they may be similar or different from one another.

- How long is it acceptable to be silent in a conversation?

In some societies, silence in a conversation suggests people have run out of ideas or lost interest in the conversation. In others, silences are a sign that people are thinking and establishing consensus with one another, or silence is a mark of respect and gives status to another speaker. What about your learners?

- What is the acceptable way to receive a compliment?

In British English it is considered impolite to imply arrogance, so one might deflect a compliment by suggesting it isn't really true. Below are some examples:

What a fabulous outfit you are wearing!
  Oh, it's just something cheap I found in the sale.
  Oh, I've had it for years.
  Oh, this old thing!

- What is the acceptable way to respond to an offer of food or drink?

In some societies it is rude to accept food the first time it is offered, even if you are extremely hungry. In other societies it is rude to refuse food, even if you are extremely full. What about in the cultures of your learners?

Task 9.6 Research task

Murray, N. (2010), 'Pragmatics, awareness raising, and the cooperative principle',
  English Language Teaching Journal, **64: 293–301**

Murray claims that pedagogic pragmatics have been 'informed by an inductive approach through which, over time, learners can infer general principles governing appropriate language use' (Murray 2010: 293). Learners have been given opportunities to observe, discuss and compare examples of authentic language exchange, arriving gradually at an understanding of governing principles. Murray argues that learners might benefit from a more explicit approach in which frameworks are put in place to give learners direct strategies for recognising underlying pragmatic principles. A valuable example of such a framework, he suggests, are Grice's co-operative principles. He suggests that explicit understanding of these principles can be transferred beyond instructed settings, giving learners a means of 'analysing and reflecting' on speech beyond the classroom context and into their real-world lives. One aspect of this learning is to acquire a 'vocabulary or metalanguage' for analysing speech events. Murray lists the following activities used by Bardovi-Harlig for generating these understandings.

Activities for pragmatic awareness

- Focus on speech acts that reflect learner needs or interests. The needs analysis questions in Table 8.2 of this book can help to establish an understanding of these needs.
- Focus on speech acts where deviation is critical to meaning and interpersonal relation. Some examples of these are listed in this section and in Chapter 7, and teachers and learners might add to these.
- Use authentic materials, such as dialogues and interaction found in corpora of natural language. Task 9.6 below invites you to explore some of these resources online.
- Translate speech acts from the mother tongue or local culture into English and discuss the differences.
- Encourage learners to become 'ethnographers' by collecting, analysing and reporting on examples of natural language heard and observed in context.
- Use film clips, YouTube and other visual recorded resources to show speech and interaction in action, and make comparisons between contexts.
- Invite students to observe a speech act of their choice in a natural setting

(Derived from Bardovi-Harlig 1996 and Murray 2010: 295)

How many of these activities do you think would be useful or viable for you or for your learners?

Task 9.7 Would you like a drink? Social and pragmatic mistakes 🖥

The link below is to clips from the comedy series Fawlty Towers which show some ways in which misunderstandings might arise between the managers of a hotel and their guests: <http://www.youtube.com/watch?v=5hWWtA7npmE>

Can you identify what has gone wrong in each situation?

How would you advise the hotel managers to repair each situation?

How could you use this clip as part of a language lesson?

9.3 TEACHING FOR INTERCULTURAL COMPETENCE

This section will consider the role of language teaching as developing the capacity to negotiate between different cultures. It will consider the way this evolving aspect of the teacher's role might impact on his or her methods and practice.

Intercultural literacy is defined by Heyward (2002: 10) as

> The understandings, competencies, attitudes, language proficiencies, participation and identities necessary for successful cross-cultural engagement – (where one has) the background required to effectively 'read' a second culture, to interpret its symbols and negotiate its meaning in a practical day-to-day context.

Byram uncovered a number of other related competences, which explore cultural competence in more detail. He described these as *savoirs* or ways of knowing. They are particularly interesting for teachers of language, to think about if and how these 'ways of knowing' can be included in the learning of a language.

- *Savoir*: knowledge of self and others, such as the understanding of how and what food is eaten and at what times of the day, how seniors or people in authority are addressed, whether to shake hands, kiss or nod on greeting someone
- *Savoir etre*: being positive, open-minded and curious, so one is open to learning. This is the difference between saying: 'I enjoy learning how things are done here,' rather than 'How strange they are!'
- *Savoir comprendre*: the capacity to analyse and interpret; for example, recognising the clues of behaviour in different settings, such as in a place of worship, in a shop or restaurant, when visiting a friend or relative, in school. When and how do people speak to one another?
- *Savoir apprendre*; the ability to make discoveries; for example, recognising the way people celebrate at a wedding, or on their day of rest, and comparing how this differs from the home culture.
- *Savoir s'engager*: the ability to make critical, informed evaluations; for example, recognising where a situation is unsafe, rather than simply culturally different; or recognising when one has mistakenly given offence.

Byram's approach takes our notion one stage further, in that here we have not a concept of culture itself, but rather of the skills and competences we might need as individuals in order to travel across borders linguistically and personally. The skills of 'being an ethnographer' described in 8.2 above, go some way towards achieving the kind of competence Heyward describes above, but what else can the teacher do? Some further possibilities are:

- Share and analyse 'critical incidents' where misunderstandings or communication breakdown occurred. There is an example on p. 206 of a framework by Storti which may be helpful for analysing and interpreting these critical incidents.

- Analyse case studies of travelling across borders and placing oneself in the shoes of the traveller.
- Provide opportunities for learning and friendship across cultural borders so that people are recognised as individuals rather than representatives of their culture or community. 'Not all British are reserved. Not all Japanese are indirect. Not all Americans are competitive' (Gebhard 1996: 125–6); hence the importance of 'getting to know one person at a time, treating each as a distinct and unique individual' (Ibid. p. 126).
- Explore not how people in a community or context are the same, but how they are different.
- Study and acknowledge one's own culture, and recognise that the complexity and diversity we appreciate within a culture we know well is equally so in cultures we know less about. **To understand another culture, study your own.**

Activities for developing intercultural competence
Problem-solving activities
Place the learner imaginatively within a number of cross-cultural settings. A needs analysis might reveal those which are authentically likely within the learner's own context.

Task 9.8 Researching cross-cultural communication
Problem-solving in cross-cultural communication
You are meeting three colleagues in Paris to discuss a business idea.
One is a Canadian who has lived in France for fifteen years and speaks fluent French.
One is Indonesian and speaks fluent English but no French.
One is French and can speak fluent English.
One is you.
Which non-verbal behaviour would be appropriate – gesture, touch, space?
Which discourse behaviour would be appropriate, when complimenting, apologising, offering, inviting?

Cross-cultural topics: Explain Yourself! – an English conversation book for Japan

The Japanese new year
Sumo wrestlng
Baseball
Funerals and weddings
Public baths
University life
Temples
Festivals

Sample questions:

How often do you use a public bath?
Why is bathing segregated? Has it always been so ?

What are likely subjects of conversation in a public bath ?
What is the most popular bathing time?
Why would it be advisable to have a hot bath if you had just eaten dinner?
Why has bathing always been such an important part of Japanese life?

(Gebhard 1996: 128; Nicholson and Sakuno 1982)

Explore critical incidents

We have discussed in earlier sections the value of a framework for developing eth-
nographic processes. Below is a framework that might be useful in interpreting
responses to cultural misunderstanding and communicative misunderstanding.

Storti's model of the process of cultural adjustment (1989)
We expect others to be like us, but they aren't
⇕
A cultural incident occurs, causing a reaction (fear, anger, surprise, embarrassment)
⇕   ⇕
We withdraw   We become aware of our reaction
⇕
We reflect on its cause
⇕
We observe the situation, which results in developing
culturally appropriate expectations

(Storti 1989)

Task 9.9 Teaching task: developing critical incidents for cultural understanding

Look at the critical incident example below in which a traveller encountered, and
failed to understand, the notion of *taarof*. Could Storti's model help you to explain the
reactions of each participant in the story?

Imagine you are the traveller in this story. What would you have done? How would
you have reacted?

How could you use stories such as these, or frameworks such as Storti's, in the
language classroom?

Critical incidents

The notion of taarof:

Taarof is a way of saying things you don't mean in order to be polite, with a shared
understanding that it is simply a social convention. For example, in response to the
phrase 'See you later', the reply might be 'I will die for you' or 'I am your servant';
when being offered payment for a service, you might politely refuse. It is a 'temporary
resistance to a seemingly sincere decline of something you intend to accept after a
couple more times of insistence' (O'Neill and Gish 2008: 18).

I had to go to a local shoe repairman to fix a small cut in my leather shoes. It took
him fifteen minutes to cover it. I asked him how much I should pay him and he

replied, 'Don't worry about it'. I kept insisting but he kept declining. Then I decided to walk away politely after thanking him, although I still did leave him with 300 romans. But he got upset and I thought it was because I gave him money. Only after he gave me a lecture about respecting the elderly did I realise that he wanted more. —Seyyed Abbas Mousani, Iran (O'Neil and Gish 2008: 18)

Task 9.10 Exploring online chat 💻
Explore the online English club: <www.englishclub.ccom/esl-chat>

- What are the benefits of using an online chat resource such as this for learners?
- Are there any problems or concerns you might have as teacher, and how would you draw up ground rules for resolving these?
- How could you use an online club such as this in the classroom?

What would you need to do as teacher? What would the learners do to consolidate their learning?

We started this book in Chapter 1 looking at Kumaravadivelu's notion of the post-methods teacher. View the clip below of Kumaravadivelu talking about the interface between language and culture. How far do you agree with his views? Do you have any examples which prove or disprove his views? <http://www.eflclassroom.com/eltinterviews/?p=283>

9.4 FURTHER READING 💻

Explore the following readings and case studies in the online resource.

Task 9.11 Teaching case study 20: a Congolese classroom
Whitehead, D. (2011), 'English language teaching in fragile states: justifying action, promoting success and combating hegemony', in H. Coleman (ed.), *Dreams and Realities: Developing Countries and the English Language*, London: British Council, pp. 333–69.

Task 9.12 Teaching case study 21: a classroom in Cameroon
Kuchah, K. (2008), 'Developing as a professional in Cameroon: challenges and visions', in S. Garton and K. Richards (eds.) (2008), *Professional Encounters in TESOL*, Basingstoke: Palgrave Macmillan, pp. 203–17.

9.5 CONCLUSION

We started with the question:

- What is the interface between learning a language and learning 'culture'? What does *culture* actually mean, and how far should this be part of the language teacher's role?

The way you responded to this question will reflect your views of what 'culture' actually means. It will be interesting for you to record whether this view remains the same as the definition you first arrived at, at the start of this chapter. For some teachers and researchers culture is a content-rich way of teaching language; for others it is a mission to open language learners to the 'adventure' of being a cultural traveller. For others again, it is part of the knowledge base that lies behind English language literary texts. Whichever position you take as a teacher of language, the key message conveyed within this chapter is that language is never culturally neutral, and teachers position themselves on this question, whether they do so consciously or unconsciously. The discussions, activities and readings in this chapter are designed to give teachers the opportunity to be fully conscious and aware of their position, so they can take a principled approach to this.

Historically, within the English language profession, 'culture' had a narrow definition as the cluster of assumptions related to the target culture. As English has become the lingua franca globally, it becomes not only reductive but unworkable to define what this 'target culture' actually is. Every speaker of the language contributes to this target culture. This makes it an imperative for teachers to be open to new information, comparison and analysis, to be ethnographers of the exchanges they engage in. Learners need to be prepared for a working adult life that takes account of all cultures and allows permeability and mobility between them. This is a challenge for the language teacher, but one which offers rich opportunity for all participants in the language classroom to learn from one another.

9.6 GUIDED READING

Alptekin, C. (2002), 'Towards intercultural communicative competence', *English Language Teaching Journal*, 56:1, 57–64

Alptekin debates the implications of English as an International Language for our understanding of communicative competence. He suggests that the four competences – grammar, sociolinguistic, discourse and strategic – had presupposed native-speaker norms as a standard of correctness and appropriacy. With our understanding of language as shared by more non-native than native speakers, this standard needs to be urgently reviewed. He suggests that intercultural competence should be a significant part of the overall competence of the language speaker, and explains this through five key implications for language pedagogy.

Look at these five implications in the list below.

What is your view of each of these positions?

Are they relevant for you in your own situation as a user of the English language, and/or as a teacher or student of the English language?

1. Bilingual speakers, with their capacity for intercultural insights, should be the 'pedagogic models', rather than the monolingual native speaker.
2. Intercultural communicative competence would entail equipping learners with linguistic and cultural behaviour relevant to their context/community, making them aware of the differences between different communities and contexts, and equipping them with strategies for coping with these differences.

3. Both global and local notions of appropriacy should be taken into account when learning a language. The learner of English should be 'equipped to be both a global and local speaker of English' (Alptekin 2002: 63).

4. Language teaching materials should take account of both local and international contexts, and these should be made meaningful and relevant to learners in their own setting.

5. Language materials should also include the discourse of both native and non-native speakers of English. Examples where native speakers are presented as the only standard should be avoided (Alptekin 2002).

Corbett, J. (2003), *An Intercultural Approach to English Language Teaching*, Clevedon: Multilingual Matters

Corbett argues that the language classroom 'trains learners to be diplomats, able to view different cultures from a perspective of informed understanding' (Corbett 2003: 2). He points out that

> the intercultural approach does not seek to replace or undermine the advances make by task-based learning or learner-centred curricula. Rather, it seeks to build on these advances and to channel them towards useful and realistic goals.

The book guides the teacher to recognise these goals through 'the skills of social observation and explanation' across all four language skills (Corbett 2003: 139). It provides examples and opportunities for making classrooms a content-rich environment, including visual images from anglophone and non-anglophone countries, literary and cultural texts, illustrating 'how a cultural approach to language teaching draws on disciplines other than mainstream linguistics.' (Ibid. p. 139).

Sampedro, R. and S. Hillyard (2004), *Global Issues*, Oxford: Oxford University Press

Sampedro and Hillyard pick up the challenge suggested by Corbett above, to generate a content-rich language classroom, by introducing global issues. Their rationale is:

- Language teaching has no defined content, so global issues offer one ready-made possibility.
- The content is not trivial, unlike the contrived content of many coursebooks. It is relevant and topical.
- Introducing global issues into the classroom expands the scope of language learning into broader educational perspectives.
- 'The English language, as the principal vehicle of global consumerism – should bear some of the responsibility for making "consumers" of English aware of some of its less desirable effects' (Sampedro and Hillyard 2004: 3).

The book offers resources and activities such as: your footprint on Earth; deconstructing bullying; our campaign against war; gender roles and you. It makes use of role play, presentations, journal writing, songs, analysing the news and choral speaking.

How practical would these content-rich ideas be for a learning situation with which you are familiar?

WINDOWS INTO TESOL CLASSROOMS: WHERE ARE WE AND WHERE ARE WE GOING?

10.1 WINDOWS INTO TESOL CLASSROOMS
with classroom examples from John Eyles

We have explored many debates, methodologies and research questions thus far, but our discussions have emphasised that the real answers to our questions about methodology come from teachers and learners themselves. What is the reality, for them, of language teaching in the twenty-first century? What answers have they found to its challenges and changes? The section that follows explores different kinds of classroom that reflect the diversity and complexity of learning settings in the twenty-first century: the low-technology class, the high-technology class, the self-access class, the large class, and the team-taught class.

The low-technology classroom

There are a number of debates surrounding what in fact characterises a low-technology classroom, and the effects that a low-technology environment has on the ability to adequately teach. The classes in the case studies below identify themselves as 'low-tech' in that they do not have adequate resources for each student in the class, and none that involve technology or digital media. However, in reading them you might like to consider for yourself how you would define low technology. What would you consider a basic requirement for teaching English to a group of students? What impact do you think the increasing prevalence of new technologies such as mobile phones, cheap laptops and tablets will have on a classroom that does not have access to these?

Teaching case study 22: a school in Koh Kong Province, southern Cambodia

In this class there are twenty students. The classroom is equipped with wooden desks for each of the students, a whiteboard that was donated by a well-meaning agency, and some old whiteboard markers that no longer work. Each student has a notepad and pen, and there is a class set of *Headway Beginner*, one of the most widely available textbooks in Cambodia. However, there are only enough books for one between two students, and so the students are required to write their answers into notepads. The textbook is seen as the core material for the course content and syllabus, and so the teacher moves through the content chapter by chapter. The students are instructed to work through Chapter 9 in pairs, which involves them

Table 10.1   Sustainable classroom resources

Student-generated resources	Resources found in the environment
Songs Skits and sketches Poems, stories, folktales, myths, nursery rhymes Home-made puppets and dolls Drawings	Natural objects: stones, leaves, fruits Household objects: labelled jars, cardboard boxes, bottles Clothing: hats, shoes, scarves Written materials: notices, flyers, leaflets, postcards, newspapers

identifying famous faces from the past. However, all the characters in the course-book are Western and therefore unknown to the students, and they are unable to complete the exercise.

This case study underlines the problem of globally published textbooks which are prescriptive in their use of images and alien to the culture they are used in. It also shows the problem of introducing new technologies without considering their sustainability within the context in which they are being used: once the initial supply of whiteboard pens ran out, the school could not afford to replace them. Resources which are expensive or unsustainable are not viable in many settings, and alternatives have been suggested in several of the case studies earlier in this book. Kuchah in the Cameroons used the folktales and stories of learners themselves: Whitehead in the Congo drew on the mother tongue of his learners, and the representation of the Congo in the newspapers (see online tasks 9.11 and 9.12).

In Table 10.1 is a list of resources which do not entail expense, training or external intervention, and which are sustainable in any classroom. You might be able to add to these from resources available within the natural world of your own learners.

The high-technology classroom

English language teaching does not require cutting-edge technology. This is not to say that the photocopier, audio player and Internet were not revolutionary when they first impacted teaching. Teachers might, however, have multiple reasons for resisting technology. It requires sustained expense, as in the case of the whiteboard pens in Cambodia described above. It also requires continuous updating, and potentially a cycle of disempowerment and deskilling as current skills are superseded by the need for new ones. However, resisting technology would be akin to resisting the trajectory of the twenty-first century; it is unrealistic to deny it, and to do so means being left behind.

Below are examples of two classrooms which have adopted technology for language learning, with differing degrees of ownership and success. As you read these case studies, you might ask yourself the questions:

- Is technology as a stimulus for learning in itself a good thing?
- What are the physical and pedagogic conditions which make technology effective for enhancing learning?

Teaching case study 23: a self-access centre in a college, Buriram Province, northeast Thailand

This class has between thirty and fifty students. Students from the English classes are required to spend five hours per week in a self-access centre computer lab using a program on Moodle, an easy-access website designed to develop their English language skills. The program they are using was created in-house by two non-native English speaking staff. Although the staff had the best of intentions by designing the online course for the students, their lack of familiarity with Moodle as a tool, with task design principles and with the language itself meant that the material was not engaging students, and in fact inducing errors and unhelpful study strategies.

In effect, the technology was leading the teachers *away* from good teaching. The responses of the learners themselves would have been apparent in the interactive classroom setting, but 'locked' into the computer room with the self-access resources, this opportunity to learn from one's learners was broken. In addition, the teachers were encouraged to believe the new technology was in itself an effective tool, irrespective of how it was used.

Teaching case study 24: a high school in Auckland, New Zealand

Faced with a disengaged class of twenty students, an English teacher realised it was time to think creatively in order to motivate his students to learn. Realising how much they used their mobile phones, the teacher utilised this as their primary tool for the lesson. The activity involved students using their mobile phones to create stories focusing on the work they had been doing in class. Working in small groups, they used their camera phones to create short videos to which they then added titles and voice-overs. They then shared the final product with each other through SD cards and Bluetooth. In another activity the students created a treasure hunt using QR codes, which led to the students writing clues for one another in English. The engagement levels of the students increased dramatically as a result of this change. By using objects the students were themselves bringing to class on a daily basis, the process was sustainable, and the content was culturally specific and determined by student choice and interest. The teacher took a risk in encouraging this activity, as he did not know how to use the technology that was now central to achieving the task. In taking this risk, he was making himself the learner, learning the technology from his students.

We saw in Chapters 2 and 3 that children taught themselves to use computers, bricked into the slum village centres in India. They did so without the intervention of adults, and were able to teach one another so that the benefit spread beyond their own learning. These examples suggest the complexity of issues surrounding the use of technology for learning. Table 10.2 introduces both considerations in the use of technology and suggested solutions for the teacher.

The large class

The notion of 'large' is clearly relative. We saw in Chapter 7 that the founder of Crazy English has classes of up to twenty thousand, whilst for some teachers, a class of fifty would be considered 'large'. One teacher defines a large class as one where it is not possible to learn all the learners' names, and where it is too large to monitor

Table 10.2   Problems and solutions for using technology in the classroom

Considerations	Solutions
Teachers are worried about using technology, as they feel they know less than students do	Engage the learners as 'teachers' so the teacher develops alongside learners.
Cost of maintenance – there are financial difficulties in keeping software and technologies up to date	Draw on the technology that is sustainable in the environment locally or already available to the learners.
Privacy and security concerns Copyright Permissions and protocols	Draw up ground-rules of how messages should be written and communicated, and with whom. These ground-rules could also be developed with learners, and where these are young children, with parents and other teachers. This may involve locking access to certain websites, or intervening in online activities.
Technology may encourage a short attention span and a tendency to jump from task to task. This has been described as the 'snack culture'	Tasks which are meaningful and focus on what learners naturally find interesting will ensure digital and online tools are used for a purpose, rather than as a series of 'snacks': for example, to solve a problem, complete a project or prepare a presentation such as a short film.
Using technology may become monotonous or unhelpful	Every activity and task in the classroom needs to be evaluated for effectiveness. Are students engaged? Are they learning? What needs to be changed to ensure these are happening?

attendance. The snapshots in Case Studies 25 and 26 below have between fifty and ninety students, but they demonstrate some of the challenges of much larger classes too. As you read these, you might wish to note what you perceive the challenges to be, and compare your ideas to those listed at the end of this section.

Teaching case study 25: Yokohama Women's College, Japan

The class has fifty students. It is a ninety-minute ESL lesson straight after lunch, on a hot summer day. The desks are in tight rows, bolted to the floor. The resources include a locally written textbook, a tape recorder, television and a video. A chalkboard is at the front of the classroom, with a lectern for the teacher. The room is filled with students speaking to each other in English, despite it not being their main subject. It is hard for students to hear the teacher, and also to hear one another, so speaking activities in pairs and groups are problematic. In addition, the room is too cramped for the teacher to move round easily to check the progress of students, and there are too many for her to do so successfully. Taking work home after class also becomes a heavy burden, with fifty scripts to mark after each lesson. The teacher also expresses her concern that she cannot have meaningful conversations on a one-to-one basis with the students while there are so many in the class, so most interactions are concerned with classroom management and the achievement of lesson objectives.

The teacher developed an activity which proved to be successful in this scenario. The television is turned on, but the sound is turned down. Students are sitting in rows working in pairs. One faces towards the front of the class, the other faces towards the back. In this task, one student is looking at the television screen and informs their partner of what they can see. They are watching the comedy show *Mr Bean*. The partner who is facing away from the screen takes notes and draws pictures of what is being described. This results in a room full of students speaking enthusiastically in English.

Team teaching

Teaching case study 26: Mukdahan, northeast Thailand

There are ninety students in a gym. They are split into smaller groups of around ten to do problem-solving tasks, involving active learning techniques such as 'running dictation' and 'jigsaw reading'. The activity that has been set by the visiting Canadian teacher relies on student-centred learning, thereby removing the teacher from his or her position as leader to become instead a facilitator. In this particular situation, one of the teachers becomes very uncomfortable with her seemingly diminished role. The students are completely engaged amongst themselves, and largely without the teacher's intervention.

The discomfort of the local teacher reminds us of the discussions which opened this book, that methods are only effective insofar as they are 'owned' by the teacher. Adopting a new 'method', as demonstrated here, is not simply a behavioural change connected with the surface activities of the classroom. A change in 'method' is only sustainable if it is owned by the teachers as something translatable and meaningful in their own context, and commensurate with their beliefs. Part of team-teaching partnerships is thus about learning from one another to negotiate a midway position in which beliefs are mutually challenged with a view to sustainable change.

However, it is interesting to note some of the characteristics which made the large class more 'successful' according to the teacher's own estimate. Note from Table 10.3 which of these worked for the two classrooms above, and identify any other strategies you think might help to resolve the challenges of the large class.

10.2 TESOL PRESENT AND FUTURE: WHERE ARE WE, AND WHERE ARE WE GOING?

Several overarching issues have been illustrated throughout this book and through the case studies in this chapter. Methods that have been orthodoxies in previous decades, such as the communicative method or the humanistic method, have been critiqued for a number of reasons. One is that most teachers prefer instead a 'principled eclectic' approach to teaching that takes from all methods and ideas whatever is most meaningful and relevant for their learners. Another is that these orthodoxies have often been based on Western approaches and idealised classrooms which do not

Table 10.3   Large class strategies

Challenges	What is possible
Communicating with each learner individually	Visual ways of checking understanding: e.g. show of hands/response to requests such as *sit down; stand up*
Hearing each learner individually	Maximise choral opportunities for the large class: half class responds to half class
Marking each learner's work	Set up situations where learners learn from one another through jigsaw and information gap activities
Ensuring learners at the back of the room are as engaged as those at the front	Change the focus of attention from the front of the room/the teacher, to the classroom in the round – e.g. posters on the wall; change the back of the room to the front

transfer smoothly into other contexts, and we thus have to find a methodology that is appropriate, rather than one that is fashionable.

An example is Case Study 23 above from Thailand, where a visiting teacher used a methodology 'imported' from his own context. Whilst this worked very well for the visiting teacher, and even for the learners, the local teacher felt very uneasy about the process. It revealed that assumptions can too easily be made about the transferability of methods from one context to another. What would your 'appropriate methodology' be, and what are your own principles for selecting what is appropriate for your learners? You may want to return to Chapter 1 to remind yourself what other researchers and teachers have thought about this issue.

The Dogme strong view described in Chapter 2 is that it is more motivating and more finely-tuned to learner needs for students and teachers to generate their own materials, rather than depend on those imposed from outside and above by others. In addition, some teachers and researchers have found that learners work very well without the intervention of a teacher at all, and especially so with a resource or stimulus they can use for themselves. Case Study 22 from Cambodia showed how unhelpful and irrelevant the coursebook was for learners, who were alienated by characters and settings which had no relevance to them. In Case Study 24, traditional materials were discarded and replaced by mobile phones and student-led activities. How meaningful are these positions for you in your own context? Do you use a coursebook/published resources, and if so, how far do these match your own learners' needs? You may want to return to Chapter 2 to remind yourself of some of the origins of these debates.

We now recognise that there are more non-native English speakers than native speakers. This has shifted our notion of who 'owns' English, as well as our notions of correctness. To answer the question of ownership, we might look to the English varieties used locally, as well as the constantly evolving language shared globally known as EIL (English as an International Language) or ELF (English as a Lingua Franca). How meaningful are these forms for you in your context? Which English do you teach, and is this choice of English imposed from above, chosen by you, or by your learners?

Is this the English that most represents the real language needs of your learners? In other words, what is your response to the debates explored in Chapter 3 of this book?

In Chapters 4 and 5 we looked at new information about how language is actually used and spoken, through the development of language corpora. This information has caused us to question many of the conventional ways we have explained grammar and vocabulary. It also suggests to us that, as a method, noticing language might be a more fruitful approach than describing or explaining it. In this process, both learner and teacher become researchers of language, with frameworks for analysing language. How far is this approach useful for you as a teacher and as a learner? Is it viable in your own learning/teaching context? What are the challenges to this? We have explored throughout this book the impact of technologies on learning and teaching. We saw in Chapters 6 and 7 that it has changed our approaches to writing and speaking, and blurred the differences between them. We also saw in Chapter 8 the multiple ways in which technologies can offer learning opportunities, exposure to global language, and interactive opportunities for learners and classrooms. Yet the presence alone of technology does not ensure effective learning; we still need to ask constant questions about how this technology is used, and when and how to make it genuinely effective for learning. An example is the Thai self-access centre described in Case Study 23 above, which appeared to be using 'state-of-the-art' Moodle technology for the learners, and yet conspired to offer the learners something inappropriate and confining. What is your position on the use of technology for effective learning? How far are these opportunities available in your context and how far are you able to exploit them for effective learning?

We have also questioned whether, and to what extent, learning a language is more than learning a system or a set of surface structures. In Chapter 9 we looked at the fact that learning another language involves exploring ways in which interaction happens socially and culturally, and how this is expressed in and outside of language. We even noted that using another language can involve a shift in sense of self and personal identity. In Chapter 3 we saw that this might cause blocks in learning if it is not understood by the teacher. How important do you consider social, cultural and intercultural competences in your own context? How far do you think it is the teacher's role to develop these, and how far do you think they emerge anyway as part of the learner's natural repertoire of skills?

New questions are constantly emerging in response to the changing dynamics of English language in the world. More people are using the language now, but will that continue, or will other languages such as Chinese replace English as a lingua franca? In 1997, Graddol predicted 'no single language will occupy the monopolistic position in the twenty-first century which English has – almost – achieved by the end of the twentieth century. It is more likely that a small number of world languages will form an 'oligopoly', each with particular spheres of influence and regional bases' (Graddol 1997: 29). We have seen that digital technologies are changing both the nature of the language, and the ways we can access this and communicate with one another. Will these changes mean the end of published hard-copy materials as we have known these to date? Does that mean eclectic classrooms picking whatever is needed from online resources, and if this is the case, will the divide become ever greater between classes that have, and those that do not have technologies? As this does happen more consistently, we need to ask more urgent questions about the best and most effective ways to use technology, and to develop mutually shared codes of practice for using this. We also need to ask about the impact of these changes on the teacher of English: how far will he or she have to be a technical expert to keep up with the expectations of the learners? Will the skills of the teacher, able to teach with nothing but a stick of chalk or marks in the sand, disappear? Is there a danger, in the march forward of technologies and methodologies, of losing some of those core qualities that made teachers memorable, or will world recession entail a re-evaluation of these?

What is interesting about much of our exploration into methods, methodologies and teacher responses to these, is that in many ways what is 'new' is also what is 'old'. Teachers have returned to (or indeed, remained with) ideas that were discarded by the mainstream, such as translation, dictation and explicit grammar teaching. Methods which appeared to be passing fashions, such as audiolingualism or Suggestopedia, have in fact left a legacy of methods and approaches which continue to be drawn upon. They have made us think about why we do still use controlled drills and repetition, or why music and low-anxiety warm-ups do work. As eclectic teachers, we should discard no method or idea that has ever entered a classroom without scrutiny; and as members of a global professional community, we now understand that what is discarded in one corner of the globe is entirely central to methodological orthodoxy in other. The critical factor in success is the commitment and belief of the teacher in the methods he or she is using, and the continuing reflection of the teacher as to whether these methods are making a positive difference.

10.3 TEACHER AS REFLECTIVE PRACTITIONER AND THE PRIMACY OF EXPERIENCE

Being a reflective teacher means asking continually: how can I improve my practice as a teacher? How can I understand my learners better? But importantly, reflection is not only about asking questions; it is critical that reflection makes a difference, and leads to some kind of positive change. For example, Kuchah (2008) in Case Study 20 in this book reflected on the fact that he adopted a 'power' relationship with his trainees even though they were older than him; and arrived at the realisation that this was inappropriate and he needed to reposition himself as a peer and co-practitioner with his peers. As a result, he adopted a more facilitative and collaborative approach to the training process which was much more successful. Hirano (2009), in the article discussed as further reading for Chapter 3, found her adult learner was not progressing in spite of all her efforts and realised that the issue was not the language itself, but the fact he had internalised the belief that he was an unsuccessful learner. This led her to reshape her lessons to focus on his sense of self and confidence, and he made significant progress as a result.

This reflective process is often conceived as a cycle, since just as questions lead to actions, so actions lead to yet more questions, and so the cycle continues. Kolb's reflective cycle leads from concrete experience to testing plans and perceptions (Kolb 1984); Honey and Mumford (1986) include in their cycle the clarification of core principles; Gibbs (1988) conceived of a cycle which leads from description of events, to feelings about events and action emerging from this. Whilst other teachers, writers and researchers might inform and enrich this learning process, they cannot provide the answers. Teachers can only find these answers for themselves. These individual teacher answers are now thoroughly legitimated within the TESOL profession. Appel's *Diary of a Language Teacher* (1995) was one of the first texts to 'tell the story' of an individual teacher and how he learnt from the daily disasters and triumphs of the school day. Since then there have been many accounts of how real teachers interface with the profession and its orthodoxies: for example, Tsui (2003), who studied second-language teachers' views of professionalism; Crookes (2009) and Johnston (2003), who have researched the values and beliefs of TESOL teachers, or Senior (2008), who researched teacher voices.

Action research is also legitimised as a way of researching practice that stands alongside more traditional approaches to knowledge. Action researchers engage in systematic study of their practice, making themselves, their learners and their actions in the classroom the subject of inquiry. See <www.actionresearch.net> for many examples of doctorate- and Masters-level educators who have achieved their status through action research enquiries. The empowering aspect of reflection and action research is that they are ways of explaining and developing what teachers such as Kuchah and Hirano do already. These approaches allow teachers to realise that their learning journeys might provide insights and opportunities for other teachers, and are therefore worth sharing.

What is exciting about the profession of TESOL is that it is constantly changing in response not only to the world outside the profession, but to its practitioners. It is a profession that includes insights from politics, sociology, anthropology, linguistics, lexicography, psychology, international relations, counselling, management; in fact, the list is ever-growing and endless. Thus, while the answers to all these questions remain unpredictable, what can be predicted is that there will indeed be multiple responses to these questions, and that the most important insights will come from practitioners working with real learners in real classrooms.

BIBLIOGRAPHY

Aitchison, J. (1994), *Words in the Mind*, Oxford: Blackwell.

Alderson, C. J. (2000), *Assessing Reading*, Cambridge: Cambridge University Press.

Alptekin, C. (2002), 'Towards intercultural communicative competence', *English Language Teaching Journal*, 56:1, 57–64.

Anderson, N. J. (1991), 'Individual differences in strategy use in second language reading and testing', *The Modern Language Journal*, 75, 460–72.

Anderson, T., B. L. Reynolds, Y. Xiao-Ping and H. Guan-Zhen (2008), *Video Games in the English as a Foreign Language Classroom*, Conference Proceedings of Second IEEE International Conference on Digital Games and Intelligent Toys Based Education, pp. 188–92.

Andrews, R. and A. Smith (2011), *Developing Writers: Teaching and Learning in the Digital Age*, Maidenhead: Open University Press.

Antenos-Conforti, E. (2009), 'Microblogging on Twitter: Social Networking in Intermediate Italian Classes', in L. Lomicka and G. Lord (eds), *The Next Generation: Social Networking and Online Collaboration in Foreign Language Learning*, CALICO: The Computer Assisted Language Instruction Consortium, pp. 59–90.

Appel, J. (1995), *Diary of a Language Teacher*, Oxford: Heinemann.

Arnold, J. (1999), *Affect in Language Learning*, Cambridge: Cambridge University Press.

Asher, J., J. A. Kusudo and R. de la Torre (1983), 'Learning a Second Language through Commands: The Second Field Test', in J. W. Oller and P. A. Richard-Amato (eds), *Methods That Work: A Smorgasbord of Ideas for Language Teachers*, Rowley, MA: Newbury House, pp. 59–72.

Atkinson, D. (2011), *Alternative Approaches to Second Language Acquisition*, London: Routledge.

Bahrick, H. P. (1984), 'Semantic memory content in permastore: fifty years of memory for Spanish learned in school', *Journal of Experimental Psychology: General*, 113: 1–30.

Bardovi-Harlig, K. (1996), 'Pragmatics and language teaching: bringing pragmatics and pedagogy together', in L. F. Bouton (ed.), *Pragmatics and Language Learning*, Monograph Series vol. 7., Urbana, IL: University of Illinois at Urbana-Champaign.

Barkham, Patrick (2011), 'Dogs listen to children reading', *Guardian* website, 28 February, <http://www.guardian.co.uk/education/2011/feb/28/dogs-listen-to-children-reading> (last accessed 17 January 2013).

Barkhuizen, G. (2008), 'A narrative approach to exploring context in language teaching', *English Language Teaching Journal*, 62: 231–9.

Barron, K. and A. Schneider (2008), *Variational Pragmatics*, Amsterdam and Philadelphia: John Benjamins.

Basturkmen, H. (2010), *Developing Courses in English for Specific Purposes*, Basingstoke: Palgrave Macmillan.

Batstone, R. (1994), *Grammar*, Oxford: Oxford University Press.

Bauer, J. and J. Kenton (2005), 'Toward technology integration in the schools: Why it isn't happening', *Journal of Technology and Teacher Education*, 13:4, 519–46.

Bax, S. (2003), 'The end of CLT: a context approach to language teaching', *ELT Journal*, 57:3, 278–87.

Beck, I., M. McKeown and L. Kucan (2002), *Bringing Words to Life: Robust Vocabulary Instruction*, New York: Guildford Press.

Bell, D. (2007), 'Do teachers think that methods are dead?', *ELT Journal*, 61:2 (April 2007), 135–43.

Bell, J. (1995), *Teachers Talk About Teaching*, Milton Keynes: Open University Press.

Benson, P. (2007), 'Autonomy in language teaching and learning', in *Language Teaching*, 40/1: pp. 21–40.

Benson, P. and D. Nunan (2005), *Learners' Stories*, Cambridge: Cambridge University Press.

Bensoussan, R. A., D. Sim and R. Weiss (1984), 'Lexical guessing in context in EFL reading comprehension', *Journal of Research in Reading*, 2: 15–32.

Bhatia, V. K. (1993), *Analysing Genre: Language Use in Professional Settings*, London: Longman.

Biber, D. (1999), *Dictionary of Spoken and Written English*, Harlow: Longman.

Blachowicz, C. L. Z., P. J. L. Fisher, D. Ogle and S. Watts-Taffe (2006), 'Vocabulary: questions from the classroom', *Reading Research Quarterly*, 41, 524–39.

Bloomer, A., P. Griffiths and A. J. Merrison (2005), *Introducing Language in Use: A Course Book*, London and New York: Routledge.

Blum-Kulka, S., J. House and G. Kasper (1989), 'Investigating cross-cultural pragmatics: an introductory overview', in S. Blum-Kulka, J. House and G. Kasper (eds), *Cross-Cultural Pragmatics: Requests and Apologies*, Norwood, NJ: Ablex.

Bolton, G. (2010), *Reflective Practice* (3rd edn), London: Sage.

Borau, K., C. Ullrich, J. Feng and R. Shen (2009), 'Microblogging for Language Learning: Using Twitter to Train Communicative and Cultural Competence', *Advances in Web Based Learning – ICWL 2009*, Berlin: Springer.

Bowen, T. and J. Marks (1992), *The Pronunciation Book*, London: Pilgrims–Longman.

Brazil, D. (1995), *A Grammar of Speech*, Oxford: Oxford University Press.

Breen, M. and C. Candlin (1987), 'Which materials? A consumer's and designer's guide', in L. Sheldon (ed.), *ELT Textbooks and Materials: Problems in Evaluation and Development*, ELT Documents 126, London: Modern English Publications.

Breen, M., B. Hird, M. Milton, R. Oliver and A. Thwaite (2001), 'Making sense of language teaching: teachers' principles and classroom practices', *Applied Linguistics*, 22: 470–501.

British Council (2012), 'Quantifiers', British Council Learn English website, <http://learnenglish.britishcouncil.org/en/english-grammar/determiners-and-quantifiers/quantifiers> (last accessed 17 January 2013).

British National Corpus (2005), *The BNC Sampler*, XML version, distributed by Oxford University Computing Services on behalf of the BNC Consortium, <http://www.natcorp.ox.ac.uk> (last accessed 17 January 2013).

Brown, H. D. (1994), *Teaching by Principles. An Interactive Approach to Language Pedagogy*, Englewood Cliffs, NJ: Prentice-Hall.

Brown, H. D. (2007), *Principles of Language Learning and Teaching*, White Plains, NY: Pearson Longman.

Bruner, J., D. J. Wood and G. Ross (1976), 'The role of tutoring in problem solving', *Journal of Child Psychology and Psychiatry*, 17:2, 89–100.

Bruton, A. (2009), 'Grammar is not only a liberating force, it is a communicative resource', *ELT Journal*, 63:4, 383–6.

Bygate, M. and C. Candlin (eds) (1994), *Grammar and the Language Teacher*, Englewood Cliffs, NJ: Prentice-Hall.

Bygate, M., P. Skehan and M. Swain (eds) (2001), *Researching Pedagogic Tasks, Second Language Learning, Teaching and Testing*, Harlow: Longman.

Byram, M. (1997), *Teaching and Assessing Intercultural Communicative Competence*, Clevedon: Multilingual Matters.

Byram, M. (ed.) (2004), *Routledge Encyclopedia of Language Teaching and Learning*, London: Routledge.

Byram, M., C. Morgan et al. (1994), *Teaching-and-Learning Language-and-Culture*, Clevedon: Multilingual Matters.

Cameron, L. (2001), *Teaching Languages to Young Learners*, Cambridge: Cambridge University Press.

Canagarajah, A. S. (1993), 'Critical ethnography of a Sri Lankan classroom: Ambiguities in student opposition to reproduction through ESOL', *TESOL Quarterly*, 27:4, 601–26.

Canale, M. and M. Swain (1980), 'Theoretical bases of communicative approaches to second language teaching and testing', *Applied Linguistics*, 1: 1–47.

Candlin, C. and S. Candlin (2002), 'Expert Talk and Risk in Health Care': A Special Issue of *Research on Language and Social Interaction*, 35: 2.

Candlin, C. and M. Gotti (eds) (2007), *Intercultural Aspects of Specialized Communication*, Bern: Peter Lang.

Candlin, C. and N. Mercer (eds) (2001), *English Language Teaching in its Social Context*, London: Routledge.

Carroll, J. B. and S. M. Sapon (1955), *Modern Language Aptitude Test, Form A*, New York: The Psychological Corporation.

Carter, R. (1998), 'Orders of reality: CANCODE, communication, and culture', *ELT Journal*, 52:1, 43–56.

Carter, R. and M. McCarthy (1988), *Vocabulary and Language Teaching*, London: Longman.

Carter, R. and M. McCarthy (1996), *Exploring Spoken English*, Cambridge: Cambridge University Press.

Carter, R. and M. McCarthy (2006), *Cambridge Grammar of English: a comprehensive guide*, Cambridge: Cambridge University Press.

Carter, R. and D. Nunan (2005), *The Cambridge Guide to Teaching English to Speakers of Other Languages*, Cambridge: Cambridge University Press.

Carter, R., R. Hughes and M. McCarthy (2011), 'Telling tails: grammar, the spoken language and materials development', in B. Tomlinson (ed.), *Materials Development in Language Teaching* (2nd edn), Cambridge: Cambridge University Press.

Carter, R., M. McCarthy, G. Mark and A. O'Keeffe (2011), *English Grammar Today*, Cambridge: Cambridge University Press.

Castagnaro, P. (2006), 'Audiolingual Method and Behaviorism: From Misunderstanding to Myth', *Applied Linguistics*, 27:3, 519–26.

Celce-Murcia, C., D. M. Brinton and J. M. Goodwin (1996), *Teaching Pronunciation: A Reference for Teachers of English to Speakers of Other Languages*, Cambridge: Cambridge University Press.

Chambers, A., F. Farr and S. O'Riordan (2011), 'Language teachers with corpora in mind: from starting steps to walking tall', in *Language Learning*, 39:1, 85–104.

Channell, J. (1988), 'Psycholinguistic considerations in the study of L2 vocabulary acquisition', in R. Carter and M. McCarthy (eds), *Vocabulary and Language Teaching*, London: Longman.

Cheng, W. and A. B. M. Tsui (2009), '"Ahh (laugh) well there is no comparison between the two I think": How do Hong Kong Chinese and native speakers of English disagree with each other?' *Journal of Pragmatics*, 41, 2365–80.

Cheng, W. and A. B. M. Tsui [2009] (2011), 'Hong Kong Chinese and English native speaker ways of disagreeing', in R. Hughes, *Teaching and Researching Speaking*, Harlow: Pearson Educational, p. 168.

Chomsky, N. (1965), *Aspects of the Theory of Syntax*, Cambridge, MA: MIT Press.

Clandfield, L. and R. B. Benne (2012), *Global*, Basingstoke: Macmillan.

Clark, J. D. (1969), 'The Pennsylvania project and the audio-lingual vs. traditional question', *The Modern Language Journal*, 53, 388–96.

Claypole, M. (2010), *Controversies in ELT: What You Always Wanted to Know about Teaching English But Were Afraid to Ask*, Linguabooks.com.

Cohen, A. D. (1996), 'Verbal reports as a source of insights into second language learner strategies', *Applied Language Learning*, 7, 5–25.

Coleman, H. (ed.) (2011), *Dreams and Realities: Developing Countries and the English Language*, London: British Council.

Compleat Lexical Tutor (2012), <http://www.lextutor.ca> (last accessed 17 January 2013).

Conole, G. (2011), 'Blue skies thinking for Design and Open Educational Resources', in L. Murray, T. Hourigan and E. Riordan (eds), *Quality Issues in ICT Integration*, Newcastle upon Tyne: Cambridge Scholars Publishing, pp. 12–27.

Cook, G. (1989), *Discourse Analysis*, Oxford: Oxford University Press.

Cook, V. (1991), *Second Language Learning and Language Teaching*, London: Edward Arnold.

Cook, V. (2008), *Second Language Learning and Language Teaching*, 4th edn, London: Hodder Education.

Corbett, J. (2003), *An Intercultural Approach to English Language Teaching*, Clevedon: Multilingual Matters.

Corbett, J. (2010), *Intercultural Language Activities*, Cambridge: Cambridge University Press.

Crandall, E. and H. Basturken (2004), 'Evaluating pragmatics-focused materials', *ELT Journal*, 58, 38–49.

Crookes, G. (2009), *Values, Philosophies, and Beliefs in TESOL*, Cambridge: Cambridge University Press.

Crystal, D. (2002), *English as a Global Language*, Cambridge: Cambridge University Press.

Csikszentmihalyi, M. (1990), *Flow: The Psychology of Optimal Experience*, New York: HarperCollins.

Cullen, R. (2008), 'Teaching Grammar as a Liberating Force', *ELT Journal*, 62:3, 221–30.

Cullen, R. and I.-C. Kuo (2007), 'Spoken Grammar and ELT Course Materials: A Missing Link?', *TESOL Quarterly*, 41:2, pp. 361–86.

Curran, C. (1983), 'Counseling-Learning', in J. W. Oller and P. A. Richard-Amato (eds), *Methods that Work: A Smorgasbord of Ideas for Language Teachers*, Rowley, MA: Newbury House, pp. 146–78.

Cutting, J. (2002), *Pragmatics and Discourse: A Resource Book for Students*, London: Routledge.

Daller, H., J. Milton and J. Treffers-Daller (2007), *Modelling and Assessing Vocabulary Knowledge*, Cambridge: Cambridge University Press.

Davenport, M. and S. J. Hannahs (2005), *Introducing Phonetics and Phonology*, London: Hodder Arnold.

Davies, D. (2005), *Varieties of Modern English*, Harlow: Pearson Longman.

Davies, R. J. (2011), 'Second-Language Acquisition and the Information Age: How Social Software Has Created a New Mode of Learning', *TESL Canada Journal*, 28:2, 11–19.

Day, R. and J. Bamford (1998), *Extensive Reading in the Second Language Classroom*, Cambridge: Cambridge University Press.

DeCarrico, J. (2001), 'Vocabulary learning and teaching', in M. Celce-Murcia (ed.), *Teaching English As a Second or Foreign Language*, Boston: Heinle and Heinle, pp. 285–99.

DeKeyser, R. M. (ed.) (2008), *Practice in a Second Language*, Cambridge: Cambridge University Press.

Deoksoon, K. and K. P. King (2011), 'Implementing Podcasts and Blogs with ESOL Teacher Candidates' Preparation: Interpretations and Implications', *International Forum of Teaching and Studies*, 7:2, 5–19.

Din, F. S. and J. Calao (2001), 'The effects of playing educational video games on kindergarten achievement', *Child Study Journal*, 31:910, 95–102.

Dörnyei, Z. (1992), 'English teaching in Hungary: how far behind?', *Studies in Educational Evaluation*, 18: 47–56.

Doughty, C. and J. Williams (1998), *Focus on Form in Classroom Second Language Acquisition*, Cambridge and New York: Cambridge University Press.

Ducate, L. and L. Lomicka (2009), 'Podcasting: an effective tool for honing language students' pronunciation?', *Language Learning and Technology*, 13:3, 66–86, <http://llt.msu.edu/vol13num3/ducatelomicka.pdf> (last accessed 17 January 2013).

Dudeney, G. (2000), *The Internet and the Language Classroom*, Cambridge: Cambridge University Press.

Dudley-Evans, T. and M. St. John (1998), *Developments in English for Specific Purposes: A Multi-Disciplinary Approach*, Cambridge: Cambridge University Press.

Duff, P. (1997), 'Immersion in Hungary', in R. K. Johnson and M. Swain (eds), *Immersion Education: International Perspectives*, Cambridge: Cambridge University Press, pp. 19–42.

Duff, P. A. and S. Talmy (2011), 'Language socialization approaches to second language acquisition', in D. Atkinson (ed.), *Alternative Approaches to Second Language Acquisition*, Abingdon: Routledge, pp. 95–116.

Duffy, G. (1993), 'Teachers' progress towards becoming expert strategy teachers', *The Elementary School Journal*, 94:2, 109–20.

Durso, F. T. and K. A. Coggins (1991), 'Organised instruction for the improvement of word knowledge skills', *Journal of Educational Psychology*, 83: 108–12.

Eckerth, J. and S. Siekmann (2008), *Task-Based Language Learning and Teaching: Theoretical, Methodological and Pedagogical Perspectives*, Frankfurt am Main: Peter Lang.

Edge, J. and S. Garton (2009), *From Experience to Knowledge in ELT*, Oxford: Oxford University Press.

Ehrman, M. E. and Z. Dornyei (1998), *Interpersonal dynamics in second language education: The visible and invisible classroom*, Thousand Oaks, CA: Sage.

Elley, W. B. (1992), *How In the World Do Students Read? IEA Study of Reading Literacy*, New York: International Association for the Evaluation of Educational Achievement.

Ellis, R. (1998), 'Teaching and Research: Options in Grammar Teaching', *TESOL Quarterly*, 32:1, 39–60.

Ellis, R. (2003), *Task-Based Learning and Teaching*, Oxford: Oxford University Press.

Ellis, R. (2006a), 'Current issues in the teaching of grammar: an SLA perspective', *TESOL Quarterly*, 40:1, 83–107.

Ellis, R. (2006b), 'Modelling Learning Difficulty and Second Language Proficiency: The Differential Contributions of Implicit and Explicit Knowledge', *Applied Linguistics*, 27:3, 431–63.

Ellis, R. (2008), *The Study of Second Language Acquisition* (2nd edn), Oxford: Oxford University Press.

Elwood, S. (2010), 'Digital Storytelling: Strategies Using VoiceThread', paper presented at the Society for Information Technology and Teacher Education International Conference, Chesapeake, VA: AACE.

Emmitt, M., L. Komesaroff and J. Pollock (2006), *Language and Learning: An Introduction for Teaching*, Oxford: Oxford University Press.

Extensive Reading Foundation, <http://www.erfoundation.org/erf/> (last accessed 17 January 2013).

Farr, F., A. Chambers and S. O'Riordan (2010), 'Corpora for materials' development in language teacher education: underlying principles and useful data' in F. Mishan and A. Chambers (eds), *Perspectives in Language Learning Materials Development*, Berlin: Peter Lang, pp. 33–62.

Ferris, D. (1995), 'Student reactions to teacher response in multiple-draft composition classrooms', *TESOL Quarterly*, 29:1, 33–53.

Ferris, D. (2010), 'Does error feedback help student writers? New evidence on the short- and long-term effects of written error correction', in K. Hyland and F. Hyland, *Feedback in Second Language Writing: Contexts and Issues*, Cambridge: Cambridge University Press, pp. 81–104.

Field, J. (2010), *Listening in the Language Classroom*, Cambridge: Cambridge University Press.

Flower, J. and J. Hayes (1981), 'A cognitive process theory of writing' *College Composition and Communication*, 32, 365–87.

Fotos, S. and C. M. Browne (2004), *New Perspectives on CALL for Second Language Classrooms*, Mahwah, NJ: Laurence Erlbaum.

Gairns, R. and S. Redman (1986), *Working with Words*, Cambridge: Cambridge University Press.

Garton, S. (2008), 'Teacher beliefs and interaction in the language classroom', in S. Garton and K. Richards (eds), *Professional Encounters in TESOL*, Basingstoke: Palgrave Macmillan, pp. 67–86.

Garton, S. and K. Richards (eds) (2008), *Professional Encounters in TESOL*, Basingstoke: Palgrave Macmillan.

Gebhard, J. G. (1996), *Teaching English as a Foreign or Second Language*, Ann Arbor, MI: University of Michigan Press.

Gee, J. P. (2003), *What Videogames Have to Teach Us about Learning and Literacy*, New York: Palgrave.

Gibbs, G. (1988), *Teaching for Understanding at University: Deep Approaches and Distinctive Ways of Thinking*, Basingstoke: Palgrave Macmillan.

Godwin-Jones, R. (2003), 'Blogs and Wikis: Environments for On-line Collaboration' *Language Learning and Technology*, 7:2, 12–16.

Goldschneider, J. M. and R. M. DeKeyser (2001), 'Explaining the "Natural Order of L2 Morpheme Acquisition" in English: A Meta-analysis of Multiple Determinants', *Language Learning*, 51, 1–50.

Grabe, W. (2002), 'Dilemmas for the development of second language reading abilities', in J. C. Richards and W. A. Renandya (eds), *Methodology in Language Teaching: An Anthology of Current Practice*, Cambridge: Cambridge University Press, pp. 276–86.

Grabe, W. (2010), *Reading in a Second Language: Moving from Theory to Practice*, Cambridge: Cambridge University Press.

Grabe, W. and R. Kaplan (1996), *Theory and Practice of Writing*, Harlow: Longman.

Grabe, W. and F. L. Stoller (2002), *Teaching and Researching Reading*, Harlow: Longman Pearson.

Graddol, D. (2001), 'English in the Future', in A. Burns and C. Coffin (eds), *Analysing English in a Global Context*, London and New York: Routledge, pp. 26–37.

Grice, H. P. (1967), 'Logic and conversation. Further notes on logic and conversation', in H. P. Grice (ed.), *Studies in the Ways of Words* (1989), Cambridge, MA: Harvard University Press, vol. 1.

Grice, H. P. (1975), 'Logic and conversation', in P. Cole and J. Morgan (eds) *Studies in Syntax and Semantics III: Speech Acts*, New York: Academic Press, pp. 183–98.

Gupta, P. and B. MacWhinney (1997), 'Vocabulary Acquisition and Verbal Short-Term Memory: Computational and Neural Bases', in *Brain and Language*, 59, 267–333.

Gusshoven, C. and H. Jacobs (2005), *Understanding Phonology*, London: Hodder Arnold.

Hall, J. K. and W. G. Eggington (eds) (2000), *The Sociopolitics of English Language Teaching*, Clevedon: Multilingual Matters.

Halliday, M.A.K. (1985), *Spoken and Written Language*, Oxford: Oxford University Press.

Halliday, M. A. K. (1994), *An Introduction to Functional Grammar* (2nd edn), London: Edward Arnold.

Halliday, M. A. K. and J. Webster (2003), *On Language and Linguistics*, London: Continuum.

Han, Z. (2000), 'Persistence of the implicit influence of NL: The case of the pseudopassive', *Applied Linguistics*, 21:1, 78–105.

Harmer, J. (2007), *The Practice of English Language Teaching* (4th edn), Harlow: Pearson Education.

Hedge, T. (2000), *Teaching and Learning in the Language Classroom*, Oxford: Oxford University Press.

Hewings, M. and A. Hewings (2002), 'It is interesting to note . . . : a comparative study of anticipatory 'it' in student and published writing', *English for Specific Purposes*, 21, 367–83.

Heyward, M. (2002), 'From international to intercultural: redefining the international school for a globalised world', *Journal of Research in International Education*, 1, 9–32.

Hinkel, E. (ed.) (1999), *Culture in Second Language Teaching and Learning*, Cambridge: Cambridge University Press.

Hinkel, E. (2006), 'Current perspectives on teaching the four skills', *TESOL Quarterly*, 40, 109–31.

Hirano, E. (2009), 'Learning difficulty and learner identity: a symbiotic relationship', *English Language Teaching Journal*, 63:1, 33–41.

Hoffman, E. (1989), *Lost in Translation*, London: Verso.

Hofstede, G. (1986), 'Cultural differences in teaching and learning', *International Journal of Intercultural Relations*, 10, 310–20.

Holliday, A. (2005), *The Struggle to Teach English as an International Language*, Oxford: Oxford University Press.

Holliday, A., M. Hyde and J. Kullman (2010), *Intercultural Communication*, London: Routledge.

Honey, P. and A. Mumford (1986), *Effective Learning*, London: IPD.

Howatt, A. P. R. (1984), *A History of English Language Teaching*, Oxford: Oxford University Press.

Hughes, R. (2010), 'What a corpus tells us about grammar teaching materials', in A. O'Keeffe and M. McCarthy (eds), *The Routledge Handbook of Corpus Linguistics*, London: Routledge, pp. 401–12.

Hughes, R. (2011), *Teaching and Researching Speaking*, Harlow: Longman Pearson.

Hughes, R. and M. McCarthy (1998), 'From Sentence to Discourse: Discourse Grammar and English Language Teaching', *TESOL Quarterly*, 32:2, 263–87.

Hutchinson, T. and A. Waters (1987), 'Needs assessment in language programming: from theory to practice', in R. K. Johnson (ed.), *The Second Language Curriculum*, Cambridge: Cambridge University Press, pp. 48–62.

Hyland, K. (2004), *Genre and Second Language Writing*, Ann Arbor, MI: University of Michigan Press.

Hyland, K. (2009a), *Teaching and Researching Writing*, Harlow: Pearson Education.

Hyland, K. (2009b), *Academic Discourse*, London: Continuum.

Hyland, K. (2012), *Disciplinary Identities*, Cambridge: Cambridge University Press.

Hyland, K. and F. Hyland (2010), *Feedback in Second Language Writing*, Cambridge: Cambridge University Press.

Hymes, D. (1972), 'On communicative competence', in J. B. Pride and J. Holmes (eds), *Sociolinguistics*, Harmondsworth: Penguin, pp. 269–93.

The Internet Grammar of English, University College London, <http://www.ucl.ac.uk/internet-grammar/home.htm> (last accessed 17 January 2013).

Ivanic, R. (1998), *Writing and Identity: The Discoursal Construction of Identity in Academic Writing*, Amsterdam: John Benjamins.

Ivanic, R. and S. Weldon (1999), 'Researching the writer–reader relationship', in C. N. Candlin and K. Hyland (eds), *Writing: Texts, Process and Practices*, Harlow: Longman, pp. 168–92.

Jackson, J. (2009), 'Game-based teaching: what educators can learn from videogames', in *Teaching Education*, 20:3, 291–304.

Janzen, J. (1996), 'Teaching strategic reading', *TESOL Journal*, 6, 6–9.

Jenkins, J. (2007), *English as a Lingua Franca: Attitude and Identity*, Oxford: Oxford University Press.

Jenkins, J. (2012), 'English as a Lingua Franca from the classroom to the classroom', in *English Language Teaching Journal*, 66:4, 486–94.

Johns, A. M. (1997), *Text, Role and Context: Developing Academic Literacies*, Cambridge: Cambridge University Press.

Johnston, B. (2003), *Values in English Language Teaching*, Mahwah, NJ: Lawrence Erlbaum Associates.

Johnstone, B. (2008), *Discourse Analysis*, Malden, MA, Oxford, and Victoria, Australia: Blackwell.

Jones, C. and D. Waller (2011), 'If only it were true: the problem with the four conditionals', *ELT Journal*, 65:1, 24.

Kachru, B. B. (1985), 'Standards, codification and sociolinguistic realism: the English language in the outer circle', in R. Quirk and H. G. Widdowson (eds), *English in the World: Teaching and Learning in the Language and Literatures*, Cambridge: Cambridge University Press.

Kachru, B. B. (1989), 'Teaching World Englishes', in D. Davies (ed.) (2005), *Varieties of Modern English*, Harlow: Pearson Educational, Chapter 4.

Kachru, Y. (1999), 'Culture, context and writing', in E. Hinkel (ed.), *Culture in Second Language Teaching and Learning*, Cambridge: Cambridge University Press, pp. 1–23.

Kellerman, E. (1986), 'An eye for an eye: constraints of the L2 lexicon', in E. Kellerman and M. Sharwood-Smith (eds), *Crosslinguistic Influences in Second Language Acquisition*, Oxford: Pergamon.

Kelly, G. (2011), *How To Teach Pronunciation*, Harlow: Longman Pearson

Khaddage, F., C. Lattemann and E. Bray (2011), *Mobile Apps Integration for Teaching and Learning (Are Teachers Ready to Re-blend?)*, paper presented at the Society for Information Technology and Teacher Education International Conference (SITE) 2011, Nashville, TN.

Kirkpatrick, A. (2007a), *World Englishes: Implications for International Communication and English Language Teaching*, Cambridge: Cambridge University Press.

Kirkpatrick, A. (2007b), 'Teaching English Across Cultures: What do English language teachers need to know to know how to teach English?', *English Australia Journal*, 23:2.

Klapper, J. (2003), 'Taking communication to task? A critical review of recent trends in language teaching', *Language Learning Journal*, 27, pp. 33–42.

Knight, S. (1994), 'Dictionary use while reading: The effects on comprehension and vocabulary acquisition for students of different verbal abilities', *Modern Language Journal*, 78, 285–99.

Koda, K. (2010), *Insights into Second Language Reading*, Cambridge: Cambridge University Press.

Kolb, D. A. (1984), *Experiential Learning: Experience As the Source of Learning and Development*, Englewood Cliffs, NJ: Prentice Hall.

Kramsch, C. (1998), *Language and Culture*, Oxford: Oxford University Press.

Kramsch, C. (2000), 'Second language acquisition, applied linguistics and the teaching of foreign languages', *Modern Language Journal*, 84, 311–26.

Krashen, S. (1981), *Second Language Acquisition and Second Language Learning*, Oxford: Pergamon Press.

Krashen, S. D. (1985), *The Input Hyothesis: Issues and Implications*, London: Longman.

Krashen, S. D. and T. D. Terrell (1992), *The Natural Approach: Language Acquisition in the Classroom*, New York: Pergamon Press.

Kuchah, K. (2008), 'Developing as a professional in Cameroon: challenges and visions', in S. Garton and K. Richards (eds), *Professional Encounters in TESOL*, Basingstoke: Palgrave Macmillan, pp. 203–17.

Kumaravadivelu, B. (1993), 'Maximizing learning potential in the communicative classroom', *English Language Teaching Journal*, 47, 12–21.

Kumaravadivelu, B. (2006), 'TESOL Methods: changing tracks, challenging trends', *TESOL Quarterly*, 40:1, pp. 59–81.

Kumaravadivelu, B. and S. Gass (eds) (1997), *Beyond Methods: New Perspectives in Second and Foreign Language Education*, Cambridge: Cambridge University Press.

Kuo, I.-C. (2006), 'Addressing the issue of teaching English as a Lingua Franca', *ELT Journal*, 60:3, 213–21.

Lado, R. (1957), *Linguistics Across Cultures: Applied Linguistics for Language Teachers*, Ann Arbor, MI; University of Michigan.

Lakoff, R. (1977), 'What you can do with words: Politeness, pragmatics and performatives', in *Proceedings of the Texas Conference on Performatives, Presuppositions and Implicatures*, ed. R. Rogers, R. Wall and J. Murphy, Arlington: Center for Applied Linguistics, pp. 79–106.

Lantolf, J. (2007), 'Conceptual knowledge and instructed second language learning; a sociocultural perspective', in S. Fotos and H. Nassaji (eds), *Form-Focused Instruction and Teacher Education: Studies in Honour of Rod Ellis*, Oxford: Oxford University Press, pp. 35–54.

Lantolf, J. P. (2011), 'The sociocultural approach to second language acquisition: sociocultural theory, second language acquisition, and artificial L2 development', in D. Atkinson (ed.), *Alternative Approaches to Second Language Acquisition*, Abingdon: Routledge, pp. 24–47.

Lapkin, S., D. Hart and M. Swain (1991), 'Early and Middle French immersion programs: French language outcomes', *Canadian Modern Language Review*, 48, 11–40.

Larsen-Freeman, D. (2000), *Techniques and Principles in Language Teaching*, Oxford: Oxford University Press.

Larsen-Freeman, D. (2002), 'The Grammar of Choice', in S. Fotos and E. Hinkel (eds), *New Perspectives on Grammar Teaching in Second Language Classrooms*, New York: Lawrence Erlbaum Associates, pp. 105–20.

Larsen-Freeman, D. (2003), *Teaching Languages: From Grammar to Grammaring*, Boston: Heinle.

Larsen-Freeman, D. (2006), 'The Emergence of Complexity, Fluency, and Accuracy in the Oral and Written Production of Five Chinese Learners of English', *Applied Linguistics*, 27:4, 590–619.

Laufer, B. (1992), 'Reading in a foreign language: how does L2 lexical knowledge interact with the reader's general academic ability?', *Journal of Research in Reading*, 15, 95–103.

Lee, I. (2009), 'Ten Mismatches between teachers' beliefs and written feedback practice', *ELT Journal*, 63:1, pp. 13–22.

Leech, G. and J. Svartvik (2002), *A Communicative Grammar of English* (3rd edn), Harlow: Pearson.

Legutke, M. and H. Thomas (1991), *Process and Experience in the Language Classroom*, London: Longman.

Lewis, M. (1985), *Practical Techniques for Language Teaching*, Hove: Language Teaching Publications.

Lewis, M. (1993), *The Lexical Approach: The State of ELT and a Way Forward*, Hove: Language Teaching Publications.

Lindsay, C. and P. Knight (2006), *Learning and Teaching English*, Oxford: Oxford University Press.

Littlewood, W. (1984), *Foreign and Second Language Learning*, Cambridge: Cambridge University Press.

Long, M. [1991] (2001), 'Focus on Form: Design feature in language teaching methodology in Candlin', in C. and N. Mercer (eds), *English Language Teaching in its Social Context*, London: Routledge, pp. 180–90.

Macalister, J. and I. S. P. Nation (2009), *Case Studies in Language Curriculum Design*, New York and London: Routledge.

McCarten, J. (2007), *Teaching Vocabulary: Lessons from the Corpus, Lessons for the Classroom*, Cambridge: Cambridge University Press, <http://www.cambridge.org/other_files/downloads/esl/booklets/McCarten-Teaching-Vocabulary.pdf> (last accessed 22 January 2013).

McCarten, J. (2010), 'Corpus-informed course book design', in A. O'Keeffe, A and M. McCarthy (eds), *The Routledge Handbook of Corpus Linguistics*, London: Routledge, pp. 401–12.

McCarthy, J. and N. Schmidt (eds) (1997), *Vocabulary: Description, Acquisition and Pedagogy*, Cambridge: Cambridge University Press.

McCarthy, M. (1991), *Discourse Analysis for Language Teachers*, Cambridge: Cambridge University Press.

McCarthy, M. (2004), *Touchstone: from Corpus to Coursebook*, Cambridge: Cambridge University Press.

McCarthy, M., J. McCarten and H. Sandiford (2005), *Touchstone*, Cambridge: Cambridge University Press.

Mackay, S. (2002), *Teaching English as an International Language*, Oxford: Oxford University Press.

Maclean, G. R. and J. A. Elwood (2009), 'Digital Natives, Learner Perceptions and the Use of ICT', in M. Thomas (ed.), *Handbook of Research on Web 2.0 and Second Language Learning*, London: IGI Global, pp. 156–79.

McNamara, J. (1972), 'Cognitive Basis of Language Learning in Infants', *Psychological Review*, 70:1.

Mawer, K and G. Stanley (2011), *Digital Play: Computer Games and Language Aims*, Surrey, UK: Delta ELT Publishing Ltd.

Meara, P. (1992), 'Network structures and vocabulary acquisition in a foreign language'. In P. Arnaud and H. Bėjoint (eds) *Vocabulary and Applied Linguistics*, London: Macmillan, pp. 62–72.

Mitra, S. (2011), 'Can kids teach themselves?', <http://www.ted.com/talks/sugata_mitra_shows_how_kids_teach_themselves.html> (last accessed 17 January 2013).

Moon, J. (1999), *Reflection in Learning and Professional Development*, London: Routledge Falmer.

Moore, M. (2011), 'What is Crazy English and who is Li Yang?', *Daily Telegraph*, 12 September, <http://www.telegraph.co.uk/news/worldnews/asia/china/8757375/What-is-Crazy-English-and-who-is-Li-Yang.html> (last accessed 17 July 2012).

Moskowitz, G. (1978), *Caring and Sharing in the Foreign Language Classroom*, Boston: Heinle and Heinle.

Moyer, A. (1999), 'Ultimate attainment in L2 phonology', *Studies in Second Language Acquisition*, 21, 109–24.

Mullany, L. and P. Stockwell (2010), *Introducing English Language: A Resource Book for Students*, London: Routledge.

Mullen, T., C. Appel and T. Shanklin (2009), 'Skype-Based Tandem Language Learning and Web 2.0', in M. Thomas (ed.), *Handbook of Research on Web 2.0 and Second Language Learning*, London: IGI Global, pp. 101–18.

Mumford, S. (2009), 'An analysis of spoken grammar: the case for production', *ELT Journal*, 63:2, 137.

Murphy, R. (2012), *English Grammar in Use* (4th edn), Cambridge: Cambridge University Press.

Murray, L. and A. Barnes (1998), 'Beyond the 'wow' factor – evaluating multimedia language learning software from a pedagogical viewpoint', *System: The International Journal of Educational Technology and Applied Linguistics*, 26:2, 249–59.

Murray, L. and T. Hourigan (2008), 'Blogs for specific purposes: Expressivist or socio-cognitivist approach?', *ReCALL*, 20:1, 83–98.

Murray, N. (2010), 'Pragmatics, awareness raising, and the cooperative principle', *English Language Teaching Journal*, 64: 293–301.

Myers, G. (2010), 'The Discourse of Blogs and Wikis', <http://www.scribd.com/doc/67859997/Myers-The-Discourse-of-Blogs-and-Wikis> (last accessed 17 January 2013).

Myskow, G. and K. Gordon (2010), 'A focus on purpose: using a genre approach in an EFL writing class', *English Language Teaching Journal*, 64, 283–91.

Nagy, W. E. (2005), 'Why vocabulary instruction needs to be long-term and comprehensive', in E. H. Hiebert and M. L. Kami (eds), *Teaching and Learning Vocabulary: Bringing Research to Practice*, Mahwah, NJ: Erlbaum, pp. 27–44.

Naiman, N., M. Frolich, H. H. Stern and A. Todesco (1996), *The Good Language Learner*, Clevedon: Multilingual Matters.

Nassaji, H. (2003), 'L2 vocabulary learning from context: Strategies, knowledge sources, and their relationship with success in L2 lexical inferencing', *TESOL Quarterly*, 37, 645–70.

Nassaji, H. and S. Fotos (2004), 'Current developments in the research on the teaching of grammar', *Annual Review of Applied Linguistics*, 24, 126–45.

Nation, I. S. P. (2001), *Learning Vocabulary in Another Language*, New York: Cambridge University Press.

Nation, I. S. P. (2004), 'A study of the most frequent word families in the British National Corpus', in P. Bogaards and B. Laufer (eds), *Vocabulary in a Second Language*, Philadelphia: J. Benjamins, pp. 3–14.

Nation, I. S. P. (2006), 'How large a vocabulary is needed for reading and listening?', *Canadian Modern Languages Review*, 63, 59–82.

Nation, I. S. P. (2007), 'The Four Strands', *Innovation in Language Learning and Teaching*, 1:1, 2–13.

Nation, I. S. P. (2008), *Teaching Vocabulary: Strategies and Techniques*, Boston: Heinle Cengage.

Nation, I. S. P. and J. Newton (2009), *Teaching ESL/EFL Listening and Speaking*, Abingdon: Routledge.

Nation, P. (2001), *Learning Vocabulary in Another Language*, Cambridge: Cambridge University Press.

Nattinger, J. R. and J. S. DeCarrico (1992), *Lexical Phrases and Language Teaching*, Oxford: Oxford University Press.

Natural Grammar website (2005), *Teaching Ideas*, <http://elt.oup.com/student/naturalgrammar/?mode=student&cc=global&selLanguage=en> (last accessed 28 January 2013).

Negash, N. (2011), 'English in Africa: an impediment or a contributor to development?', in H. Coleman (ed.), *Dreams and Realities: Developing Countries and the English Language*, London: British Council, pp. 165–87.

Nesi, H. (2012), *Genre Across the Disciplines*, Cambridge: Cambridge University Press.

Nicholson, P. and R. Sakuno (1982), *Explain Yourself! An English Conversation Book for Japan*, Kyoto: PAL.

Nikolov, M. (2000), 'The CPH reconsidered: successful adult learners of Hungarian and English', in *International Review of Applied Linguistics*, 38, 109–24.

Nikolov, M. and J. M. Djigunovic (2012), 'Recent research on age, second language acquisition and early foreign language learning', *Europe Platform Online*, <www.europeesplatform.nl/sf.mcgi?3859&cat=769> (last accessed 17 January 2013).

Nitta, R. and S. Gardner (2005), 'Consciousness-raising and practice in ELT coursebooks', *ELT Journal*, 59:1, 3.

Norris, J. M. and L. Ortega (2000), 'Effectiveness of L2 Instruction: A Research Synthesis and Quantitative Meta-analysis', *Language Learning*, 50:3, 417.

Nunan, D. (1989), *Designing Tasks for the Communicative Classroom*, Cambridge: Cambridge University Press.

Nunan, D. (1991), *Language Teaching Methodology: a Textbook for Teachers*, Hemel Hempstead: Prentice-Hall.

Nystrand, M., A. Doyle and M. Himly (1986), 'A critical examination of the doctrine of autonomous texts', in M. Nystrand (ed.), *The Structure of Written Communication*, Orlando: Academic Press, pp. 81–107.

O'Keeffe, A. and M. McCarthy (eds) (2010), *The Routledge Handbook of Corpus Linguistics*, London: Routledge.

O'Neill, R. (1978), *American Kernel Intermediate*, Harlow: Longman.

O'Neill, S. and A. Gish (2008), *Teaching English as a Second Language*, Oxford: Oxford University Press.

Orkeny, I. (1998), *One Minute Stories* (trans. Sollosy), Budapest: Corvina.

Oxford, R. (1990), *Language Learning Strategies: What Every Teacher Should Know*, Boston: Heinle and Heinle.

Oxford, R. (2011), *Teaching and Researching Language Learning Strategies*, London: Longman.

Ozkan, Y. (2011), 'Blogging in a teaching skills course for pre-service teachers of English as a second language', *Australasian Journal of Educational Technology*, 27:4, 655–70, <http://www.ascilite.org.au/ajet/ajet27/ozkan.html> (last accessed 17 January 2013).

Palfreyman, D. and R. C. Smith (eds) (2003), *Learner Autonomy Across Cultures*, Basingstoke: Palgrave Macmillan.

Parent, K. (2009), 'The Teacher as Intermediary between National Curriculum and Classroom' in J. Macalister and I. S. P. Nation, *Case Studies in Language Curriculum Design*, New York and London: Routledge, pp. 190–4.

Parrott, M. (2010), *Grammar for English Language Teachers* (2nd edn), Cambridge: Cambridge University Press.

Pavlenko, A. and J. P. Lantolf (2000), 'Second language learning as participation and the (re) construction of selves', in J. P. Lantolf (ed.), *Sociocultural Theory and Second Language Learning*, Oxford: Oxford University Press.

Pennycook, A. (2000), 'The social politics and the cultural politics of the language classroom', in J. K. Hall and W. A. Eggington, *The Sociopolitics of English Language Teaching*, Clevedon: Multilingual Matters, pp. 89–103.

Perifanou, M. A. (2009), 'Language Micro-gaming: Fun and Informal Microblogging Activities for Language Learning', in M. D. Lytras (ed.), *Best Practices for the Knowledge Society: Knowledge, Learning, Development and Technology for All*, Berlin: Springer.

Peterson, M. (2012), 'Language Learner Interaction in a Massively Multiplayer Online Role-Playing Game', in H. Reinders (ed.), *Digital Games in Language Learning and Teaching*, Palgrave Macmillan, pp. 70–92.

Pickett, D. (1978), 'The foreign language learning process: an occasional paper', London: British Council.

Pienemann, M., M. Johnston and G. Brindley (1988), 'Constructing an acquisition-based procedure for second language assessment', *AILA Review*, 5, pp. 40–72.

Pimsleur, P. (1966), *The Pimsleur Language Aptitude Battery*, New York: Harcourt Brace Jovanovitch.

Prensky, M. (2001), 'Digital Natives, Digital Immigrants', *On the Horizon*, 9:5, <http://pre2005.flexiblelearning.net.au/projects/resources/Digital_Natives_Digital_Immigrants.pdf> (last accessed 24 January 2013).

Prensky, M. (2006), *Don't Bother Me Mom – I'm Learning*, St. Paul, MN: Paragon House.

Pollard, A. (2008), *Readings for Reflective Teaching* (5th edn), London: Continuum.

Prabhu, N. (1987), *Second Language Pedagogy*, Oxford: Oxford University Press.

Prabhu, N. S. (1992), 'The dynamic of the language lesson', *TESOL Quarterly*, 26:2, 225–41.

Raith, T. (2009), 'The Use of Weblogs in Language Education', in M. Thomas (ed.), *Handbook of Research on Web 2.0 and Second Language Learning*, London: IGI Global, pp. 274–91.

Randall, M. and J. Mirador (2003), 'How well am I doing? Using a corpus-based analysis to investigate tutor and institutional messages in comment sheets', in *Assessment and Evaluation in Higher Education*, 28:5, 515–26.

Reinders, H. (ed.) (2012), *Digital Games in Language Learning and Teaching*, Basingstoke: Palgrave Macmillan.

Renandya, W. A. and J. C. Richards (2002), *Methodology in Language Teaching: an Anthology of Current Practice*, Cambridge: Cambridge University Press.

Richards, J. (1984), 'The Secret Life of Methods', *TESOL Quarterly*, 18:1.

Richards, J. (1990), *The Language Teaching Matrix*, Cambridge: Cambridge University Press.

Richards, J. C. and T. S. Rodgers (2001), *Approaches and Methods in Language Teaching*, Cambridge: Cambridge University Press.

Richards, J., J. Platt and H. Platt (1993), *Dictionary of Language Teaching and Applied Linguistics* (3rd edn), London: Longman.

Richardson, W. (2006), *Blogs, Wikis and Podcasts, and Other Powerful Web Tools for Classrooms*, California: Corwin Press.

Risko, V. J. (2000), 'Preparing Teachers to Teach With Understanding', in A. W. Pailliotet and P. B. Mosenthal (eds), *Reconceptualising Literacy in the Media Age*, Oxford: Elsevier Science Ltd, pp. 91–104.

Roach, P. (2009), *English Phonetics and Phonology* (4th edn), Cambridge: Cambridge University Press.

Robinson, P. (2008), 'Aptitudes, abilities, contexts and practice', in R. M. DeKeyser (ed.), *Practice in a Second Language*, Cambridge: Cambridge University Press, pp. 256–86.

Rodzvilla, J. (ed.) (2002), *We've Got Blog: How Weblogs are Changing Our Culture*, Cambridge, MA: Perseus Books.

Rogers, C. (1994), *Freedom to Learn*, London: Prentice Hall.

Rost, M. (2011), *Teaching and Researching Listening*, Harlow: Longman Pearson.

Rourke, A. J., and K. Coleman (2009), 'An emancipating space: Reflective and collaborative blogging', paper presented at *Ascilite: Same Places, Different Spaces*, Auckland.

Rubin, J. (1987), 'Learner strategies: theoretical assumptions, research history and typology', in A. Wendeon and J. Rubin (eds), *Learner Strategies in Language Learning*, London: Prentice Hall, pp. 15–30.

Russell, R. A. (2005), 'Acquisition and Attrition of -wa and -ga in Japanese as a Second Language', in C. J. K. McAlister, K. Rolstad and J. MacSwan (eds), *Proceedings of the 4th International Symposium on Bilingualism*, Somerville, MA: Cascadilla Press, pp. 2020–36.

Sampedro, R. and S. Hillyard (2004), *Global Issues*, Oxford: Oxford University Press.

Savery, J. R. and T. M. Duffy (1996), 'Problem Based Learning: An Instructional Model and its Constructivist Framework', in B. Wilson (ed.), *Constructivist Learning Environments: Case Studies in Instructional Design*, Englewood Cliffs, NJ: Educational Technology Publications, pp. 135–48.

Sayer, P. (2010), 'Using the linguistic landscape as a pedagogical resource', *English Language Teaching Journal*, 64: 143–54.

Schmitt, N. (2000), *Vocabulary in Language Teaching*, New York: Cambridge University Press.

Schön, D. (1983), *The Reflective Practitioner: How Professionals Think in Action*, London: Temple Smith.

Scrivener, J. (2010), *Teaching English Grammar* (2nd edn), Oxford: MacMillan Education.

Seidlhofer, B. (2001), 'Closing a conceptual gap: the case for a description of English as a Lingua Franca', in *International Journal of Applied Linguistics*, 11:2, 133–58.

Seidlhofer, B. (2005), 'English as a lingua franca', *ELT Journal*, 59:4, 339–41.

Seidlhofer, B. (2011), *Understanding English as a Lingua Franca*, Oxford: Oxford University Press.

Selinker, L. (1972), 'Interlanguage', *IRAL*, 10:3, 209–31.

Senior, R. (2006), *The Experience of English Language Teaching*, Cambridge: Cambridge University Press.

Shawcross, P. (2011), *Flightpath: Aviation English for Pilots and ATCOs*, Cambridge: Cambridge University Press.

Sheen, Y. (2004), 'Corrective feedback and learner uptake in communicative classrooms across instructional settings', *Language Teaching Research*, 8:3, 263–300.

Sidnell, J. (2010), *Conversation Analysis: An Introduction*, Chichester: Blackwells.

Simpson, J. (2007), 'Review of Holliday, A.: *The Struggle to teach English as an International Language*', in *Applied Linguistics*, 28:1, 147–50.

Sinclair, J. (2004), *Trust the Text: Language, Corpus and Discourse*, London: Routledge.

Skehan, P. (2002), 'Theorising and updating aptitude', in P. Robinson (ed.), *Individual Differences and Instructed Language Learning*, Amsterdam and Philadelphia: John Benjamins, pp. 69–93.

Skinner, B. F. (1961), *Verbal Behaviour*, Appleton-Century-Crofts.

Slobin, D. I. (1971), 'Universals of grammatical development in children', in G. B. Flores d'Arcais and W. J. M. Levelt (eds), *Readings in Child Language Acquisition*, New York: Holt, Rinehart and Winston.

Spada, N. (1997), 'Form-focused instruction and second language acquisition: A review of classroom and laboratory research', *Language Teaching*, 30, 73–87.

Spada, N. (2010), 'Beyond form-focused instruction: Reflections on past, present and future research', *Language Teaching*, 44:2, 225–36.

Spada, N. and Y. Tomita (2010), 'Interactions Between Type of Instruction and Type of Language Feature: A Meta-Analysis', *Language Learning*, 60:2, 263–308.

Spiro, J. (2004), *Creative Poetry Writing*, Oxford: Oxford University Press.

Spiro, J. (2007a), *Storybuilding*, Oxford: Oxford University Press.

Spiro, J. (2007b), 'Teaching poetry: writing poetry – teaching as a writer', *English in Education*, 41:3, 78–93.

Spiro, J. (2010), 'Crossing the Bridge from Appreciative Reader to Reflective Writer: The Assessment of Creative Process', in A. Paran and L. Sercu (eds), *Testing the Untestable*, Bristol: Multilingual Matters, pp. 165–90.

Spolsky, B. (1999), *Sociolinguistics*, Oxford: Oxford University Press.

Spratt, M. (1996), *English for the Teacher*, Cambridge: Cambridge University Press.

Stahl, S. A., J. L. Burdge, M. B. Machuga and S. Stecyk (1992), 'The effects of semantic grouping on learning word meanings', *Reading Psychology*, 13, 19–35.

Stapleton, P. (2000), 'Culture's Role in TEFL: an attitude survey in Japan', *Language, Culture and Curriculum*, 13:3, pp. 291–305.

Stapleton, P. and P. Radia (2010), 'Tech-era L2 writing: towards a new kind of process', *English Language Teaching Journal*, 6:2, pp. 175–83.

Stevick, E. (1983), 'Interpreting and Adapting Lozanov's Philosophy', in J. W. Oller and P. A. Richard-Amato (eds), *Methods that Work: a smorgasbord of ideas for language teachers*, Rowley, MA: Newbury House, pp. 115–47.

Storti, C. (1989), *The Art of Crossing Cultures*, Yarmouth, ME: Intercultural Press.

Stubbs, M. (1996), *Texts and Corpus Analysis*, Oxford: Blackwells.

Swales, J. (1990), *Genre Analysis: English in Academic and Research Settings*, Cambridge: Cambridge University Press.

Swales, J. and C. Feak (2000), *Academic Writing for Graduate Students: Essential Tasks and Skills*, Ann Arbor, MI: University of Michigan Press.

Swan, M. (1985), 'A critical look at the Communicative Approach', *ELT Journal*, 39:1, pp. 2–11.

Swan, M. and B. Smith (2001), *Learner English: A Teacher's Guide to Interference and Other Problems*, Cambridge: Cambridge University Press.

Thomas, D. (1995), *Teachers' Stories*, Milton Keynes: Open University Press.

Thomas, M. (2012), 'Contextualizing Digital Game-Based Language Learning: Transformational Paradigm Shift or Business as Usual?', in H. Reinders (ed.), *Digital Games in Language Learning and Teaching*, Palgrave Macmillan, pp. 11–31.

Thornbury, S. (1996), 'Teachers research teacher talk', *English Language Teaching Journal*, 50, 279–88.

Thornbury, S. (1997), 'Reformulation and reconstruction: tasks that promote "noticing"', *ELT Journal*, 51:4, 326–35.

Thornbury, S. (2001), *Uncovering Grammar*, Oxford: Macmillan Heinemann.

Thornbury, S. (2002), *How to Teach Vocabulary*, Harlow: Longman.

Thornbury, S. (2004), *Natural Grammar*, Oxford: Oxford University Press.

Thornbury, S. (2005), *How to Teach Speaking*, Harlow: Pearson.

Thornbury, S. (2009), *Teaching Unplugged*, Surrey: Delta Publishing.

Thorne, S. L. and J. S. Payne (2005), 'Evolutionary trajectories, internet-mediated expression, and language education', *CALICO Journal*, 22:3, 371–97.

Timmis, I. (2005), 'Towards a framework for teaching spoken grammar', *English Language Teaching Journal*, 59: 117–25.

Tognini-Bonelli, E. (2001), *Corpus Linguistics at Work*, Amsterdam and Philadelphia: John Benjamins.

Tomlinson, B. (ed.) (2011), *Materials Development in Language Teaching*, Cambridge: Cambridge University Press.

Travis, P. (2007), 'Podcasting', *English Teaching Professional*, 52, 62–4.

Travis, P. and F. Joseph (2009), 'Improving Learners' Speaking Skills with Podcasts', in M. Thomas (ed.), *Handbook of Research on Web 2.0 and Second Language Learning*, London: IGI Global, pp. 313–30.

Tripp, D. (1993), *Critical Incidents in Teaching: Developing Professional Judgement*, London and New York: Routledge.

Tsui, A. B. (2009), *Understanding Expertise in Teaching*, Cambridge: Cambridge University Press.

Urponen, M. I. (2004), *Ultimate Attainment in Postpuberty Second Language Acquisition*, Boston: Boston University Press.

Valdes, J. C. (2001), *Culture Bound* (11th printing), Cambridge: Cambridge University Press.

Van Ek, J. A. (1973), *The Threshold Level in a Unit/Credit System*, Strasbourg: Council of Europe.

Vygotsky, L. S. (1978), *Mind in Society: The Development of Higher Psychological Processes*, Cambridge, MA: Harvard University Press.

Wajnryb, R. (1990), *Grammar Dictation*, Oxford: Oxford University Press.

Walsh, S. (2011), *Exploring Classroom Discourse: Language in Action*, London and New York: Routledge.

Wardhaugh, R. (1970), 'The contrastive analysis hypothesis', *TESOL Quarterly*, 4: 123–36.

Warschauer, M. and M. Liaw (2011), 'Emerging technologies for autonomous language learning', *Studies in Self-Access Learning Journal*, 2:3, 107–18, <http://sisaljournal.org/archives/sep11/warschauer_liaw/> (last accessed 17 January 2013).

Warschauer, M. and H. Shetzer (2000), 'An electronic literacy approach to network-based language teaching', in M. Warschauer (ed.), *Network-Based Language Teaching*, Cambridge: Cambridge University Press, pp. 171–85.

Watcyn-Jones, P. (1995), *Vocabulary Games and Activities*, Harmondsworth: Penguin.

Watkins, J. and M. Wilkins (2011), 'Using YouTube in the EFL Classroom', *Language Education in Asia*, 2:1, 113–19, <http://www.camtesol.org/Download/LEiA_Vol2_Iss1_2011/LEiA_V2_I1_09_Jon_Watkins_and_Michael_Wilkins_Using_YouTube_in_the_EFL_Classroom.pdf> (last accessed 17 January 2013).

Wharton, S. (2011), 'Critical text analysis: linking language and cultural studies', in *English Language Teaching Journal*, 65:3, pp. 221–9.

White, R. V. and V. Arndt (1992), *Process writing*, London: Longman.

Whitehead, D. (2011), 'English language teaching in fragile states: justifying action, promoting success and combating hegemony', in H. Coleman (ed.), *Dreams and Realities: Developing Countries and the English Language*, London: British Council, pp. 333–69.

Widdowson, H. G. (1988), 'Grammar, and nonsense, and learning', in W. Rutherford and M. Sharwood-Smith (eds), *Grammar and Second Language Teaching*, New York: Newbury House.

Willis, D. (1990), *The Lexical Syllabus: A New Approach to Language Teaching*, London: Collins ELT.

Willis, D. (2003), *Rules, Patterns and Words: Grammar and Lexis in English Language Teaching*, Cambridge: Cambridge University Press.

Willis, J. (1996), *A Framework for Task-Based Learning*, Harlow: Longman.

Willis, D. and J. Willis (2001), 'Task-based language learning', in R. Carter and D. Nunan (eds), *The Cambridge Guide to Teaching English to Speakers of Other Languages*, Cambridge: Cambridge University Press, pp. 173–9.

Wong, J. and H. Z. Waring (2010), *Conversation Analysis and Second Language Pedagogy*, Abingdon: Routledge.

Wood, D. (1998), *How Children Think and Learn*, Cambridge, MA and Oxford: Blackwell.

Wray, A., K. Trott and A. Bloomer (1998), *Projects in Linguistics*, London: Arnold.

INDEX

Note: numbers in *italics* refer to tasks in the online resource